Island Fever

Life Adventures in Search of Island Paradise

CHARLES PFLUEGER

iUniverse, Inc.
Bloomington

Island Fever
Life Adventures in Search of Island Paradise

iUniverse books may be ordered through booksellers or by contacting:

iUniverse
1663 Liberty Drive
Bloomington, IN 47403
www.iuniverse.com
1-800-Authors (1-800-288-4677)

Because of the dynamic nature of the Internet, any Web addresses or links contained in this book may have changed since publication and may no longer be valid. The views expressed in this work are solely those of the author and do not necessarily reflect the views of the publisher, and the publisher hereby disclaims any responsibility for them.

Any people depicted in stock imagery provided by Thinkstock are models, and such images are being used for illustrative purposes only.

Certain stock imagery © Thinkstock.

ISBN: 978-1-4502-8792-0 (pbk)
ISBN: 978-1-4502-8794-4 (cloth)
ISBN: 978-1-4502-8793-7 (ebk)

Printed in the United States of America

iUniverse rev. date: 4/14/2011

About the Author

 Charles Philip Pflueger (Charlie) was born in Miami, Florida on May 23, 1931 and attended Miami Senior High School, the University of Florida and graduated with a B.B.A. from the University of Miami in 1958.

He was proud to serve in the U.S. Air Force during the Korean War, after a stint in the Florida National Guard. Charlie was married twice and in his autobiography, 'Island Fever,' he takes us on life's journey through many exotic locations, for almost 80 years.

He has been heavily committed to Bahamian tourism for many years, having held positions of President of the Bahamas Out Island Promotion Board, Vice-President of the Bahamas Hotel Association, a Director of the Caribbean Hotel Association and Bahamas Hotelier of the Year 1991. In addition, he has been General Manager of one of the oldest out island hotels, Club Peace and Plenty on Great Exuma Island, for decades.

Charlie hopes 'Island Fever' is amusing and informative, although he advises it contains some mildly salacious adventures that might not be suitable for minors and the overly sensitive.

Mr. Pflueger spends his time between his seaside home on Great Exuma Island and Plantation, Florida.

Interested readers may contact the author at his email address: cpp42@hotmail. com

DEDICATION

The early part of this autobiography is dedicated to my Mother, who provided a happy childhood and shared my life well into her 90's.

The later part is dedicated to my dear friend Stan Benjamin, who made many wonderful adventures possible.

Premise

When you near your 80th birthday and you have anything to say ... you had better get it said! So........

'The time has come, the Walrus said, to talk of many things:

Of ships and shoes and sealing wax and cabbages and kings –

And why the sea is boiling hot, and whether pigs have wings'

Lewis Carroll
Alice in Wonderland
1865

Preface

Some people think their lives have been interesting and worthy of recording... others drudge in boredom and obscurity and never seem to really live. As I mentally flipped through the decades of jobs, travel, projects and life in general, I also came to the conclusion that it would be amusing and hopefully interesting to relive my many years managing an out island hotel in the Bahamas. That being decided, my thoughts ran amuck like stampeding mustangs and enveloped the premise of putting to paper events of my life from day one and lifes' lessons learned along the way. So be it and let the chips fall where they may!

I was blessed with a caring Mother that enjoyed growing up with me through my early years. In later life I had the good fortune, through no special thought or planning, to have three talented sons... Tom an Architect from Auburn University, now residing in Birmingham, Alabama; Paul the Orthopedic Surgeon from Tulane University, now residing in Prescott, Arizona; and Chris the Real Estate Manager from the University of Florida, with a masters from South Florida and now residing near Denver, Colorado. They are all educated... married with wonderful wives.... and two lovely children each. Obviously, I am proud of them, their accomplishments and their life style. Good fortune also smiled with three wonderful step-daughters and their familes who I cherish as my own.

As you will note in the book, I have enjoyed the company of various ladies over the years but only married twice to Joan Fraser of Montego Bay and later Jean Steder of Miami. I respect both and still enjoy a friendly relationship with fond memories of life's challenges, children, family, shared travels and adventures.

With a restless soul, the book follows my adventures from childhood to its near conclusion in the Bahamas Out Islands.... well past the Biblical allotment of 'Three Score and Ten'. Stops along the way include a U.S. Air Force hitch during the Korean War, a Station Manager stint with Pan American World Airways in the Caribbean and Latin American, a crack at the retail business with Sears, Roebuck and Company, real estate land development in Central Florida, adventures in Costa Rica, around the world travel and of course, hotel resort management in the Southern Bahamas.

Has my life been interesting? I think so... but it's for the readers to make up their own minds. Give it a try!

Charlie Pflueger
George Town, Exuma
Bahama Islands

Table of Contents

The Magic City

Weather reporting in the 20's was a little sketchy at best ... no satellites to pinpoint tropical disturbances and communications primitive, particularly from the islands, so little notice was given to the approaching black thunder clouds and sprinkling rain. As the wind increased, my Grandmother, with a mother's concern, took the children across the street to a neighbor's house, itself little more than a wooden shack set on concrete blocks, but offering more security than a canvas tent that had provided temporary shelter to the family since their arrival from Montana. Grandfather had rejected the idea of 'a little wind and rain' causing any problems and refused to join the family at the neighbor's across the street.

As the story unfolded, the infamous 1926 hurricane[**] roared over nearby Biscayne Bay hitting the Miami-Coconut Grove area like a battering ram with extremely high winds and blinding torrents

---

[*] Wikipedia reports that the 1926 Hurricane started on September 6 off the Cape Verde Islands and moved westward, lashing the Bahama Islands with winds clocked at 150 MPH (on a side note: this is one of only a couple hurricanes to hit Exuma in the 20th Century). On September 18th the hurricane came ashore between Coral Gables and South Miami rated a Category Four, with a 15' surge and an advanced warning by the National Weather Bureau of only a few hours. The passing 'eye' was of thirty-five minutes duration, creating a false impression that the storm was over.

1

of slashing rain. As the onslaught continued to gain strength, Grandmother crawled back across the street and dragged her husband, in his underwear, to the relative safety of the cottage, where the children were laying on the floor of a wildly shaking building. When the wind and rain finally subsided, the family loaded into the tile truck and drove to nearby Dinner Key on Biscayne Bay, eager to see the resulting storm damage to the bay front area. They were stunned by the massive devastation of buildings and score after score of sail and power boats scattered like toys all over the highway and hundreds of yards inland. Many of these battered hulks coming to rest against multi-million dollar mansions, reposing far back from the highway on higher land, as a testimony to the power of the storm's surge.

While marveling at the destruction of natures' fury, few of the sightseers paid any attention to the sudden increase of wind velocity until a hard, piercing rain began pelting the crowd, announcing the arrival of the second half of this catastrophic hurricane.....The storm's eye had passed! With the sudden realization that there was more to come, there was a mad dash back to the truck, stinging rain peppering those that couldn't fit in the cab, and a race back to the house before another onslaught.

With the wind at well over 100 MPH rotating from another quadrant, the rickety cottage blew off its block foundation and crashed to the ground. The frightened occupants narrowly escaped serious injury when the stump of a massive Australian Pine Tree under the house smashed through the flimsy wooden floor, knocking everyone off their feet, but effectively anchoring the building to the ground preventing a major catastrophy.

When the storm finally subsided, the family returned to their tent site to view what little was left of their canvas home. My Mother said they were astonished to see nothing but the main tent cross beam which had fallen and pinned my grandfather's pants to his broken cot along with his intact wallet. Welcome to Miami, Briggle family!

It wasn't long before the family found and purchased a suitably large house, solidly constructed of a local wood (Dade County pine) that resisted rot and termites, well located, and with a huge double garage Grandfather could use for his tile business. It was built in1912 and is still standing well into the 21ˢᵗ Century.

In 1931 the 'Magic City' of Miami, jewel of the Sunshine State, claimed only 175,000 sun-drenched, year around citizens, spread out over a vast area of bays, canals, beaches, Indian villages along the Miami River, horse and dog tracks, luxury beach hotels, and wealthy winter visitors. Miami was rapidly becoming a beacon for snowbirds seeking to escape the harsh northern winters in relative warmth and glitz of south Florida.

Near Eight Street (later famous as 'Little Havana's 'Calle Ocho') I was born at Riverside Hospital on a bright, Saturday morning on May 23ʳᵈ… only child of Philip Pflueger and Ethel (Doll) Mae Briggle Pflueger.

Philip Pflueger was one of the three sons of the Pfluegers' that emigrated from Hamburg, Germany, landing on Ellis Island in 1895, settling in Elizabeth, New Jersey. An enterprising man, Grandfather Pflueger soon opened a saloon and eatery and settled down to raise their family of three children… the eldest John, middle son Philip and the youngest Al.

When the United States entered the First World War, John enlisted in the army to join the raging European inferno, suffering a service ending gassing by the Kaiser and after a hospital stay returned to civilian life. In 1919, when Phil turned 18 he joined the Navy and spend a few years serving on a battleship, where he was a boxing champion. Meanwhile, Al left the cold confines of New Jersey for sunny south Florida, finding a job with a local fish taxidermist. Learning the taxidermist trade, Al and bride Louise set up their own business on Miami Avenue near the old Sears Biscayne Boulevard store on U.S. 1 and the McArthur Causeway, the first road leading to the south Miami Beach area.

Figuring that Al had something good going, John moved to Miami and went to work in the Al Pflueger Taxidermist business. As soon as Philip's navy hitch was up, he too beat a fast track to Miami and joined his brothers.

Philip Pflueger with Barracuda
at Al Pflueger Taxidermist plant 1935

With Miami rapidly becoming the winter playground of North America (lets not forget the vast numbers of Canadians that ritually headed south in the winter) and the proximity of the fish filled Gulf Stream, it's little wonder that Al Pflueger Taxidermist would soon become the largest marine taxidermist in the world, drawing business worldwide. In addition to becoming wealthy, Al became a respected expert, along with Dr. Rivera of the University of Miami, as final authorities on the classification of fish species. Upon his untimely death in 1962 from a stairway fall at his North Miami home, Al was honored by having a new species of Longbill Spearfish (Tetrapturus pfluegeri) he discovered, named after him.

While the above was playing out, my mother, her two brothers and two sisters were living in Great Falls, Montana, where their father owned and ran a tile business and a boat rental on the Missouri River. During the early 1900's Spanish Flu and other dreaded diseases ran roughshod throughout the medically deprived rural west, wiping out entire families. My Mother and her four siblings contracted a deadly diphtheria strain, which proved to be fatal to the oldest child, 16 year old Cecelia. My Mother always maintained that eating vast amounts of fresh, raw onions helped to keep the windpipes open on the remaining children and saved their lives.

Whatever the case, the death of Cecelia proved to be the last straw in a rugged life style of the early twenties in northern Montana. Devastated the family soon sold their assets and journeyed south to a booming Miami and to support the family, start one of the first ceramic tile installation companies in the area.

Upon arriving in the Promised Land, the first obstacle for the family of six was to find accommodations in a real estate mad south Florida. This difficulty was soon solved with the purchase of a plot of land near Coral Way and southwest 27th Avenue, where they erected two huge wall tents to provide at least temporary shelter. Life for the new arrivals seemed to be settling down with Grandfather finding ample tile jobs in an expanding economy. My Mother, now in her late teens, secured employment with Burdines Department Store in downtown Miami and the three younger children attended school. All seemed to going well when a little thing like the patter of a few drops of rain on the tent roof, was the harbinger of a major hurricane, as reported in the first few pages.

In 1929 romance blossomed and my father and mother, having met at a local dance, were married and I arrived a few years later.

In Miami the motion picture industry was all the rage in the 30's. The Great Depression was in full swing, creating a huge demand for inexpensive entertainment and Hollywood gave it to them, cranking out hundreds of movies a year to fill the seemly insatiable market. Many, of course, were 'A' pictures featuring well hyped big name studio stars (MGM publicized that their studio 'had more stars than were in the heavens'). Others were of the 'B' variety, cheaper and with lesser known players, such as one of my favorites, Charlie Chan the Chinese detective from Honolulu with his sidekick 'Number One' son (what kid could resist the shiver of dread when the villain delivered a fatal blow gun dart to the neck of his victim form behind heavy drapes). Other 'B' favorites were Boston Blackie and of course, the unending stream of cowboy movies staring Charles Starrett, Lash LaRue, Buck Jones (who unfortunately, died at he height of his career in the Copacabana fire in New York in 1941), Hopalong Cassidy, Gene Autry and lets not forget the 'King of the Cowboys,' Roy Rogers.

Saturday nights at Gram's house, which was happily located four blocks from the Tower Theater, meant all Saturday afternoon at the movies. From the age of seven, Gram and I would pack a lunch and head for the theater. My Mother did not send me empty handed, but with a carefully clutched quarter which Gram and I dutifully slipped into a Piggy Bank to grow until it reached the vast sum of $18.75 for the purchase of a $25 government bond. It was a great revelation to discover 'interest' and if you saved money someone would pay to borrow it....Wow! The concept of compound interest and dividends would come later.

Gram and I enjoyed these many golden days in the air conditioned theater where she paid for my 15 cent ticket and threw in a big 10 cent box of popcorn to boot....We always timed our arrival to catch the noon program which usually started with a cartoon, news of the world, a Three Stooge comedy short, a Buck Rogers or Flash Gordon serial and for the kids main attraction, a 'B' or cowboy movie. This line-up carried us through the popcorn and into the packed sandwiches, before the first of the weekend's adult 'A' film screenings came on, which of course, we felt obligated to attend. After some five hours in the theater, with the sun low in the sky, we would, on wobbly legs, stroll back to Grams with a satisfied feeling that we certainly received our money's worth.

Later, when I was a little older and Gram's legs couldn't make the walk, I went by myself, and many an evening I ran like the wind back home only a few steps ahead of Count Dracula… keeping an ear to the sky for the dreaded flutter of giant bat wings or the rasping breath of a howling Werewolf with flashing and snapping fangs, dripping an innocents blood! I didn't worry; however, about Frankenstein....I figured I could out run him! Golden days, indeed!

Kids like to swim and we were no exception. The closest water was one of the feeder canals leading to the Miami River near the Seminole Indian tourist exhibition encampment. The canal was reasonably clean and drew a daily crowd of local lads, splashing and horsing around. One frightful day I swallowed a large gulp of water and panicked, while swimming in the middle of the canal. I let out a horrific 'I'm drowning' scream which the kids on the bank found to be extremely funny and gave me a big laugh while I sputtered my last breath away. By some great chance or perhaps a guardian angel, my wildly flaying hand clutched the very end of a fallen Australian Pine Tree and was able to pull my limp, shaking body to the bank. I did not mention this episode to my mother, who almost lost her only child and who would probably not be amused. I promptly gave up swimming in the canal (good call), but later learned to swim well enough to spearfish offshore and avoid drowning.

During this time my dad worked for my Uncle Al at the taxidermist plant. In the height of the depression this proved to be a very good job paying him a reported $50 a week and the use of a pick-up truck. On Sundays, when the regular employees were enjoying a day off, Dad used to collect fish for mounting at the city's charter boat fleet headquarters at Bayfront Park's famous Pier Five. On many of these Sunday excursions, Dad would take me with him and while he talked with the captains, tagged the fish to be mounted, and loaded the truck, I would engage in some of South Florida's finest bottom fishing around the docks heavy pilings.

The captains were monetarily encouraged to talk the lucky (until he got the bill) fisherman in to mounting that huge trophy sailfish (or whatever) to commemorate the epic battle. Six months later, the proud fisherman hung the beautifully mounted fish on the living room wall, often to the consternation of a whining spouse who reluctantly had to remove her Aunt Sophie's Butterfly print to make room for the new addition. With married life being what it is, it usually wasn't long before the loving spouse swam his prize off the wall and onto a shelf in the garage to await the next garage sale or trash collection.

None the less, it was a good job for Dad and a lot of Sunday fun for a kid that could throw his line in bay waters churning with a feeding frenzy of Mangrove Snapper, dining on a multitude of bits and pieces of large, freshly cleaned fish... I caught my first Bonefish at the pier on a hand line one unforgettable afternoon... proud as any fisherman... with Dad and a few charter boat captains shouting a jumble of contradictory instructions to a deaf ear.

One evening while fooling around in the back yard, it seemed like a good idea to build a bonfire and boil some water in an old coffee can. This sound thinking carried right along to catching some grasshoppers and throwing them in the boiling water for the fun of watching them jump around. Unfortunately, a miss-step dumped the boiling water on the top of my right foot, providing third degree burns and numerous doctors' visits. Here was a lesson well learned... that cruelty to living things might soon bite you in the backside!

After school on most afternoons we could be found playing touch football on the street in front of my house. I usually proclaimed myself as 'captain' in virtue of owning the ball, scruffy as it might be from bouncing off the asphalt a zillion times. The traffic was light but added an extra element of skill to follow the odd Chevrolet over the chalked goal line, through a scattering defense. When five o'clock came, no matter the score, it was time to hang it up for the day and retire to the console radio in the living room and listen to 'I Love a Mystery'. This daily 15 minute serial adventure told the story of Jack, Doc and Reggie, solving mysteries and battling huge vampire bats in Mayan ruins in Central America! Other afternoon favorites were 'Hop Harrigan', some sort of a pilot, and 'Jack Armstrong, the All American Boy'.... all good stuff for kids.

Night time, after dinner, I did my homework, still in front of the radio tuned to my favorite station, WIOD, which stood for 'Wonderful Isle of Dreams,' according to their announcements, whispered over background music of 'Moon Over Miami.' I listened to the likes of Bob (whatever base he was visiting) Hope, Fibber Magee and Molly, Eddie Cantor, George Burns and Gracie Allen, and sometimes classical music, when Dad was listening, to the Firestone Hour. Radio was (and still is) a mystery to me, not to mention television which would not enter the picture (no pun here) to further boggle my mind until many years later.

The 1930s

I can't remember much of the early 30's ... just hanging around the house learning to walk, talk and use the potty... all useful things for later in life. Mrs. Mahoney, our landlady, gave me a miniature bible, which I just had to have and remained mostly unread, even when I learned to read. One thing I will always remember was dressing up in my 'Buck Roger's' suit complete with a deadly raygun, skulking around corners of my house hoping to get a clear shot at imagined aliens. All I got, however, was when Dad would come home from work and call out in a falsetto, "Yoo Hoo... Buck Rogers!" accompanied by a limp wristed wave. I laugh now ... but I remember how it used to send me into a rage... 'Yoo Hoo... Buck Rogers' your ass!

In the 20's Henry Flagler brought the Florida East Coast Railroad to Miami and on thru to Key West. To increase the availability of hotel rooms to support the railroad, he built the much hyped 'largest wooden hotel in the world' at Bayfront Park and the Miami River. This hotel was quite a famous attraction until one night in 1934 when it caught fire and burned to the ground. In my child's minds-eye, even though still little more than a toddler, I can still remember my father taking me down town to see one of the greatest bonfires in Florida history... lighting up the sky for miles around.

In 1936 we moved to a house on N.W. 6th street and around 14th avenue, just in time to watch the Roddy Burdine Stadium being built...day and night.... rivet by pounding rivet....The new steel stadium replaced the old wooden bleachers where Dad took me to watch the home games of the best football team in south Florida, the Miami High Stingarees... and the worst team, the University of Miami Hurricanes (on a side note: its mascot was the Ibis, a waterfowl, selected after the 1926 hurricane. Folklore said it was the last bird to leave an area before a hurricane and the first bird to return after it was gone).

The new stadium was soon named the 'Orange Bowl', and was home field to the Hurricanes until 2008 when it was demolished to make room for a new baseball stadium. The Orange Bowl was also the venue for the annual New Year's college game, before it moved to Dolphin Stadium, along with the 'U,' after the City of Miami failed in efforts to raise the necessary funds to refurbish this tired old lady.

In 1938 we moved a mile or so to the west into a nice 3 bedroom stucco home my Grandfather gave to my Mother, where from our front porch, I could hear the loudspeakers at the Orange Bowl. Many a night the neighborhood kids and I would walk the four blocks to the stadium, slip through a small orange grove at the east end zone and sneak in over a fence. Other nights we could wait until the half when they left the gates unmanned and enjoy the second half in seats of our choice. A great second half was not always in the cards but 'free' was good. One night in the stands, I learned a valuable lesson when one of the smart-ass fans put a quarter on a piece of ice cream vendors discarded dry ice and offered it to me if I would pick it up... I wanted the money, but my keen intellect decided that burned fingers was too high a price to pay... not so for my school chum, Oliver, who also wanted the quarter, and with a smirk, quickly picked up the coin and flipped it rapidly from hand to hand until it warmed to the air, at which time it disappeared into his pocket. I guess I didn't want it as badly (nor was as calculating) as Oliver!

As the 30's moved along, I got a little bigger and settled into a pleasant home-school life until just before Christmas 1941 when something happened that even a 10 year old kid could understand as a world altering event. The family huddled around a huge radio console to listen to President Roosevelt proclaim a "state of war with the Empire of Japan!" Being a budding humanitarian, the first thing I asked was "does this mean I won't get any presents for Christmas?" So much for my social sensibilities. I guess my motto was to look out for 'Number One'!

It wasn't long before my maternal uncle, Frank, Jr. went back into the navy (his pre-war hitch was on the Battleship Arizona sunk at Pearl Harbor). He was later seriously injured in the South Pacific from a snapped, recoiling towing cable resulting in many months in the hospital, a medical discharge and a life long disability pension. My other maternal uncle, Vernon a first class tile setter, joined the SeaBees, a construction arm of the navy, building airfields across the Pacific Islands. He made it through the war unscathed, but died of a heart attack at the V.A. Hospital in Coral Gables, when he was only 54 years old.

Before television, my favorite leisure activity, after sports and listening to the radio, was reading. On Saturday mornings I would take the bus to downtown Miami and browse a few used book stores for a treasure like the Hardy Boys Detective series. There were over 30 novels in the series, full of mystery and adventure and what a thrill when I would discover an un-read title. I would savor the moment, then march up to the cashier and plunk down .50 cents like I was buying some exotic diamond. Ah! On the rare day when I found two novels (even if one of them was a Nancy Drew – Girl Detective, who, in her defense, had mind-boggling and dangerous adventures of her own) I felt like I had won the Irish Sweepstakes (no Lotto in those days). I later gave the collection to my cousin, who I hope enjoyed them as much as I did.

When I was nine, Mom sent me to summer camp in the North Carolina Mountains. I was miserably lonesome and wrote daily imploring her to come and get me. I recently found a few of the tear stained letters she kept all these years and relived the twinge of homesickness. She and my Aunt had planned to drive to Wisconsin to visit friends, picking me up on the way back, but my whining letters gave her a guilty conscience and they stopped on the way up to take me with them. By the time they arrived, I had already adjusted to camp life, making new friends and was busy fishing in the lake as they pulled up. I would have just as soon stayed another couple of weeks at camp until their return trip, but after all the moaning and groaning, I had to put on my 'thank God, you're here to get me' face and headed to Wisconsin, while waving a sad farewell to my fellow campers. I learned to be careful what you wish for!

The Fabulous Forties

As 1942 got underway and we were at war, my Mother feeling her patriotic juices flow, joined the 'McAllister Volunteers,' a quasi-military medical support group in the Miami area. Meetings were held once a week in the park, where various simulated injuries were administered, first aid practiced and procedures polished., along with a bit of marching and passing of the colors. It was not so far fetched to prepare for an enemy attack, in light of oil smoke almost daily billowing high in the tropical sky from sinking Allied cargo ships torpedoed by the ferocious U-Boat wolfpacks that plied the nearby Gulf Stream off South Beach.

McAllister Volunteers,
Charlie between flags, Mother far right

Attending the weekly meetings with my Mother put me in a position to volunteer as 'cannon fodder,' where I dripped ketchup from serious simulated head wounds and mangled limbs. I think that wearing a uniform was my main motivation, since I had little or no knowledge of first or any other kind of aid (except maybe Kool-Aid). I did, however, consider myself a first class casualty, flag barer and un-official mascot of the troop.

This activity went well until the weather forecasters predicted a possible hurricane direct hit, trigging a call-out of the Volunteers to man various area hospital emergency rooms. Since children were not encouraged to accompany a parent trooper to the hospital, Mom took me to the Commander's place of business, which turned out to be a funeral home. I blanched at this unhappy revelation, accompanied by the sweet scent of copious amounts of flowers (a popular 'dearly departed', I mused) surrounding a mahogany casket (hopefully empty), perhaps for a funeral postponed as a result of the impending storm..

When my Mother tried to seat me in a pew with a blanket and a pillow, I had had quite enough and when she turned to retreat back up the aisle, I was right behind her, wailing at the top of my lungs. As daylight broke over dark and windy skies, I was well ensconced in a comfortable bed on the hospital's fourth floor, enjoying a delicious (ok, I know its hospital food but I was starved by that time) breakfast in bed... the darling of all the attending nurses. I decided I could handle disaster like this any time.

A Scout is trustworthy, friendly, courteous, kind, etc., or so one of my young friends told me and I thought it described me to a tee! Joining the Boy Scouts of America sounded like a splendid plan (I was at the age that I would have joined the 'Blackshirts'), so I promptly signed up. I was assigned to the Sea Gull Patrol (disappointingly not the Tigers, Lions or even Bears... but Sea Gulls?) and a finer bunch of misfits and malcontents would be hard to find. Even now it boggles my mind, but I must admit I had the time of my young life playing 'Capture the Flag' every Thursday night and camping in pup tents in the bush (in areas long since urbanized).

A few of the Sea Gull denizens are still close friends well into the final chapter of life. I reflect how lucky we were to grow up in South Florida before it sprawled out of control, and marvel on how wonderful a place it was for kids to spread their wings. In those days we could camp at Haulover Beach and Sunny Isles, or sneak over to exotic Key Biscayne being developed from a coconut plantation to a park (Crandon). The war delayed, unopened causeway and bridges provided access to enable us to sample some of the finest bay fishing and shrimp netting anywhere. Sometimes it was a little dicey while carefully edging out along the wooden bridge fenders, fighting a fish, as torrents of water rushed in from the ocean to the bay... and in the dark... where a slip or miss-step would spell disaster or at least a serious swim. As an adult, I marvel at what we got away with.

While scouting occupied much of my youthful free time, going to Miami Senior High in my sophomore year proved to be the end of my 'boy' scouting and the beginning of 'man' scouting. In 1946 Miami Senior High School was thought to be one of the best schools in the south: college prep in scholastics and state champions in football and basketball. In 1947 we played the champions of Atlanta, Joe Brown High, in football at our Orange Bowl home field and won 48 to 14. We also played the champions of Pennsylvania in the annual post season Kiwanis game and nailed the coalminers 34 to 14. Many college stars emerged from the Miami 'Stingaree' teams, such as Army's Arnold Tucker, Navy's Pete Williams, University of Miami's and Chicago Bears tight end Jim Dooley (later head coach) among many others. Miami Senior also produced U.S. Senators, Governors and high powered men of business and the arts, and shamefully, an assortment of swindlers, con men and world class drug runners. So....the school was good, the girls pretty and the new found social life boggling for a well groomed and mannered tenth grader who had been voted 'Best

Dressed' in junior high school. I can't remember what I wore that made me the best dressed, but maybe it was because the other kids dressed like slobs and I was one step up... thanks to a caring Mother, rather than a keen personal sense of sartorial splendor. I stepped up the accolades and was voted 'Best Looking' in my graduating class from Miami High in February 1949. It was never proven the committee vote was rigged!

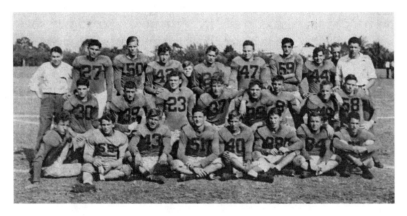

Miami Senior High intramural, Charlie #40, 1947

A neighbor and school buddy of mine, Bob Woodrich, well over 6' tall and something like 220 pounds confided in me that he was going out for the football team (he later played for Florida State), an idea that appealed to me even at 5' 11" and 145 pounds. So with false courage, I asked one of the assistant coaches if I could come out for the first year junior varsity or 'B' team. Apparently the coach was happy enough to have some additional cannon fodder and assured me that I would be most welcome. This was the introduction to the life of a third string high school would be jock, who eventually got a front tooth pushed in (no sissy mouthpieces nor face guards in those halcyon days), a vertebra knocked out of place stopping a leaping linebacker's right foot which caused my Mother to almost faint as teammates carried me home, dragging one leg.... and the final blow in practice when another linebacker gave me a helmet shot to the upper body, dislocating my right shoulder. This injury proved to be the finish of an improbable athletic career, rendering it painfully difficult to raise my right arm to match the left when delivering a block, allowing the opponent to slip off the right side. The line coach thought I was 'dogging' it and lined the team up for head-on blocking and kept them coming for the better part of twenty minutes until I could only get to my knees to receive the next onslaught. I really took a beating that afternoon which prompted me to advise the coach (it might have been more prudent to advise him BEFORE the drill) that I was unable to raise my right arm to hold a block. After a second's thought his response was, "put a little liniment on it!" No coddling of athletes here!

Early in my sophomore year I was hot for a girl named Marie, who lived a few miles from me and near my best friend from the Boy Scouts, Charlie Callahan. In those days their neighborhood was rural with truck farms and open pasture within blocks of their homes. A classy neighborhood it was not, sporting a three story house close by, where one night I was talking to detectives that apparently had the house under surveillance.

"Move along, kid," one growled. "We're going to get the goods on them tonight!" He also mentioned something like 'swooping down on the unsuspecting johns and their ladies of the evening!' I figured whatever John and his lady friends were doing; it was not going to be an enjoyable night! But I digress... one Saturday night Charlie and I set up a pup tent not too far from his house for an over night in the bush. We amused ourselves with my bb gun shooting (actually 'trying' to shoot as we rarely hit anything) swooping Nightlarks. During a lull in the action to re-load, Charlie had one of his better ideas when he offered, "if I can use your gun I'll ride my bike over to Marie's house and bring her back!" This sounded like an idea whose time had come, although I was not 100 percent sure what I was going to do with her when she got here.

In a short time he arrived with my current crush on his handlebars and claimed his reward of unlimited use of my air rifle (like winning the lottery to a 14 year old kid). Marie was not against joining me in the tent where we fumbled around for awhile before finally figuring out what part goes where and for how long (although that was not an exact science at this state of the game... or any other time for that matter), The good news was that with great relief and joy I had joined the ranks of ex-virgins and now had the right to brag and exaggerate my exploits to my cronies (only partially kidding). The bad news of this scenario was that Charlie shot up all my bb's ... an early lesson that nothing is free!

As high school progressed, I joined an unsanctioned athletic fraternity (described by school officials as 'an illegal social club') called the 'Gremlins'. Hazing and stupid pranks were the order of the day... one popular prank was the 'bare mile', where pledges were required to report to the school track at nine o'clock on a dark night, stripped of all clothing and present their private parts for a liberal dash of Sloan's Liniment generously applied to the scrotum (reminds me of the song 'baby light that fire!'). Once properly prepared, we were encouraged by members wielding belts to the backside, on a four lap run around the track. While the sniveling pledges were occupied with the exertion of the dash, a burning groin from the Sloan's and trying to dodge slashing belts, a few of the members, under the cloak of the aforementioned darkness, were busy tying up the discarded clothing and shoes into a giant bundle of confusion. As the 'mile' ended, the members shouted "scatter...here come the police!" Apparently watching the mad scramble of the exhausted, pain crazed pledges trying to find their clothes and shoes from the jumbled pile, in the dark, before the imagined arrival of the paddy wagon, amused the twisted sensibilities of the membership.

Other idiotic foolishness included a group of pledges I goose-stepped (with a dandy Nazi salute that would make the recently deceased Furher proud) across the cafeteria patio during lunch recess. My heart skipped a beat when I spotted the very strict study hall teacher glaring down from the second floor balcony (I assumed that a bunch of Nazi Bund members goose-stepping across the patio would not find much favor in her book), but relaxed when her myopic eye sight misinterpreted our nonsense as a friendly and affectionate wave from her beloved students, which was returned with relish.

My all time favorite was 'hell night' the last humiliation before acceptance as members of the Gremlins. Taken to the edge of the everglades on a cold night, stripped, blindfolded, garbage pelted, given a 'golden shower' (the warmth actually felt good), and culminating with a long walk home... a final entrance 'fee' to the school's 'in group'. God, it was fun!

During all this activity, girls were not ignored. We went to the usual sock hops, beach and house parties, the usual run of sports events and school functions. By the eleventh grade, most of us had a steady girl friend that we were sleeping with (or more likely, hoping to sleep with)....changing partners on occasion, with the usual anguish, gnashing of teeth and heartbreak. Contrary to popular belief, I can't recall any known pregnancies, alcohol or drug use at Miami High in those days, in fact my first beer was at the University of Florida campus a few years later.

During my junior year in high school, a few of my closest friends pondered the lure of joining the University of Miami branch of the Florida National Guard's 211 Infantry. What a wonderful idea... getting into uniform (shades of the McAllister Volunteers), drilling once a week, field-stripping M-1 rifles and re-assembling blindfolded... spending two weeks in the summer at Ft. Fort Jackson, South Carolina's infantry school... running through the bushes blasting away with real guns and... get this.... actually getting paid for it! This proved to be stupidity at its worst.

Our first two week 'paid vacation' to Ft. Jackson started well with a fun train ride from South Florida to Columbia, South Carolina, with lots of singing and the usual horseplay young guys in a group seem unable to resist.

Charlie middle of back row,
211th Infantry Florida National Guard 1948

Once on the base, we were kept busy doing a few overnight marches, sleeping in pup tents in heavy bush, going to the firing range and blasting away with the M-1, the main infantry rifle, the smaller carbine, and the Browning automatic rifle, until the barrels were red hot. The rush of hitting a 'bulls-eye' and the shame of getting 'Maggie's Drawers', a red flag waved by the pit crew when you miss the entire target. My favorite was the skirmish line where our platoon would space ourselves across the field in a skirmish line... walking fast, while firing as rapidly as possible at pop-up targets. This was one exercise that it did not pay to lead the pack unless you enjoyed the sound of bullets whizzing past your ears fired by 17 and 18 year old kids. Parrish the thought!

My most bizarre and exciting night started with our company taking positions along a ridge overlooking a saw grass meadow. Our commander selected me as the advance scout to man a foxhole a few hundred yards away in the meadow, to prevent a surprise attack by the 'Aggressor' force manned by regular army troops. I was well ensconced in the foxhole with walkie-talkie in hand, peering into the dark night for any sign of oncoming enemy ....half adrenalin rush and half scared... I missed the advancement of the Aggressor scout who silently moved with the periodic rustle of the saw grass in the breeze. The first time I became aware of the situation, I was facing the muzzle of a carbine and listening to the chilling words, "you're captured!".

Somewhat embarrassed, I reacted quickly enough to throw the field phone into the bush. As the Aggressor fumbled around trying to find the phone in the darkness, madness must have come over me as I leaped on his back and was treated to a hell of a flogging clinic! As it turned out, he was a very seasoned karate and judo instructor who had little problem throwing me all over the saw grass field. Finally, bleeding from numerous grass cuts, full of sweat caked sand and with quivering lip (actually, I think I might have called out for my Mama) I gave up to fight (or more likely hide) another day.

With me in tow and a full troop of the enemy that had moved up while I was getting thrashed, we continued to moved up the ridge where shouts of our secret (apparently, not anymore) password and countersign, 'Thunder and Lightening' and 'the games are over,' brought most of our gallant defenders out of their positions and on their way to a field prison camp. One of the lessons I learned here was not to jump a martial arts expert, bigger than you and in the dark... Surrendering at the drop of a hat seems like a wiser decision.

My busy schedule allowed just enough time to pass all of my subjects and soon it was time to attend graduation from high school. Reflecting ... I had a great time in school, but was ready for the excitement of adult challenges. On graduation night, a bunch of us headed to South Beach, blankets in hand, with roaring fire, for an all night session to celebrate our right of passage! Alas, around 1:30 AM with visions of our nice, comfortable beds, we said to hell with it and headed home... so much for our grand gesture!

It was a pleasant summer in 1949, filled with beach outings, lazing around, meeting classmates in front of Burdines Department Store on Saturday mornings, movies, fishing and living the good life. Ah yes... life was good until my girl friend's father offered me a job as a 'printers devil' in his printing shop. Mopping up gobs of ink from the nooks and crannies of printing machines did not seem fitting for a recent high school graduate (you would think I had graduated from Harvard with a PhD), not to mention it was damn hard work. A few months into this fiasco my mother advised that a letter had arrived from the University of Florida, the state's premiere school, accepting my application for the fall semester. Since I did not recall (in those days there was no qualifying test and graduates from approved state high schools were automatically accepted) actually applying, I was numb with shock. I was further stunned with the seriousness of the situation when Mom handed me a Greyhound Bus ticket with my name on it and a destination of 'Gainesville, Florida' in bold letters. What about my budding printing career, I asked, stretching a bit, hoping to defuse this nasty turn of events.

"Stop the nonsense" she snorted, handing me a packet of school documents (looking ahead to the possibility that I might need to sleep somewhere and have an occasional meal). We suppressed a sniffle or two, and this stout lad boarded the 'Hound' and was off to seek the bounty of higher education in 'Gatorland!'

With the war years in the not distant past, hordes of ex-G.I. students poured into the nations' universities to reclaim stolen college delights (if not to seek higher education for career advancement and personal satisfaction). This influx, along with the normal recent high school graduates, put a strain on all facets of the university life, including utilization of alternate freshmen housing. My first dorm room was twenty minutes down the highway toward Jacksonville, in an abandoned army barracks. It was not terribly convenient bussing back and forth to classes, but before long enough would-be students flunked out or in the case of some of the older veterans, decided college was better left to the younger students and went in pursuit of more adult activities, i.e....getting a real job and marriage, thereby releasing a number of campus dorms where one could cop a quick afternoon nap without a long bus ride.

This first year at Florida was filled with new things, such as going to my first fraternity rush, where I drank an improbable five beers (my first). About half way through the evening, a few of the 'brothers' decided it was time to serenade some of the favorite sorority houses that were deemed to be in dire need of our musical talents. So, arm in arm, we climbed into cars and with other like minded drunks, proceeded to grace the ladies with a few slobbering, but stirring fraternity songs (which I faked). It usually took only a minute or so for the girls to get out of bed, put their robes on and turn out on the balconies to wave and applaud encouragement. This was usually short lived when an alert (or music loving) house mother would appear and nip it in the bud with threats of campus police intervention, a thought not well received by the ensemble of inebriated louts. Not withstanding a scuffed up lawn, no serious damage was done and panty raids were some time in the future.

I decided to pledge a fraternity, which did not turn out to be an enjoyable activity, requiring the wearing of a Florida 'rat cap' .... a kind of freshman's baseball cap, attending meetings, getting whacked on the ass with a paddle for imagined infractions, constant pranks, feuds with other frats, social functions and late night weekend boozing behind the frat house (the last two items were tolerable).

One night, during a round of drinking, some of the booze besotted members burned the outside patio bar to the ground, accompanied by rousing college songs. The local fire department did not seem too happy, which translated to a stern warning by school officials suggesting that the next incident would require a relocation of accommodations as the house would certainly be kicked off the campus. Fortunately, the next caper must not have qualified as an 'incident' when a few of the members, imbibing a few cool ones, decided that a 'drink on the house' could be taken literally and proceeded to climb out of the top floor windows and onto the sloping roof with accompanying idiotic giggles, while waving to amazed passer-bys! High spirited lads... all!

Some of the anticipated highlights of the school year was the annual 'Gator Growl', held at Florida Field for students and supporters, featuring funny skits, music and well known, paid comics and entertainers. The Fall and Spring Frolics also offered nationally known dance bands such as Harry James, Clyde McCoy, Wayne King the 'Waltz King', and Charlie Spivack, to name a few. This was a good excuse to invite your hometown girl to Gainesville and party the weekend away, hoping to get a little sex for your trouble. Finding a decent looking and friendly (i.e., wiling to sleep with you) girl on campus was a long-shot at best, since Florida only recently converted from an all boys school to co-ed. Florida State in Tallahassee also recently went from an all girls school to a co-ed one. Unfortunately, it takes time to fully integrate, so when I attended Florida most of the student population was male and most of the good looking girls were attending Florida State. This brought home the old adage that 'life is not fair!'

Disaster struck after Spring Frolics my freshmen year, when I invited my hometown love, Donna Lea to come to Gainesville for the party weekend. She hitched a ride with a girl friend that was driving up. As fate would have it, a slightly older, ex-army fellow accompanied them and Donna fell in love with him, resulting in a 'Dear John' (read 'Dear Charlie') letter, sadly, not my last, and a thoroughly crushed heart as only a first love can deliver. A sad tale, indeed!

Donna Lea Post and Charlie Pflueger, Military Ball University of Florida 1949

While I usually maintained decent grades in high school, I had never been mistaken for a scholar. Excuses included a very active social life, athletic demands and my favorite, a lazy streak... all partially offset by a decent I.Q. Nothing changed at the university level, except a more difficult curriculum and no football, leaving only an active social life and a lazy streak to shore up the 'poor grade excuse folio' for my less than sterling academic results. Racking my brain, I threw in the demanding 'keeping up with the domestic requirements of eating, laundry and such' that faces a young fellow away from the conveniences of home for the first time.

I was cheered when at the end of my disappointing first year, one of my room mates invited two of us to spend a few days at his father's citrus grove in Kissimmee on our way to Miami. He promised the opportunity to go on a wild boar hunt before heading home. In the days before Disney World and its purchase of thousands of rural acres of land, the area was noted for its orange groves and its rednecks living in shacks with wild boar skulls decorating almost every fence post, wearing bib overalls and topped off by the nice touch of a wild turkey feather protruding from their jaunty caps.

Perhaps you can imagine cartoon like hillbillies running through the thick bush, hooping, hollering, and guzzling home made 'white lightening' from mason jars and shooting pistols into a full mooned sky.....Well, around Kissimmee in those days, it wasn't Fantasyland.... it was really life in the slow lane.

After a quick unpacking, the three room mates loaded an old, flea-bitten hound in the back of the pickup truck and drove winding dirt roads to rendezvous with a half dozen locals (as described above) with a couple hounds per man, howling and snapping at each other.... keen to get the 'catch a wild boar' show on the road. A stiff slug of 'lightening' was prescribed for all....my slug burned a new trough as it made its fiery way to my stomach. With the unsnapping of the leashes, the howling pack of 'hounds from hell' tore off into the bush, followed by the hunters with the three students bringing up the rear (after calculating the odds, I thought that chances of not getting shot, bitten or gored was better if not too closely associated with the hounds snapping teeth, muzzle blasts from the heavy artillery being generously applied into the powder laden air, or the razor sharp tusks of a, so far, invisible,vicious wild boar).

From time to time, some of the hounds would corner something and bay and howl until we raced after them, hearts pumping like a jackhammer, expecting to see a blood-shot eyed monster boar, snorting fire (the vision probably augmented by the 'lightening' we consumed) and froth from its nose, while pawing the ground like some crazed bull. Actually what we really saw was some wretched possum hanging from a tree branch or lying on the ground in a fake death like pose. The hounds granted no reprieves, leaping on the poor animals as they were blasted out of the trees or caught on the ground, fighting each other to see which one could tear it to pieces first. This 'sport' paled in a hurry with the college boys and after a few hours with no boar in sight we begged off 'one for the road' and headed back through the groves toward the house.

Suddenly, as we slowed through my friend's grove, the dog leaped out of the truck and raced to tree a huge raccoon in a tall grapefruit tree. Since we had no pistol and wouldn't have used it anyway, we threw large pieces of wooden limb supports to dislodge the poor beast. To this day, I don't know why we felt compelled to assist the dog in having a go at the coon, as the evening had already been a little stomach wrenching. On one toss, the outraged daddy coon lost his perch and came down, wildly flaying, on one side and the 2X4 on the other with me in the middle. Barely escaping having to wear a 'coon-skin cap' with the coon still in it, I watched the terrified coon scamper into the thick swamp boarding the grove, one step ahead of the snapping dog and disappearing into the thick trees. The howling became fainter as the antagonists moved deeper into the swamp. Our host suggested that we might as well retire as the smart old raccoon will lull the hound into believing he has his prey treed, as he skips tree to tree. Eventually, the hound will give up and go home, tail between his legs. Maybe if there is a moral to this saga, it might be a smart, old coon doesn't have to learn new tricks since the old tricks were working just fine!

Off to War

I arrived home from school that summer of 1950 to the reality of the Korean War and a step-up of National Guard activities. A new urgency permeated our up and coming two week trip to Ft. Jackson. Was there a chance that playing soldier might result in being a real soldier in a shooting war? As a sergeant in the Florida Guard infantry it sure as hell was looking that way with the specter of winding up in the trenches with a group of semi-literate nitwits. The thought of becoming a 'real' soldier had questionable appeal and not nearly as attractive as when it was 'just for fun.' With a war on, it was small wonder our two week training period was packed with all phases of an infantryman's responsibilities and a new dedication was quickly evident.

Returning from camp, pal Marshall Nembach and I decided to take a couple weeks vacation before enrolling at the University of Miami, having opted to continue school at home under the current clouds of war. Marshall's parents and sister had moved to Atlanta a year or so before and invited us to visit them before we were due to attend the fall semester. Realizing that the possibility of this being our last chance to take a break, along with Marshalls' need to pick up his car and three weeks to fritter away before the fall semester, had us jumping at the opportunity.

The plan had one serious flaw, we needed a car to drive the 600 miles to Atlanta and in 1950, decent cars were expensive for a couple of school kids. A quick visit to a used car lot on southwest eight street, we asked a salesman what he had available that would run and was cheap? He thought for a moment then said through his dangling toothpick, "Got a nice one for you boys. It runs like a dream and is very affordable." He was probably thinking 'that at last I'm going to unload this old bucket of bolts on a couple of rube kids,' as he pointed to a 1936 Chrysler Airflow four door sedan.

We thought it looked beautiful, sporting a sheet metal roof instead of its original canvas of some 15 years ago and with a radio that actually worked. "Get in and see how well it runs", he suggested. A quick run around the block disclosed a slightly rough engine, but we were in love with it and reached deep in our wallets to drag out the full price of $30. It actually ran well enough to proudly motor to my house, where we filled the radiator with water and topped off the engine oil, to see what might leak first in the next few days before our departure.

One glaring obstacle to our euphoria and an affront to our finely tuned artistic temperment was the drab paint job. After a trip to Western Auto where we selected a couple cans of pea green car paint (we couldn't figure out how this great color was heavily discounted), we hand brushed it on. Outstanding, was our conclusion and with no leaks we were ready to roll. In love with our car...yes... but not being complete idiots (the jury was still out on that one), we packed light and planned to abandon the vehicle and hitchhike the rest of the way in the event it faltered enroute. No fools here!

To our surprise, the engine, while not hitting on all cylinders until we reached Jacksonville, settled down and purred the rest of the way. We rolled into Atlanta, like fat cats with the radio blaring, where we sold the Chrysler for $50 to some lucky guy (?) that lived near Marshall's Dad. You can't say that we don't know how to make a big buck!

Marshall and I took one of the couple dozen tourist cabins (as they called the motels in the South) and settled down to make ourselves useful by replacing the vacationing night clerk, sometimes keeping the 'Vacant' sign lit late into the night. In a quick orientation, Mr. Nembach, partly in deference to Marshall's impressionable 15 year old sister, instructed us with, "we don't want to rent to the 'quickie' trade from the nearby army base. This is a respectable family oriented establishment!"

"Parish the though," we chimed, "that we would even consider a despicable act like that." (I thought I could feel my nose getting longer). .

That very night, when the family was fast asleep, including of course, the adolescent sister, we rented the most remote cottage to a lipstick besmirched soldier with a young beauty draped around his neck. Ignoring a base sticker on the windshield, we quickly concluded that the customer was a legitimate tourist driving thru and thus felt no betrayal of trust. Since the customer left after an hour, we had plenty of time to clean the room and still get a good night's sleep. For the rest of our stay we did a 'land office' late night 'tourist' business, making enough to finance our vacation after splitting with the company.... If Mr. Nembach wondered how we managed to rent rooms late almost every night, I guess he chalked it up to our dedicated work ethic and a good tourist season... or maybe it was hard to complain when you're counting all the extra money.

The Korean War was building in intensity, and with the Fall semester at Miami looming, we packed Marshall's car and took our leave. It's been a long time, but I think we shed a tear as we left our lucrative 'mid-night express' business. The '34 Chevy coupe ran well and sported a pull -open 'rumble seat' in the rear, where passengers could enjoy fresh wind in their faces (along with having to pick bugs out of their teeth). It was slow going in the days before super highways, but it did allow time to enjoy the scenery and get a peek at every crummy little town between Atlanta and Miami.

Back at home in Miami, I immediately contacted my girlfriend who worked as a legal secretary for my National Guard Company Commander. Actually, I was interested in a little feminine companionship, but instead received some disappointing, if not shocking, news that my unit, the 211th Infantry, was on alert for a possible deployment to the Far East. Rats! It looked like my fat was in the fire. As a college student, I would probably be able to get a educational deferment from the draft, but the 'catch 22' was my commitment in the Guard. Marshall and another pal, Bob Castleberry and I got our nerves under control with a bottle of the cheapest wine available.... Thunderbird ... and tried to come up with an alternate plan to what possibly be a short career in a shooting war in Asia. One attractive solution, rejected after a lengthy discussion, was booking an extended fishing trip to Canada.

After filtering through the alternatives, we came to the conclusion that although we abhorred the idea of our fine, young bodies peppered with Korean bullet holes, we couldn't evade service to our country. This epiphany lead us down a trail of reason to the conclusion that we needed to join a branch of the service that held minimum danger like the Navy or the Air Force (the Coast Guard never came up). I mentioned that I had little appeal for the bell bottom sailor suits with neckerchief and round hats, so the Navy was out. Obviously, the Marines were in the same dangerous frying pan along with the Army... that left the Air Force by default.

After reading the comic strip,' Smiling Jack' and listen to the radio serial, 'Hop Harrigan,' planes had some sizzle in my book. Being a member of a flight crew with fur lined flying jackets and aviator sun glasses grabbed my imagination.... so after much gnashing of teeth and soul searching we came to the conclusion that joining the U.S. Air Force was the thing to do. By mid-December we had taken physicals (no luck here, we all passed), was sworn-in, and scheduled to take a train from Miami to Lackland Air Force Base near San Antonio, Texas on January 3, 1951.

I spent the evening before departure at home with my Mother, trying to soothe her tears of anguish, peppered with an occasional sob or two of my own.

On a cold early January day, we boarded one of the Pullman cars for our three day journey to San Antonio. We were assigned sleeper compartments, making our trip out comfortable, except for Bob, who after a few hours of booze in the club car chatting up a very pretty young lady, enticed her to join him in whiling away each night in his compartment. I admit, I was envious and pouted away the time bemoaning my fate and wishing I was somewhere else (maybe fishing in Canada?).

The conductor rousted us out of a warm bed in time to dress, grab out bags and disembark the train at an uncivilized hour of 1:00 AM. The cold night got colder when we boarded open army trucks and sped thru town to the base. Directly upon arrival, we were ushered into the mess hall where a waiting breakfast of powdered, greenish scrambled eggs, hot lumpy oatmeal, and the universal military 'piece de resistance'- hamburger in gravy, fondly known by generations servicemen as 'shit on the shingle,' was offered. Our first dining experience registered about 2 on a scale of 10, which we thought was as low as it gets. This rapidly changed when we reached our living quarters which were quickly exposed as 16 man wall tents, with one pot bellied wood burning stove, military issue folding cots and boasting one blanket, a thin pillow and one mattress cover, sans the mattress. Our mythical accommodation satisfaction indicator quickly made the breakfast chow look good... as it plunged out of sight.

While some of the massive numbers of incoming airman (most were avoiding the army draft) were housed in regular barracks, the rest of us had to suffer through the on and off zero Texas temperatures. On one occasion the temperature dipped to an attention grabbing eight degrees, freezing the fire fighting water barrels and motivating the various denizens of 'Tentville' into monumental battles as firewood was pushed off the back of trucks a couple times a day. Melees between tent gangs got ugly in competition for all the wood they could snatch in a desperate quest to keep a canvas tent warm enough to keep from freeing to death.

Little organization seemed present in the early days of mobilization. Most days were under utilized and spent just hanging around. Close order drills were dialed up when things really dragged. Slipping away to the Post Exchange to drink a beer and try to warm up was a popular.pursuit. Bob and I spent as much time as we could at the PX, trying to warm up and survive head colds. This activity earned us the nick-name of the 'Vicks Twins,' as we shared a big jar of the Vapor Rub. We credited the salve with saving our live… since going to the clinic seemed a poor option in that chaotic environment and a sure way to have to repeat the training.

One of the few bright spots in this miserable existence was my portable radio. It's batteries were carefully conserved for use every Saturday night, when we all huddled around listening to the national top ten songs on 'Your Hit Parade' with Frank Sinatra. Talk about being desperate for a little entertainment!

We endured week after week of sitting in an open- fronted latrine (often with icicles hanging from the sloping roof) using letters from home for toilet paper (girlfriend, keep those letters to your lonely airman coming!), eating slop in the chow hall, and the occasional march to the firing range to shoot a few clips. One of the favorites was to rouse out the troops in the early morning cold (2:00 AM was popular) to march a mile or two to the hospital for a chest x-ray and back to the tent by 5:00 AM, in time to fall out for morning calisthenics… a nice touch! Another time we did an early morning march back to the hospital for a blood test (with the faint of heart less than bravely responding to the sight of a needle… by sliding down the wall in a dead faint).

Finally after 7 weeks of a 13 week boot camp, the 'powers that be' came to the conclusion that they needed to shrink the ranks as rapidly as possible, as the program, not to mention the rampaging flu and assorted maladies laying waste to the troops, was suffering serious overcrowding problems. Tech school assignments were accelerated and much to my pleasure, I received notice that I was selected to become an Airborne Radio Operator, since my near-sightedness precluded pilot training. Normally, the radio operators school is located at Kessler Air Force Base in Mississippi but due to over crowding, I was assigned to the Signal Corps School at Ft. Mommouth, New Jersey. You will soon see why this was quite a blessing in disguise.

It was cold in New Jersey in late February, but moving into a real, well heated barracks was a big upgrade in living accommodations from the previous tent-city fiasco. A first peek at television in the recreation room was gripping! When I left Miami in early January television had not yet arrived. A quick look around the area confirmed that this part of Jersey had an abundance of natural beauty, if presently marred by the usual winter vistas, including my first snow fall (the only snow in Miami was on a cone!). All considered... things were looking up!

During my first week at Ft. Monmouth, I had the opportunity to attend a television broadcast sponsored by Chesterfield Cigarettes starring Vaughtn Monroe and his orchestra (remember his signature song, 'Racing with the Moon?'). As luck would have it, sitting next to me were two cute, teenaged girls, daughters of ranking officers living on the base. True to form, I chatted the young ladies up before the show, starting with the mandatory 'where are you from' routine. When I mentioned that I was from Miami, one of the girls gushed, "Oh, we know someone from Miami living on the base. Maybe you know him?"

Having gone down the road before and have never known anyone suggested, particurlarly in a city with a population of well over a million people. I had little expectation of making this connection. I was shocked when she mentioned Willard Bowsky, my old Miami

High and University of Florida freshman year buddy... and it got better! Apparently Willie was living with his bird-colonel father who was the Adjacent Base Commander, in a large, two story house on the base.

Vaughn finally finished the show, giving us a taste of 'Racing with the Moon', touted Chesterfields and we started filing out, chatting all the way. "We will tell Willard we met you", she gushed as we parted.

When I returned to the barracks after a day of elementary Morse code training, I had already forgotton the conversation from the evening before. I was stunned to see Willie, sitting in his sleek Ford Victoria hard-top, waiting patiently to take me home to have dinner and meet his Dad. Wow! What a reunion we had and meeting Colonel Bowsky, the second most powerful officer on the base was particularly memorable when the Colonel put his arm around my shoulder and pledged, "any friend of Willard's is a friend of mine. Is there anything I can do for you?" Overwhelmed with this turn of events, I mentioned that my pay records had been lost in the shuffle and I had not been paid in some time and with seemingly little effort to rectify the situation.

The next day during the lunch break, I received word to report to the First Sergeant... a meeting that went something like this, "Pflueger, report immediately to the Pay Master to receive your back pay!" I had to hand it to the Colonel; he didn't let grass grow under his feet. This was the first in a series of helping hands from this fine man, and put the jingle back in my fatigues.

Radio School

While learning to type and at the same time master Morse code, proved to be absorbing, as we progressed from 3 words a minute to our graduating goal of 25 five letter words per minute. At this speed the operator is listening to a word in code while writing a couple of words back, franticly trying not to lose concentration. At the final exam we had to correctly copy 25 words per minute. During my supervised exam, the paper I was typing rolled over the keyboard causing me to keep flicking it up to be able to see the keys…. talk about a 'one armed paper hanger'! There was little doubt in my mind that under the circumstances, I flunked the test, but I guess the instructor gave me a 'pass' for effort. The fastest code taker I saw during my time at the school was an Iranian officer on detached assignment, who was unbelievably fast… its baffling to see how fast a mind can process and fingers can execute at these high speeds.

I had a roommate by the name of Robert Herring (it was inevitable he would be called 'Fish') from somewhere in Alabama. Fish had been in baseballs' Cardinal farm system and was an excellent catcher on the Ft. Monmouth baseball team. He played in several games with Yankee Ace, Whitey Ford, along with a bevy of professional baseball players filling the roster and riding out the war.

Another note worthy character was a lanky lad named Foxworthy, I think from Kentucky, who had a serious love affair with bourbon.

One night when checking in with the Charge of Quarters in the office, a bottle concealed in his shirt slipped out and broke on the floor. Foxworthy, almost in tears over his loss, croaked, "you have to keep up with your drinking.... .'Cause they're making it while you're sleeping!" A useful bit of wisdom I interpreted as 'in life you need to keep focused!'

In any event, since I met Willie, my social life took a giant leap forward. He picked me up almost every night in his car, which sported high officer license plates, and fielded sharp salutes from the base guards as we were waved thru the gate (without the inconvenience of showing ID and passes). Our evenings usually consisted of sorties into the surrounding communities to date the local young ladies, dance, dinner, movies and such. On weekends I rarely stayed in the barracks. This caused some curiosity among my classmates who laughed when I would reply, when questioned, as to my weekend plans, "I am going to spend the weekend at the Colonel's house." For a PFC student this was some cushy and unbelieveable gig!

As graduation loomed, the Colonel sprung a little surprise one evening at his house. While relaxing with a pre-dinner cocktail, "Charlie," he beamed, "I have made arrangements for you to be accepted in the Officers Candidate School once you graduate. Of course, you will have to take the entrance exam, but that shouldn't be a problem."

Shocked! My mind was reeling.... flashing to a scene where a young infantry Second Lieutenant is shot all to hell leading his troops into the teeth of enemy fire! Another scene popped up where I was part of a proud air crew, with silver wings on my chest and a silk ascot, (ok, this might be a tad melodramatic) tucked into my starched shirt, flying to exotic foreign capitals! It didn't take long to select the most appealing option!

The idea of becoming an officer was powerful and this gesture on the Colonel's part was genuine and much appreciated. When asked, however, if he could arrange for me to join the Signal Corps after OCS, he admitted that although he did have a certain clout, he could not absolutely guarantee it, the Army being what it was. At that point, after kicking it around for a few days, I had to disappoint him and turn the opportunity down. I often wondered if I made the right decision, but I guess the fact that I lived through the war was proof enough for me.

Soon it was time to join the pool of newly graduated High-Speed Radio operators in selecting duty assignments from a list of openings. Our Air Force graduates had the option of a 3 year assignment to Germany, 2 years to the Far East and 18 months to Alaska. I figured that 3 years to Germany was too long to leave my girlfriend (actually six months was too long as it played out), and going into a war zone in the Far East, where the shooting was going on, conflicted with my basic strategy of avoiding an early demise. So I opted for Alaska with visions of fabulous hunting and world class fishing and for only 18 months..... a winning combination for sure! Unfortunately, by the time I finally decided, the 3 year tour to Germany was booked by fellow airmen that were smart enough to realize 3 years in Europe was like a paid vacation..... fraternizing with some of the most beautiful women in the world, touring ancient capitals, and an opportunity to learn a useful language, and not a war in sight. The rest of us losers now had to scramble for Alaska, drawing names out of a hat. Of course, I lost the draw for Alaska and wound up in the dreaded Far East group but salvaged some cheer when it was reveled our destination was Clark Air Force Base, 40 miles north of Manila in the Philippines. Not too bad, I thought, considering that just a little farther north one could get his ass shot off.

Willie and the Colonel took me to the train station in New York to catch Florida East Coast to Miami. Reluctantly we took our leave, with tears in our eyes and promised we would meet again after the war.

With a 30 day leave to look forward to... it was back to the good times. Old pals, Roscoe Needham and Bob Neumann joined me in working in a five day visit to nearby Cuba, running amuck in Havana. My Mother worked for National Airlines at the time, providing me with almost free airline tickets and a big discount on one of Havana's best hotel. In Pre-Castro days it was party time in Cuba. Plenty of rum, pretty Cuban girls, a visit to a cockfight and a few X-rated live shows (one featuring 'Superman', touted as having the world's largest male member, and a weather-beaten woman in her 30's, who accomplished an improbable coupling with a randy donkey). All very educational for young fellows. An evening at the famous Tropicana night club, featuring long legged show girls and plenty of hot Cuban music was also a highlight of this great tourist country.

We made it back to Miami one step ahead of a hurricane that swept Cuba, just in time to board my charter flight to Oakland, California and a date with a miserable troop ship for the trip across the Pacific to Manila... and what a trip it was!

Across the Pacific

We had a chance to do a little sightseeing around Oakland and San Francisco before boarding the troop ship in early October 1951, and heading for Honolulu, Guam Island and ending in Manila. Our ship had clearly seen better days and gave new meaning to the words, 'Rusty Bucket.'

Going under the Golden Gate Bridge was a thrill, but we soon hunkered down to develop a workable routine for survival. Sleeping in five high, canvas bunks in stuffy, crowded compartments, was not what I had in mind when joined the Air Force. After a few restless nights with my nose almost touching the bottom of the bunk above, we found that if we took our thin mattress to the library we could sleep on the floor under the air conditioning vents, with the added advantage of books and magazines to peruse.

After a little less than a week we docked in Honolulu and were finally permitted to get off the boat for a day of sightseeing, a decent lunch and a long planned tattoo. Why a tattoo you might ask? After we found out that we were going to the Far East via Hawaii, Fish and I decided it was a super idea to get a tattoo to commemorate the occasion. While its one thing to sit around the barracks and think of future nonsense, its quite another to actually put the plan in action.

Finding a tattoo parlor in the waterfront district of Honolulu was a cinch, but finding one that was air conditioned and not fit for pigs, was a challenge. When we finally realized the problem would remain unsolved, we settled for a shop that appeared the least filthy out of five or six hovels, if oven hot. As Fish sat in an old barber's chair and mumbled a shaky, "lets do it!", a thought crossed my mind that this might not be the best idea I ever had. I suggested that perhaps I could put this off for another day and another place, but my companion suggested in return, that he would not be happy if he got a tattoo and I chickened out!

Once in the chair, sweat poured down my flushed face and I bit my lip to keep from whimpering, as I toughed it out. I deduced that a whole rose with 'Hawaii' scrolled under it was better than an unfinished rose... if I climbed out of the chair and ran screaming down the road (probably with Fish in hot pursuit with blood in his eye). The only thing that came out of this fiasco was that the artist did not have a skull with aviator helmet, goggles, and crossed propellers for bones....that I thought would be really neat! On the other hand, at least it didn't say 'Mother'.

During the journey, work assignments were allocated according to the branch of service, with the Air Force doing the kitchen police, the Navy running the ship, and the Marines pulled the watch. A few of us were assigned to the kitchen for cleanup after dinner, and this proved a decent gig with perks of all the food you wanted, plus it helped keep boredom at bay.

As we crossed the 180th Meridian, the Navy boys put quite a bit of effort to induct the landlubbers into the most sacred 'Order of the Golden Dragon'. 'King Neptune' sat on his throne and mermaids (using mops for wigs and half a coconut for bras, the 'mermaids' were a scurvy lot at best) were in attendance. Blindfolded and in our skivvies the tormentors threw garbage and oil on us, selecting a few shaking novices to 'walk the plank' (climaxing with screams of terror and a 2" drop to the deck and not into a pounding sea, bringing howls of laughter by the assembled). After all was over, we had a mug of grog (rum and water) and received a fancy certificate to remember this day. There is another right of passage connected with crossing the equator, which I did not experience until much later and happily, not on a troop ship.

While continuing the journey, we stopped at the U.S. base in Guam to pick up 500 Filipino kitchen workers returning home after the exporation of their contracts. Our usual dinner operation was to feed these workers after the U.S. troops were fed and before we cleaned up the kitchen. The first night out of Guam, we forgot the 500 new arrivals and after the troops were fed we felt free to start the cleanup. This night, bored to tears, we started fooling around, donned chef hats, picked up a couple of stirring paddles, and with phony French accents started dumping a wide variety of condiments into a large half full pot of spaghetti sauce before dumping it in the garbage. Our cleanup gang was howling with glee as I swished around more hot sauce and unknown condiments. Actually it was hilariously funny even looking back some fifty plus years, but it was probably due to the fact that we were easily amused.

Our amusement ended abruptly with a steward shouting from the kitchen door, "Hold up on dumping the spaghetti sauce.... the Filipinos haven't eaten yet!" I broke out in a cold sweat and wondered if the U.S. Navy still flogged miscreants? I forced back an urge to confess that the sauce was a tad tainted, but the options for replacement at this hour was very questionable.....so we poured this murderous brew on the pasta and held our collective breaths. Listening for screams of agony, we kept our fingers crossed and as far as we know, no serious problems resulted from our outrageous behavior. The next day what our sauce couldn't accomplish, giant waves crashing over the bow and a wildly rolling ship did, when all 500 Filipinos (and not a few of our troops) threw-up all over the decks in a massive seasickness episode. A pleasure cruise this was not!

With a prayer of thanks, we finally docked in Manila Bay and boarded busses for the 40 mile trip north on the main island of Luzon to Clark Field. Just before we reached the base we went thru the town of Angeles, complete with dirt streets, roaming pigs and fowl, 105 bars, houses of ill-repute, and untold numbers of prostitutes. This proved to be a very popular destination for base personnel. On weekends and any rainy day when the usual daytime heat abated somewhat, vast numbers of the troops would take the day off and head for Angeles for a little R&R, i.e., drinking and some feminine companionship. Most bars were Filipino owned, but a few were owned by discharged U.S. Air Force personnel who did indeed, find a home away from home.

I was assigned to the Base Flight squadron on the flight line, a short walk from our two story, concrete block barracks. Our job was to provide radio operators to a fleet of four twin engine C-47 aircraft (civilian version was the DC-3, first built in 1935 and the work horse of the Air Force for many yeas), that were used for various missions around the Philippines and the Far East. Posted on the wall of the radio shack was a list of operators for daily flights and another 'per diem' list for flights of more than one day. In a normal week of flights scheduled for trips around the Philippines, an operator might be flying three or four days out of seven, visiting places like Cebu City, Baggio, Porta Princessa, Manila and Zamboanga (the most southern city in the islands and where the aircraft commander warned us that while strolling the streets that we do not attempt to chat up any of the ladies since the local lads carried long, curved knives ground out of old jeep chassis springs and honed to razor sharpness. The U.S. Army developed the .45 pistol for stopping power when fighting the Moros in Zamboanga after the Spanish American War).

The flight assignments we looked forward to was the per diem list that would send us for days and on occasion a week or more, to exotic locations. Tianan and Taipei, Taiwan (Formosa in those days) was a regular monthly trip to pay our air support airman, where twenty dollars exchanged on the local black market would return more Yen than you could stuff in your pocket and spend in a couple days dining, drinking and entertaining young Chinese women. I still have a business card from Taipei that proclaims, "House 29 Pretty Women. We make you comfort and satisfy!" Talk about another home away from home.... When you went to House 29 they did make you comfortable with a huge living room set up in half a dozen sofa-easy chair-cocktail table groupings, one of which was spacious enough to accommodate our crew.

Charlie and Wanda, House 29 Taipei, Taiwan 1952

Once seated, we were brought set-ups for our usual bottle of Canadian Club (purchased from the local U.S. Commissary for around two dollars a bottle), we would instruct Alex, the male Madame, to 'bring on the girls!' This resulted in a line-up of some ten to twelve very pretty, Chinese women, who would stand until a companion was selected for the evening. At that point, the girls would sit with us while we had a few drinks and talked about home, old girlfriends, sports, our jobs, or whatever drivel young military guys talk about when halfway around the world from their homes. The girls did not speak English and were unable to join in our conversation. This did not present a problem as we were quite happy to have them just sit there, sip their drinks, giggle on occasion, and best of all...smile.

Eventually, when we would run out of conversation and Canadian Club, we would take our girls and wonder upstairs to turn in for the night. Beds were non-existent, but mats on the floor seemed to do as well (although hell on the knees). As I recall, the cost of all this hospitality was a fist full of Yen totaling around $3.00 U.S. and a tip of $1.00, which we felt put us in the category of 'big time spenders'.

As you might surmise, protection was something most of us kept in mind even after a few drinks. In the military it was mandatory to attend disease prevention seminars and when you have seen enough films of horribly infected soldiers you want to keep the family jewels in the vault. Failing that, we used condoms as a matter of course with a back up pro-kit (a tube of anti-bacterial salve injected into the urethra after intercourse) to use in case the condom broke or slipped off. I never caught any disease using these precautions, but often watched a few of my barracks mates with their penises in peanut cans (which I presumed was full of liquid medication, since you can't eat peanuts with your penis), and which I further presume was the result of throwing caution to the wind in fits of inebriated passion.

On a cold, sunny afternoon in Taipei, a few of our crew had our Chinese driver take us to the commissary for the customary bottle of CC. When we entered one narrow street we were met by an angry mob mulling around a wooden cart being pulled by a couple of rag clad Chinese. In the cart, with hands tied to the rails, was a young man crying through his screams, with face lifted toward me as I sat in the front seat of the Jeep. His right arm had what looked like a white strip of tape wrapped around about half way between wrist and elbow. Since no one could pass between the cart and our Jeep, I felt the full impact of his obvious despair, with little understanding of the magnitude of his distress. At that point, we edged on past the cart and angry throng, and when clear I asked the driver what the problem was? He thought for a few seconds....then made a chopping motion on his arm and with a chilling explanation said, "they take thief to square and chop arm off! He steals no more with that hand!" The driver further said that if he had friends that could help seal the missing appendage, he would probably live through it.....if not, he would probably bleed to death. In those days in the Orient, justice was swift and brutal!

I enjoyed many trips to Taipei while at Clark Field and will always remember the sight and smell of the East, 'honey' carts (carrying human excrement in large drums, used to fertilize their rice patties) being pulled by coolies, the smoky smell of thousands of cooking fires, the aroma of ducks, geese and parts of unknown animals dried and hanging in shops all over the city, and the popping of motor scooters on pedestrian crowded, narrow street. There seemed to be a general joy of life in this ancient and exotic culture, much of which was soon to pass into the modern world.

On one flight to Taipei I met my first celebrity! We were offering a lift from the Philippines to Taipei on our regular pay run, to the publisher of Time Magazine, Henry Luce and his wife (and later a U.S. Ambassador) Claire Boothe Luce. They were very pleasant and interesting people.

Another time, I was lucky enough to be selected for a trip on the Manila Embassy C-47, when the regular radio operator fell ill. We were bound for the then British island colony of Singapore. An extra plus was a quick look around Kelung, Borneo while refueling, stirred by the notoriety of the old circus attraction, the 'Wild Man from Borneo'.

Singapore was a lovely old city, which showed little sign of the recent occupation by the Japanese during WWII. Our crew booked rooms in the Hotel 'de la Europe, which conjured up visions of the British 'Empire'. We spent a week there with very little to do except visit the 'New World' and 'Old World' amusement parks, sample various food carts with such delicacies as fried prawns, see a Chinese

'Opera', enjoy local Chinese cuisine and fine English piano bars and dining.

Arlene, a lovely Australian radio station singer I was dating had an apartment a block up a steep hill from my hotel. Late one evening after a foray on the town, I took her home and started back down the hill to the Hotel 'de la Europe. With each step I seemed to gain a little more speed until I was galloping flat out thru the hotel lobby and right out the French doors to the gardens, winding up in a well trimmed ledge. Extracting myself from the hedge and slightly bleeding from nicks and cuts, I collected my key from an amazed desk clerk and made it upstairs to my room, where my key had a problem finding the keyhole (I think the keyhole was moving). Every time I made a thrust and missed… the recoil would bounce me across the narrow corridor and off the wall on the other side. Since the thumping was not silent, it attracted the attention of night security in the form of a giant Indian Punjab type complete with turban and a serious scowl! Fortunately, he recognized me….took the key out of my shaking hand, easily inserted it into a suddenly stationary keyhole and ushered me into the room with a sensible suggestion (more like "don't let me see you out again tonight!') to get a little sleep.

For me, one of the highlights of the trip was a visit to 'Raffles' the world renowned colonial hotel, with its period furniture and a long, sweeping bar. The only disappointment was the bartender didn't know how to make their famous drink 'Singapore Sling'!

Soon the week was over and I sadly took my leave from Singapore and Arlene, suppressing a sniffle, while trying to remind myself that…. after all ….'There was a war on,' although up to this point, you couldn't prove it by me!

In early 1953 my name came up on the per diem board for a first time trip to French Indo-China (later called Viet Nam), some 750 miles across the South China Sea. The destination was Nha Trang, where the French borrowed six C-47 aircraft presumably to jump paratroopers in their war with the Vietnamese. The contract had now ended and major maintenance was due. Our Colonel's mission was to make this arrangement and set a convenient pickup date to return the aircraft to our base in the Philippines.

Charlie at Nah Trang airfield, French Indo-China 1952

We landed at the airport that was constructed by the French, boasting old hangers and old Tri-Engine German Fokker Aircraft with corrugated fuselage (American Ford Aircraft also built one very similar). It was like a time capsule from the 1920's.

It was a short drive to town where we checked into a posh, beach hotel and set out to tour Nha Trang. Checking out the local bars we met a lot of the French military, including the French Foreign Legion troops represented predominately by Algerians and other African nations. We enjoyed drinking a few beers with them and they seem happy to meet some American flyers. We chatted in broken English and a smattering of French, as arm in arm, they showed us some of the more rustic bars in the town. It reminded me of an old Foreign Legion film....plenty of atmosphere here!

One night, our assigned guide in response to a request of "where's the action?", informed us that nearly every early evening a beautiful Chinese woman would be driven in a pedi-cab (a rickshaw with an

attached bicycle) along the sea road in front of our hotel. If one was so inclined, an arrangement could be negotiated for a quickie, using a hollowed out shrub along the edge of the beach. He barely got it out of his mouth when the lady came peddling along and pulled to a stop. A quick conversation with our guide proved fruitful and she happily accommodated a few of our horny lads and in the shrub with a grass mat, as advertised! It was certainly a novel and interesting venue and even if you got a branch in the rear on the upstroke, it seemed to work.

Charlie on the beach
at Nah Trang 1952,
French Indochina

A month or so later six of our air crews boarded a four engine DC-6 for a quick trip back to Nha Trang to pick up the C-47's we lent the French. As we landed it was obvious that the situation had changed and the Foreign Legion was engaged in battle with Viet forces. It seemed that the enemy was attacking the perimeter of the airport, which was defended gallanty by French troops, some using the guns in rusty, old Japanese tanks strategically located since the end of WWII, to provide fire power. The noise of machine gun and rifle fire assaulted our eardrums, along with odd stray bullet humming thru the heavy noon air! It didn't take a conference to understand that we were in a precarious position in the middle of a full blown Viet attack and with the unsavory possibility of being shot (a condition I have tried to avoid since National Guard days). Another almost equally appalling scenario was capture by Viet forces while aiding the French, particularly since we were not, at that time, at war with the Vietnamese. Potentially a very embarrassing and sticky wicket, indeed!

With obvious urgency we jumped in our assigned aircraft, urged on by our commander shouting 'lets haul ass!'" and, without a warm-up, roared down the runway and wheels up, headed back across the South China Sea. We ignored the air whistling through the scattering of bullet holes in the fuselage, but since the C-47 was not pressurized they posed little hazard in that regard. Once safely back on the base, we spent a few hours sipping 'Lucky Lager' California beer at ten cents a can and nervously tittering about the day's near miss. Fortunately, as dicey as it was…this was the extent of my combat experience!

Another memorable trip took us to Hong Kong in 1952, before it became known as a famous tourist attraction. Hand fitted clothing was popular even then and it was difficult not to buy a cashmere sport coat for $15.00 U.S. I still have the coat in my closet and I can still get it on, if a tad tight. We visited the Tiger Baum Gardens build by a Chinese tycoon famous for a tinned salve touted to cure most anything you have wrong with you. The Gardens, depicted in statutes, features the pitfalls of life and the eventual rewards of a moral existence and the peril of a sinful life and its punishment in the hands of a devilish persona of evil.

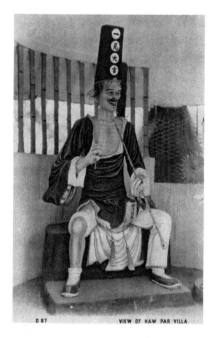

VIEW OF HAW PAR VILLA

Eternal Judgment Hong Kong

For a little sport, a couple of the crew hired rickshaws and after consuming considerable alcoholic beverages, they persuaded the runners to sit in the passenger seats while they took over pulling, amid hoots of laughter and screams of encouragement, in a downhill race. The good citizens were treated to a sight probably never been before (or ever again) on the streets of Hong Kong. As you might imagine, the local cuisine was excellent, but for breakfast I used to drop in to the British Army-Navy Club and have steak, eggs, chips and tea for a whopping fifty cents.

When I first arrived in the Philippines, I had the common view that the country was mostly jungle and tropical beaches.....that was largely true, but with some startling changes. The north end of the main island of Luzon was mountainous with the provincial capitol of Baggio over a mile high, with rolling hills, pine trees and crystal pools fed by cold waterfalls, much like some areas of North Carolina. The Air Force operated a R& R camp snuggled in the mountains, with roaring fireplaces in cozy barracks, overlooking a well manicured golf course and country club. I played my first golf there and it was probably my best, since I was relaxed and had no bad habits to break. The next time out, my golf mates were generous with their suggestions on how to improve my swing, putting, club selection and everything except how to doctor the score…I learned that myself by discovering the caddies were apparently was not above dropping a new ball in a better spot after a slice into the rough in hopes of a bigger tip. Maybe that assessment was unfair since there were deadly snakes living in the bush around the course and one searched for lost balls very gingerly, if at all. I saw one picture of King Cobra killed on a golf course somewhere in the Far East being held up by 18 men, on display in the club house with a note urging caution ….a suggestion taken quite seriously.

A three day pass was available each month and if you were off over a weekend you could tie it in with the pass and milk the system for five days. A free bus was available daily to the Baggio base, and of course, everything was free once you arrived. In order to further stretch the personal funds, we could buy a maximum of two cartons of American cigarettes daily for $1.00 a carton, In the evening before we would call for a taxi to take us to town, it was common practice to stick one carton in each expandable sock, pull the pant leg down and ride out the gate. Stopping at one favorite watering hole or another, we were rewarded with $7.00 per carton, providing enough spending money for a reasonable night of fun and games, including a taxi back to the base at the end of the evening.

I became friendly with a lovely local lady in her mid-thirties, and saw her when I made my monthly visit to Baggio. She was educated and not the average run of the mill lady of easy persuasion. We had a lot of fun together until her daughter of around 8 years old and a son of 6 years old were kidnapped and apparently taken out of Baggio and possibly out of Luzon. Fearing a life of sexual slavery for the children (which I understood was not unusual in the Philippines at the time), she left Baggio on a search mission….a mission from which she never returned. I often said a silent prayer for her and hope that she did eventually find them.

Another troubling scene that I have never forgotten, took place one night at a popular Madam's cabin in Baggio. After dark a cold breeze sprang up and a large bon-fire was started in the yard. A few of us were stand around drinking a few beers, warming ourselves at the fire and trying to decide whether we needed a little feminine companionship, or to go back to the base for a night cap at the country club. A heated conversation focused our attention on the male madam with his arm protectively around an obviously young, slim Chinese girl, who was loudly crying and trying to pull away. Two Chinese men were apparently negotiating with the madam for the services of the girl. This was not terribly novel in that environment for young girls to be pressed into the trade (usually sold to a pimp or brothel by their penniless parents), but this seemed off the norm by the excessive distress exhibited as the girl continued to try to pull away and make a run for it.

With a final agreement between the madam and the two customers, they dragged her along....moaning and crying....to disappear inside the cabin. While horribly fascinated, we felt that we should have intervened, but at night in a questionable area of a foreign country, it was probably prudent to ignore the situation and move on. Before we left, however, and while the madam stood counting his money in the light of the blazing fire, we asked him what actually transpired. He replied, with candor, "I know her family and have been watching her for some time, waiting until she was old enough. I buy her from her father to work in my business! The Chinese men own a business in town and pay big dollar for a young virgin, and since she will be one of my girls anyway, it's a profitable way to start her!" It was troubling to see human nature at its cruelest and degrading.

In general, life on the base was interesting. We had a movie theater that had reasonably current films (although they offered a lot of Roy Rogers Westerns for the simple minded troops). The U.S.O. put on an occasional show with mostly unknown talent (how I hated the jugglers and half-assed magicians with card tricks whose saving grace was usually a leggy assistant). The only name entertainer I can remember was Raymond Burr, known at the time from a few movies like the 'Jester' with Danny Kay, but before TV's 'Perry Mason' and 'Ironsides'.

We had an American Legion Club whose main feature was a big bar, lounge area and dance floor. It could be a little rough when the boys tied one on. I filled in a few nights as the bouncer for a friend on leave. My heart was in my mouth one evening when I had to escort a couple of nasty guys out. One of them snarled, "Are you a Mick?" I smartly denied being one, whatever it was. It was probably the right answer since they left with out pounding me to a pulp. It's hard to believe, but growing up in Miami, I had never heard the word, since we had few people of Irish decent in the population. Try Boston!

When not flying, my night time activities were not all amusements. The University of Wisconsin at Madison, provided various creditable educational courses for the U.S. Military, and for something constructive to do a few nights a week, I took three 3 hour elective courses. Later at the University of Miami, they gave me the nine credits, happily saving me time and money.

On a boring day a group of us checked out a personnel carrier truck and drove a few hours to a lovely, coconut fringed beach. A large family of Filipino's lived there in stilt raised huts. They invited us to swim in the crystal water of the Layte Gulf (close to where General McArthur waded ashore to reclaim the Philippines from the Japanese). Enjoying the day and chatting with the girls of the village, we were invited to a chicken dinner which started with a mad dash by all, after wildly scampering and clucking chickens on the 'hoof' so to speak. It gave new meaning to 'working for your dinner,' which involved the exhausting chase....killing and plucking.....cooking them on a hot, coconut husk fire....and finally eating the poor devils. Actually, it turned out to be one of the best meals I had in the Philippines, and when washed down with copious amounts of local San Miguel Beer, it was pure bliss.

Two or three times a month, I used to visit Angeles for a little female companionship in the 'Twilight Bar', a slightly upscale dive with good music and good beer. I hooked up with the very attractive owner, Lennie, partly for the companionship but more for the great Tango dancer she was. She taught me many things, but the best was teaching me to dance. With the 'Blue Tango' wailing away, we plowed through the crowded dance floor, cheek to jowl...dipping and spinning for half the evening. The second half was spent with squadron mates, drinking with Lennie and her bevy of decent looking girls, an hour of lovemaking and a race back to the check point before the bewitching (and AOWL) hour of mid-night. A well spent...miss-spent youth!

Our radio shack was run by Master Sergeant Jack Barton, (a Texan and a regular Sgt. Bilko) who was a fair and sensible young man, wholly committed to making a dollar by any means possible. He sold C-47 radio parts to the Philippines Airways for a handsome profit (particularly since he got them free from the U.S. Air Force after filing a defective report).

Another successful scam was having the doors re-constructed in his 1949 Plymouth coupe' to hold countless cartons of PX cigarettes, which he boldly drove off the base at least once a week to Angeles and occasionally on a pass to Manila for volume black market. He always said 'think big'.

As the Air Force at Clark Field paid the personnel in military script the Angeles bar owners had a problem in exchanging it for U.S. Dollars. Jim came up with a plan to collect the script and on his trips to Taipei legally exchange it at the paymaster there. To the delight of the bar owners and a generous commission to Jack, it worked well for a few trips, but one day he threw in an extra wrinkle. Unknown to the bar owners, Jack's rotation orders to a base in the

States came in, hatching a brilliant if outrageous plan for one final swindle. He went to Angeles and told the bar owners he found a way to triple his usual allotment of script for dollars on his next trip.

Indeed, he had found a way to exchange almost an unlimited amount of script (presumably his savings for the last two years) since he had orders to return to the States and could only use dollars. A week later the bar owners were getting a little nervous and started asking when Jack was coming back from his flight? Finally one of the squadron told them "why Jack was ordered back to he States a week ago. He won't be coming back!" I guess when the light bulb was switched on, the bar owners could hardly be expected to be amused and I understand there was some discussion of sending an envoy to his next base for a little knee capping. I think in the final analysis, though, they did nothing but lick their financial wounds, since it just wasn't worth the effort. I often thought of Jack and his drive and ingenuity (with that touch of larceny) and figured he probably wound up as Governer of Texas.

Homeward Bound

Although my tour of duty was 24 months, the buzz around the base was that the three radio operators closest to completing their tours would be selected to join the three flight crews preparing to transport three WWII B-17 Bombers to Mobile, Alabama for final retirement. The aircraft were used years ago to photomap the Philippines and now sat with pickled engines waiting for their last flight. The maintenance crew was required to drain the pickling solution and re-oil at Clark Field. We were then scheduled to fly out together for the trip across the Pacific, stopping on Quaduline Island, Guam, Hickham Field, Honolulu, and Sacramento, California and finally deliver them for target practice to Mobile, Alabama.

Sounds good, huh? Leave at least three months early, go home on an aircraft not a rust bucket freighter, for a well deserved leave and relax. Looking at the down side, it's a hell'va long way across the Pacific and half of the U.S., in a WWII aircraft whose engines have been in pickled storage for years. When you're young you feel immortal and ready for adventure, of course, being a nitwit certainly helps!

It must have been some sight from the ground... three B-17's flying in formation over Manila in the summer of 1953. The first day's flight did not go without incident. Upon landing at Quaduline in twilight, we could see one of our sister ships taxiing in, showing a feathered propeller, signaling engine failure. Upon closer inspection, I watched their crew chief take out a sump bolt under the engine and allow the oil to flow onto his hand. We were shocked to see bits and pieces of the piston rings and metal shavings accompanying the oil. It was obvious, even to a radio operator, that this particular aircraft would not be joining us on the following morning flight. The crew chef called the aircraft commander over with, "Major, it doesn't look good! I don't think a partial rebuild is possible. We need to order a new engine!"

The Major replied with anguish in his voice, "Sergeant, I shutter to think how long it might take us to bring a new B-17 or rebuilt engine all the way out here, even if there is one readily available. I hope you guys like fishing and throwing rocks at gooney birds!"

After a few minutes of trying to figure out what happened to trigger this calamity, we came to the conclusion that the pickling solution was not fully nor properly drained at Clark Field. This made for an enthusiastic, if exhausting couple of hours of labor re-draining our four engines into oil carts and disbursing it in the bush (certainly an environmental faux pas at the least). We fell into our visiting airmen's quarters at the Navy Base and passed out from exhaustion. I felt like I was going to a firing squad, when at dawn our remaining flight of two bombers refueled and rolled wheels up into a rising sun. Our confidence that we had headed off a serious engine problem at the proverbial pass, was shaky at best.

After a long day of droning engines in the non-pressurized cabin, facing a massive rush of air pushing up through an open camera hole where bomb storage used to be, we finally landed at Guam Island. With groans from our crew, the second bomber proved to have the same problem with disintegrating piston rings, putting paid to our last companion. Spurred on with little desire to remain in Guam, we did another couple of hours on draining and re-oiling our engines, allowing us to proceed with the next day's long flight to Hawaii.

All went well as we over flew Johnson Island... a speck in the vast ocean, and on into Hickham Field, on a blanket of beautiful, pink clouds... a little prayer of thanks was in order and a hope that our luck would hold awhile longer.

Civilization, or a reasonable facsimile, took away some of the stress and a couple of days rest prepared us for the big jump of some 2,400 miles from Hawaii to Sacramento. There was some conversation about remaining at Hickham until belly tanks could be shipped out via sea freight. This was not well received by our aircraft commander, nor with the rest of the crew who were tired and keen to go home. The Colonel assured us that we did not need belly tanks to provide extra fuel reserves, as our standard tanks could hold enough gas to allow a carefree flight to California. A few days later, we topped the tanks at dawn and took off for the 14 hour flight.

The crew was aware that this was going to be a very long flight over open water and contrary to the Colonel's optimism, knew this had the potential to be very dicey. Any unusual headwinds, storms or mechanical problems could be catastrophic, but as the morning wore on and we reported our position, ground speed and fuel consumption on each hour, all seemed to be going well.

When Hawaii Control received our report on the fifth hour... thing changed! The Command suggested that due to fuel consumption, we should consider returning to base. I advised the Colonel of the suggestion and in response he snorted, "Tell those people we are doing fine and proceeding with the mission!"

As we droned on into our sixth hour, I received a terse radio message directing us to return to Hickham immediately due to dangerously high fuel consumption. With shaky hands, I handed the Commander the message and got a repeat of his 'doing fine' speech... adding, 'you tell them our fuel consumption is not excessive and we are pressing on!" At this point, I could have grabbed the yoke and turned the damn plane around myself, but reason and visions of an extended vacation at Leavenworth Federal Prison prevailed and I mumbled, "Please notate on the message that you received it from me, if you will?" He did as I requested and understood, as I slipped it into zippered flying jacket, that if in the event of an incident, I wanted proof that he did, indeed, receive the directive. Looking back, I wonder how well the paper message would hold up after some hours treading water in the Pacific... but it was all I could come up with at the time. I started wondering how raw seagull tastes.

The crew's stress level raced into overflow. The Navigator, a seasoned flyer, kept his nose buried in the maps, consumption charts and such, stuttering a promise of a bee-line directly to Sacramento. The Colonel's confidence seemed to lose some of its luster, as he pointed out the slim margin for error, increasing the tension from 'were cool' to cut it with a knife!' I suspected the Colonel had second thoughts on the wisdom of his rash (to me) decision to proceed in the face of a direct order to return, and if we pronged the aircraft in the ocean, his career would certainly be in shambles, provided we survived the crash. I kept sending hourly messages to a largely unsympathetic Hawaiian Command Control, until receiving orders to transfer jurisdiction of our aircraft to California Air Control. This gave us a bit of encouragement knowing that we were in range of the U.S. mainland air/sea rescue in the event of the worst scenario.

Finally the Golden Gate Bridge appeared in the far distance and we all let out a collective breath, whipping up another 'Hail Mary.' At least from this point on, rescue would be more dependable and not the 'crap shoot' we had been operating under. A short time later, our wheels touched down at the base in Sacramento, prompting our crew chief to whisper, "Charlie, I think I'm going to pass out! My gages are only showing 15 minutes of fuel left in the tanks!" I think 'chalk white' replaced my gorgeous island tan.

We all looked forward to an early morning flight across the mountains headed for Mobile and the conclusion of this hair-raising adventure. It was a bright morning with fantastic alpine vistas raising our morale to recent unseen levels, as visions of home danced in our heads. Suddenly, the pilot reached up and feathered number one engine, due to a precipitous drop in oil pressure. I had a brow full of instant sweat over this current crisis, not only from the immediate danger factor, but realizing that if this had happened a few hours earlier over the Pacific, this story would have been a couple of pages shorter... or not at all!

Flying over the mountains on a beautiful day was breathtaking. Thinking about going home after almost two years in the Far East was wonderful until the Colonel came on the intercom with, "for those reading comic books, I have to tell you we had to feather an engine... but the good news is that we have three left!" A nice touch, but bad news is still bad news. What I really wanted to hear was that we were going to make it somewhere that had a landing field and hold the comedy routine for tonight over a beer at the club... laughing over our 'close call!'

I was encouraged however, that the Colonel did not sound ruffled, but after all, any pilot who could fly across the Pacific and land with a teacup full of gas left, would probably not give too much concern to losing one lousy engine when he had three more remaining. He continued with, "we could probably fly all the way to our drop off base, but if we should lose another one, it could get a little sticky... so put your 'chutes on just in case (didn't like the way this briefing was going)... we are going to land in El Paso!" He had my vote! The balance of the flight to this southwest Texas base was uneventful, but sprinkled with the usual set of prayers reserved for Indo-China and the middle of the Pacific... so far they worked just fine!

As we touched down at El Paso, some thousand miles short of our final destination, I thought it was a fitting end to the three B-17's that took off from Clark Field with so much promise only a week ago. While none of the aircraft made it to the drop-off, at least they did not leave us paddling around on a raft or in a pile of smoldering ruins. What a lot of aggravation, anguish and expense to bring the aircraft back over half the world, only to fly one more time for target practice (if this was indeed the case). In my opinion, the Air Force should have shot hell out of them in the Philippines and saved us all a lot of trouble.

Being stuck in a hot, dry and dusty El Paso in the summer of 1953 was not a pleasant experience, particularly with home so close. We were now faced with the same old story of trying to obtain an engine for an WWII bomber. It soom became apparent that it was going to be a challenge, even in the United States…so I got my courage up and talked (read 'pleaded') with the Colonel.

Putting on my sadest face, I sobbed, "Sir, I don't think I can be of much help changing an engine, if and when we get one. I would really appreciate getting on with my leave!"

"Charlie, we have been through a lot together and we enjoyed having you as part of the crew, but I know you're chaffing at the bit to get home. We'll cut you some orders and let you get on with your life," he replied, with a kindly pat on the shoulder. "Oh! Don't forget to take your parachute to your next base…it's signed out to you."

As my spirits soared, I gave him a snappy salute and babbled, "My Mother will be happy to see me. " Less than snappy dialog I fear, to go along with the salute. I raced to pack my few belongings and headed to the flight line, fresh orders in hand. MATS (the Air Force's Military Air Transport Service) had a flight leaving for Tulsa almost immediately and since I had my own parachute (I knew it would come in handy), I jumped aboard and flew my first leg home.

A few hours later I lucked out on a flight from Tulsa to Mobile, where I arrived just in time to see a DC-6 rolling down the runway bound for Miami. Drat! Foiled again! Well, what the hell, since I was really motivated to get the show on the road, I bummed a ride to the local bus station and with parachute over my shoulder, bought a ticket on the 'Grey Dog' to Miami. My usual good humor was tested however, when I suffered a plethora of caustic remarks from the local wags, going something like this,"Hey, flyboy! You all planning on bailing out of that bus?"

I smiled and told them…"Not unless I have to! I'm going home!"

Strategic Air Command

Coming home after years of service in the Far East was a joyful affair and seeing family and old friends was certainly a valid excuse for celebration, which we exercised with abandon. Since I had received a 'Dear John' letter from my fiancée while I was in the Philippines, who explained she met her 'soul mate' at the University of Florida, I preceded flank speed to uncover some willing replacements. Like wind through the willows, my 30 day leave slipped through giddy fingers and soon it was time to load my previously mentioned parachute into a newly purchased 1950 Olds 88 and headed north.

When I reported to my new air refueling squadron of the Second Bomb Wing of the prestigious 'Strategic Air Command' at Hunter Air Force Base near Savannah, Georgia, I couldn't help but notice a stack of personnel records on the First Sergeant's desk.

"More incoming airmen?" I asked the First Sargeant, thumbing the manila envelopes.

He hesitated for a moment, and then slowly answered, "I guess you didn't hear about the air tanker we lost last week. One of the converted WWII B-29's (seems like I couldn't get away from Second World War bombers), lost engines and with a full fuel load had the glide ratio of an anvil. It seems like these old war horses are having one problem after another." Shaking his head in sorrow he continued, "Fortunately, we are slated to get the new KC-97 air tankers and they can't come soon enough! We can't afford to lose any more SAC air crews like this one... scattered all over the landscape," he concluded, pointing at the stack.

I jerked my thumb off the pile as I felt the bile rise in my throat ....picturing the monstrous fireball that must have resulted in a crash of a large four engine aircraft with fully loaded jet fuel tanks. Our squadron was the air to air refueling arm of a prominent bomb wing of B-52, high flying jet bombers that carried our ultimate atomic bomb response to a Russian attack. These long range deterrents had the capacity to remain aloft for days if necessary, with the support of our air to air refueling capabilities. The SAC mission was to have a portion of the Command's bombers aloft at all times, armed with atomic weapons and prepared to head for Russia at a moments notice....talk about a deterrent! General Curtis LeMay, head of SAC, was an astute commander who demanded first class aircraft and highly trained air and ground crews. One of his major contributions was in the development of this air refueling concept, enhancing our ability to protect the United States under a doomsday nuclear retaliation threat.

My job function on an air crew was obviously to send and receive radio messages pertinent to the success of the refueling exercise, however, during the actual refueling I would take a position behind the 'boom operator' and act as an observer in the event of other aircraft straying dangerously close. The boom operator layed prone on a mat, peering out a back window under the tail section and manipulating the controls of the 'flying boom' (literally a gas pipe, with wings), had the ultimate responsibility of placing the nozzle of the fuel delivery system into the fuel receptacle located near the nose of the receiving aircraft. This was the tricky part of the operation.... both aircraft on a shallow dive to allow our slower tanker to keep up with the faster jet receiving aircraft, while buffeted by high winds.... staring into the eyes of the pilot below and all depending on the combined skills of others.

Air refueling was a dicey occupation without having to worry about whether our refueling aircraft was fit to continue flying. As an enlisted airman, I was not required to continue on flying status and could, at my option, 'stand down' and opt for an assignment on the ground. On the other hand, if your squadron had a surplus of your particular job function, you could be reassigned to another area of expertise. The First Sergeant, as luck would have it, apologized that there was no openings on an air crew at that time and he would have to re-assign me, temporarily of course, to the radio repair section (not withstanding that I had no clue how radio actually worked). I thought I could, however, pull an inoperative unit out of its case and plug a new one in ...figuring it can't be rocket science, could it?

"Like I said, the Second is one of the first wings to get the new KC-97' air tankers (civilian name was 'Strata-Cruiser, as used by Pan American Airways in the early 50's, and easily recognized by its unusual double cabin) and as soon as that happens we'll get you back on a crew," he continued, feeling sorry to have to cut me out of the extra flying pay.

Remembering the stacked personnel records of the dead crew and suppressing a great sigh of relief, I magnanimously replied, "it's disappointing, of course, but maybe it won't be too long." I felt that I had just dodged a bullet and had a new lease on life, without having to voluntarily opt out of flying status....thereby showing my true reluctance to 'going down in a blaze of glory.' I forced a brief chicken dance of glee out of my mind and skipped out of the office.

Life around the flight line for a radio repair mechanic was pleasant, even if I was still amazed and mind boggled over Marconi's achievements. My expertise improved to being able to wipe the dust off the electronic equipment and swapping a defective unit for a repaired or new one. I wondered if there was a high paying civilian job swapping units waiting for me upon discharge? Nah! You better hope you can get back into the university, I rapidly concluded.

We received one 3 day pass a month which we dragged out to the usual 5 or 6 days, allowing plenty of time to drive home to Miami or visit friends in Brunswick or Atlanta. On one such trip, I hit a black cow in the twilight with the '88, bashing in my left fender and sending the cow back from whence it came, probably with a tenderized rump. Life was easy, but I was looking forward to my discharge, preferably an honorable one, and a return to scholastic pursuits at the University of Florida.

Four months later Sarge called me back into the office and gave me the 'good news.' "Charlie, it's your lucky day!" he boomed. Not convinced, I didn't interrupt in an effort to get him to 'spit it out!' The new tankers have arrived and you're back on flying status!" Oh, goody, but like beauty....good news is also in the eye of the beholder! With a tight simile of simulated joy, I thanked him and with mixed emotions headed for the flight line to meet my new crew.

As I reported to my new assignment, I expected to be thrust into a whirlwind of air crew training, but soon found that everyday life of a crew member was pretty much showing up at our recreation room, putting updated NOTAMS (Notice to Airmen) in loose leaf notebooks and playing volley ball. Most of the training was of the 'on the job' variety and conducted on frequent refueling missions over the Atlantic. My first take off from Hunter Field's medium length runway with a full load of jet fuel and topped off aircraft tanks, was an attention grabber. I stood just behind the pilot and the copilot....with wheels still on the pavement and watching the remaining runway dwindle at an alarming rate. Finally we hit V-2 and the pilot, with all four engines howling under full throttles, pulled the KC-97 off the ground within a few yards from joining highway traffic. If I thought this was all the heart pounding I was going to receive this day, I was mistaken, as we headed out over the Atlantic and a rendezvous with our first B-52.

With the thumping in my chest slowing down, I sent our 'engaged' report, closed down the radio and sat down at an observation window near the boom operator. It was disconcerting trying to figure the odds that the boom operator would make one wrong swipe and lots of things could happen... all bad! Watching the boom operator maneuver the flying fuel pipe sent my heart into a 'race' mode again. Fortunately, whether thru skill or perhaps divine intervention the procedure went flawlessly. In actual fact, our wing only lost one aircraft during my entire tenure, but more about that later.

After a leisurely lunch one boring afternoon, I strolled into our rec room, facing another session of volley ball, when I noticed a group of airmen crowding around the bulletin board. This was unusual, since not too many guys ever seemed interested in announcements, except for the three day pass listings. Pushing my way closer, I heard mumblings like, "we're screwed!" and "this is the worst!" along with assorted cursing that would make a stevedore blush.

Tippy-toed....trying to peek over the crowd, with my mind awhirl conjuring wild scenarios ... war with Andorra or South Florida attacked by Canadians (wait! That's done very winter!) I pleaded with someone to enlighten me, 'I can't read the board from here!' I whined. A kind soul snarled, "They finally got us! Those bastards have scheduled our Wing for the Air Crew Survival Course in Reno, Nevada."

Off hand, a week in Reno didn't sound bad to me, at least it should stave off our present monotonous routine, but it didn't take too long to be informed of the ramifications of this week in Reno. Leave your loaded dice at home....this training consisted of parachute instruction at the base, and then seven days of survival in the bush. The premise, as I was informed, was to drop off at point 'A' in the mountains with a compass and very little food or equipment and successfully make our way to point 'B'. On the surface, this didn't sound too difficult until you figure in the 'food' factor, which obviously demanded a certain amount of living off the land, as if we were forced to bail out over enemy territory and make our way to a neutral or friendly country. I could see where living off the land could put a hurting on any flora or fauna in the way. One circulating horror story was the fate of a poor, little faun that fell prey to one bloodthirsty (read 'starving') crew and wound up as a venison stew. In addition to a strenuous mountain forced march, we had to learn some rudimentary Russian and assimilate escape tips, such as approaching only older Russian farmers, not younger people, if help is needed. Still doesn't sound too tough? Well, as an extra incentive to spice up the program, a group of 'Aggressors', simulated 'enemy' troops were roaming the area with instructions to capture any crews they could find before the crews reach point 'B' which promised a helicopter pickup and return to base with the exercise successfully completed. Captured crews were taken to a mockup of a Russian prison camp and roughly interrogated....certainly not a happy thought by any means.

Many 'cat and mouse' games were played, including one crew that was said to have slipped back to the base under the cover of darkness and broke into the P.X., loading up on warm clothing and various food items, before vanishing back into the mountains. I understand that this caper was not viewed with much amusement by the base commander.

The day after arrival at the base, we were in parachute training, consisting of dragging the crew member in harness on the ground requiring him to roll over on his shoulder and scramble to his feet to rush and collapse a simulated billowing 'chute.'

This maneuver shouldn't be a problem for a young and reasonably athletic guy, right? Wrong! Unfortunately, when my turn came, I followed instructions and rolled over on my previously mentioned dislocated shoulder....knocking it out again, but this time it didn't pop back in the socket when my arm was raised. In excruciating pain, I was taken to the base hospital where a doctor tried to rotate the shoulder manually, but met with no success. Taking his shoe off, the medic placed his stocking foot in my arm pit and gave it another try. After a few minutes of this torture and screams that could be heard on the parade field, I was whisked off to the downtown Reno V.A. Hospital for more sophisticated (I hoped) procedures. As for the charms of downtown Reno....I guess all cities look the same from inside an ambulance!

I was deposited in one of the beds, sans shirt, covered in dirt and sweaty grime, when a nurse came in and unlaced my jump boots and in a 'no-nonsense' order, "take off your pants and put this gown on, "throwing it on the bed, and continuing with, "opening in the rear!" Oh! Oh! That didn't sound reassuring!

Still clutching my arm to help ease the pain, I managed to squeak out, "I can't manage it!" at which she asked if I was bashful. Receiving a muffled curse, which she rightly took as a 'no', she unbuttoned my pants and slid them off....now we're getting somewhere I thought. As she slipped the gown on, the nurse revealed that in a couple of minutes a gurney would arrive and take me to the operating room, where, one way or the other, the shoulder would be returned to its rightful place.

At this time she deftly administered a shot of Demerol, rending my destination moot, since all of a sudden like Brett Butler in 'Gone With the Wind'....I didn't give a damn!. On the way out.... strapped to the gurney, I even gave a cavalierish wave to a bevy of WWI patients, who kindly responded with a spattering of applause in a salute to a brave warrior (at least that's how I saw it through a haze of Demerol). Once in the OR, I was hooked up to the sodium phenathol and instructed to count to a hundred backwards. I think I made it to 95 when the lights went out. Later the doctor told me once I was under and the muscles relaxed, it only took a few seconds to rotate the arm and slip it back in the socket. The arm was then taped across by body to hold it firmly while the three weeks healing process took place.

A few days later my crew-mates were starving to death in the mountains, while I was heading back to Savannah, licking my wounds. While happy not to be beating myself up in the bush, I did miss the camaraderie and loss of the adventure aspect of the exercise. The good news was my crew managed to complete the training and return to base with only minor cuts and abrasions, without complications and no murder of a Bambi on their collective consciousness.

In July of 1954, our Wing was sent on TDY (Temporary Duty Assignment) to Morocco in northwest Africa. Our route took us over Bermuda and into one of the Portuguese Islands of the Azores, in the middle of the Atlantic. The flight was uneventful and an evening on the town, visiting interesting bistros and sampling the charms of some of the local debutants (read 'professional ladies not bound by social mores'), made for a pleasant visit to these historic islands.

The next leg of the flight took us to a temporary home at a seaside U.S. base at Port LeOty, Morocco, for a week's joint 'maximum effort' of the various assembled air wings. Every night we flew missions out of our new base. On most nights our support cadre, i.e. mechanics, ground fuel personnel and such, would sign on the flight and use this time to play a few wicked hands of poker with some of the air crew members during periods when not actively engaged in the operation of the mission.

On one of the flights, a sister tanker developed a problem with faulty gages (the official story) allowing the tanker to pump out most of its own fuel along with the normal refueling commitments. The night was black and when it became apparent that the aircraft would run out of fuel short of a safe landing at the base, the captain engaged the auto-pilot, steered away from the cold, wet Atlantic, to a bailout area over the desert.

The rag-tag crew was shocked when the bailout order was barked over the intercom, creating a chaotic scrambling to find and buckle on parachutes (they had obviously ignored regulations requiring the wearing of a 'chute at all times when in the air).... poker players must have felt immune to such nonsense, but when the 'chips' were down....they knew when to hold 'em and when to fold 'em! With little time to assess their plight, they shuffled to the rear hatch and fell away into an alien night sky!

It was amazing that only an assortment of bruises were suffered by the entire extended crew, gamblers and assorted hangers-on, even when bailing out at night over unknown territory. It seemed that the group had barely been picked up and returned to base before they were bragging about their exploits and looking forward to receiving the customary 'Golden Caterpillar' pin from the parachute company to commemorate the perilous occasion of having to bail out to save ones life.

The real punch-line to this story is almost unbelievable! We heard the report the next day that the aircraft, still on auto-pilot, crash landed, wheels up, on the flat desert surface with little evidence of major damage....amazing! Bent props and battered underbelly was basically, the only visual damage evident. The theory presented was that the outboard engines lost fuel supply and stopped, while apparently the inboard engines continued to sputter, resulting in a gradual decline until it slid onto the fairly smooth desert surface.

Our crew had some reservations and did not completely buy the 'miracle' landing theory. We convinced our aircraft commander to do a slight deviation from our daily refueling mission to do a fly-over of the downed aircraft. We wanted to see the 'miracle' for ourselves. The story was not exaggerated! The tanker was intact and what appeared to be excellent condition.

Later, one of the downed crew-members was re-assigned to our crew and told me his take on the events, "Charlie, it happened so fast! One moment we were engrossed in a hot poker game, when the crew chief threw me a parachute and frog marched me to the hatch, where he gave me a quick 'good luck' accompanied by a boot to the backside, followed by a terrifying fall into a very dark night! You know we left in a hurry, when we left all the money on the table."

"I didn't even feel the jolt of the 'chute opening. Floating down was not too bad until I hit the ground with considerable impact, stunning me for a few seconds. I could barely see my hand in front of me in the dark. I fumbled and found the flashlight and whistle clipped to the harness, which was a big help in locating the rest of the crew that was spread out over a couple hundred yards or more. There was a lot of nervous chatter going on when air rescue picked us up in a helicopter and whisked us back to the base." He licked his lips and continued the narration, "it was hard to believe, but the next day we 'coptered back to the crash site and retrieved our personal items and tried to sort out who belonged to the money strewn around the aircraft. Talk about 'found money'....who would have imagined that the plane would still be in one piece? Go figure!"

On a side note: a few months later word filtered down that the downed aircraft was repaired and actually flown off the desert and back to the base. This was hard to believe, but probably no harder than the miraculous crash landing crewless, in the first place.

As the monotonous routine ground on, our crew got a break in the form of a TDY for a week at one of our Mediterranean bases, Wheelis AFB near the historical city of Tripoli, Libya. It was a huge base with all the facilities, i.e. big theater, huge PX, comfortable barracks, a swimming beach and pretty good food. Scheduled buses to Tripoli were an added perk, giving us ample opportunity to explore this ancient and interesting city.

At that time, the population was very friendly to Americans and partially thanks to a strong dollar, the restaurants and clubs were inexpensive. I imagined that one day I would return and explore the area at my leisure, but during my later traveling days, there was a developing animosity toward Americans making any effort along these lines not very appealing.

It was a clear day as we flew back to Morocco. It seemed like you could see the whole Mediterranean southern coast, including Algiers, another city I though would be interesting but never had the chance to visit. We landed in Port LeOty without incident just in time to pack up and head for our next assignment.

Our wing moved a few hundred miles south and inland to a new, but as yet unfinished base about 40 miles from Marrakech called Ben Garier (my memory does not guarantee the spelling after 56 years). The base only had two concrete block buildings.... the mess hall and the airport terminal building. Our barracks consisted of eight man tents with plywood sides. Sleeping accouterments consisted of a pitifully thin mattress and mattress cover (it seemed that the Air Force is going to make damn sure you get a mattress cover if you get nothing else), a pillow and a couple of military issue woolen blankets, probably left over horse blankets from the calvary. The tents had screen window openings with plywood shutters that encouraged cross ventilation during the day and helped keep the desert cold out at night. Another use for the shutters was to prevent the occasional dust devil (little tornado-like spinning air, picking up sand and dust) from depositing sand all over the cots and floor.....if you were nimble enough to shut them before the damage was done. Needless to note, woolen blankets full of sand certainly create a nasty sleeping environment and for the slow of foot, it demanded considerable sweeping and shaking .

On the desert, recreational amusements were hard to find and consisted of sitting on folding chairs in the searing sun in front of the tents, flyswatters in hand, in 'hot' competition for the 'fly-killing championship' of the squadron. I claimed the championship with a kill of over 900 flies in an hour, after beating a charge of cheating on the count. In my defense, I put it to the judges, "would a man of my caliber cheat on a fly-swatting contest?" A few of the louts voiced some reservations, but my honest face carried the day and I was finally declared the winner! Mom would be proud!

Another activity we looked forward to was a nightly presentation of fairly recent motion pictures. A few minutes before sunset we would grab a blanket and troop over to the rear of the mess hall where we would fold the blanket, making a temporary pillow to spare our rear ends from the hard planks of wooden benches. As darkness fell, the movie would be projected against the white plaster walls of the mess hall, making for a pretty effective movie screen. Usually about half way through the film, the cushions would turn into shawls, proving warmth against the increasing cold of the open desert air. By the end of the movie, it was almost teeth chattering time as the lack of cloud cover allowed ground level heat to rapidly evaporate. During the walk back to the tents in the dark, crystal clear evenings, we were constantly amazed at eye-popping vistas of a million stars shining through the dry, cloudless desert sky.

To shake the lethargy and to help while away the time between missions, we played our usual game of volleyball (of course, we brought the net with us!), swatting flies and reading. In addition, our crew went wild when we were selected (our Aircraft Commander was also the Squadron Leader and apparently had some extra clout) to take a group to England for a five day R&R session. Since most us had never been to Europe, morale soared as we lined up at the paymaster to draw per diem and personal spending money. Compared to today, England was definitely an inexpensive tourist destination in 1954, partly due to an economy that was less than a decade from the end of WWII, and the previously mentioned worldwide strength of the U.S. Dollar.

After a clear flight over Western Europe, we landed at Upper Hayford Royal Air Force Base a hundred miles or so north of London, where we boarded a train for the trip to the 'big city'. Our crew checked into a charming three star hotel near Piccadilly Circus in the heart of the West End and all its theater and entertainment opportunities. Most of us had no warm civilian clothes suitable for this English climate, lending some urgency to a visit to Marks and Spence Department Store for the purchase of a jacket and a few long sleeved shirts, before we began any serious sightseeing.

A few of us found our way to famous Trafalgar Square with its tall pillar and statue of Lord Nelson, commemorating his huge victory at the 'Battle of Trafalgar' on October 21, 1805, between the Royal Navy and a combined Spanish and French naval force. As a side note: the British Fleet of 27 ships of the line, under Admiral Lord Nelson, sunk 22 of the 33 ship French and Spanish armada, however, Lord Nelson was fatally wounded by a sniper and died between decks on his flagship, the HMS Victory. Many years later I had the opportunity to tour the Victory at its final resting place at Bristol, England, and marveled at the huge size of this wooden ship.

Today's Trafalgar Square is a favorite tourist venue and a gathering place for 'birds', both the feathered kind (a zillion pigeons) looking for peanuts sold by local entrepreneurs and the female kind....some of which are looking for a friendly companion for a few drinks and dinner at one of a thousand pubs scattered around the Greater London area.

We managed to charm a few lasses and enlisted their sightseeing expertise for the cost of a pub visit. We started our tourism efforts with the National Art Museum, which so happened to be located on the corner right across the street from the Square and worked our way down to Madame Toussards Wax Works on Oxford Street. We left few major attractions unscathed and even threw in an evening at the theater, featuring an 'English farce' for good measure. What an exciting old city for a first time visitor, not to mention the pleasure of a pretty escort and the change of cooler weather. This was definitely a place I vowed to return to at the first opportunity, which, unfortunately, was not to come for another six years.

Almost every weekend the base ran buses into Marrakech for the day. The city, with its multitude of Minarets, Islamic prayer towers with the Muezzins calling the faithful to prayer five times a day, lent an exciting Middle East flavor. Date palms lined the wide streets and Arab style architecture made for fascinating photo opportunities.

For most visitors the high point of a trip to Marrakech was spending an afternoon exploring the fabulous 'Medina,' a ancient shopping mall of stores fronting narrow, winding streets catering to a vast variety of merchandise, jewelry and restaurants. It was exciting fare indeed....blaring Arab music on loudspeakers while security guards wearing traditional Arab burnoose headdresses with flowing white robes complete with a curved dagger in waist sashes and carrying 1903 Enfield bolt action rifles (right out of a 1930's Hollywood Foreign Legion film) cast a sharp eye on the passing parade of shoppers. Hawking shop keepers wearing the picturesque Fez hats added to the din by offering their 'best deals' in gold, jewelry, fine carpets, leather, produce and my favorite....camel saddles! Oh! To complete the picture, throw in a few baskets of cobras dancing to the hypnotic music of a handler's flute! All we needed was Charles Boyer skulking thru the Kasbah!

I don't think we had any incidents involving our troops while in Marrakech, perhaps partly due to the briefing we received at the base where we were advised to wear our U.S. uniforms with the flag on the sleeve to identify us. Apparently, the French that controlled Morocco at that time were not held in high esteem by the local Arabs and being mistaken for a 'Frenchie' was a questionable idea.

After haggling in various 'best deal' shops, I settled on an attractive, silver ring featuring scroll writing in Arabic on the face. In halting English, the shop keeper told me that the message meant 'Long Life and Good Health!' I always suspected, however, it actually meant 'Death to the Infidel!' or something like that.

As we made our way out of the Medina onto the huge open plaza to board our return buses, we got another dose of snake charmers fluting the cobras out of the proverbial baskets to the delight of crowds of tourists. As our visit came to an end, the amplified calls to prayer from the many towers seemed a fitting conclusion to the overall mystique of this fabulous Arab city.

With our TDY assignment almost completed, our crew was chosen to leave a week early (maybe it was rigged, since our crew seemed to get all the perks) to return to home base in Savannah to prepare the Wing's grand homecoming. Stopping in the Azores once again, I bought a case of single malt Scotch Whiskey at a really cheap, no tax price and hid it in the electronics compartment under the flight deck and away from the prying eyes of U.S. Customs. Generally, Customs did only a cursory inspection of the aircraft back at the home field (this was before smuggling drugs into the country became popular) and probably figured 'what the hell!' if the flight crew brought in a few extra bottles of booze it caused no harm, except, perhaps to the individual's liver. I once again, took the Greyhound bus (sans parachute this time) back to Miami to pick up my car and return to the base for another few months until my enlistment was up.

During my last week in the service I was flying almost every day due to a Wing Max Effort. The weather was overcast and less than 20 degrees when I gratefully took my last flight. I was Honorably (did you ever doubt?) discharged on December 20, 1954 and made it home in time for the best Christmas in a long, long time....what did Reverend Dr. King say about being 'Free at Last?...Thank God Almighty....Free at Last!' I figured two years in the National Guard and four years in the Air Force was enough for me.

Back to School

Being home, with the military behind me and visiting with family and old friends, along with the added prospect of going back to my university studies in February, was a joyous time. After a relaxing holiday I decided that with over a month before enrollment I could put a few dollar sin my pocket by getting a temporary job. I called my Uncle, Al Pflueger and asked him if he had a job I could do before going back to school. Gracious as usual, he told me to "go down to the shop and ask Dommic to find a job for you."

I really appreciated the job but after a few days standing around sanding various areas of giant marlin, sharks and the like..... sniffing dust, decaying fish and formaldehyde, I thought that getting in some beach time was the better part of valor. In any event, after a quick tussle with my conscience, I thanked Uncle Al and weaseled out of the job he so kindly gave me.

I had been reluctant to return to the scene of my freshman year grades crime at the University of Florida....afraid that I might be jailed for pretending to be a student....so I opted for a year or so at the University of Miami. The rational being that it would be nice to stay home after the four year air force tour and while it was more expensive at Miami, a private school; it was a cheaper alternative living at home with Mom and my stepfather Jack, than living alone. I applied and received the G.I. Bill, providing funds to apply to tuition and books and proceeded to register at the 'U' for the February 1955 semester.

The first semester of my sophomore year was proceeding nicely, when in April I read a notice advising that Pan American World Airways was offering a cooperative Station Manager training program at Miami for the first time. This struck a cord and when I checked it out it had a tremendous appeal. The program was in cooperation with the university and provided for the prospect of going with the airline every other semester for at least three semesters and with the possibility of a job offer at graduation.

The initial orientation at the business school had over a hundred interested students in attendance, but when grades and other issues were factored in the group dropped to around forty. The next step was a personal interview with the Pan American Latin American Division headquarters senior management personnel. My interviewer was Santos Chiantos, Maintenance Chief of LAD, who, as luck would have it, knew my Uncle Al and in addition, seemed impressed with my air force background, or at least the fact that I had completed any military obligation.

In due course, the dean of the business school called me in and advised that Pan Am had selected me as one of the students for the training program. He touched on my responsibility to keep the grades up while at school and to do my best not to embarrass the university while with the air line. I promised the 'moon' and meant it! He shook my hand and told me to report to Pan Am Field in mid-September for my first semester, which would be in Miami at their Ground School for Station Manager Trainee's... Although I had figured my chances were pretty good that I would be selected in the top twenty, I literally jumped for joy at the news and counted the days until I was expected to report.

Finally the day came. I presented myself to the Superintendent of Stations office at Pan Am Field on 36 Street in Miami Springs, took a seat and when I looked around the room I saw only two possible students (from the dazed look). Introducing myself to Bob and Jim, we wondered where the other 17 trainees were. The answer soon became apparent that there were no other 17 trainees... the three of us were 'it'.

A quick briefing informed us that we could wander around the Pan Am offices and hangers to familiar ourselves but to return in an hour to meet the Superintendent of Stations and receive instructions on the Station Manager course. We gawked around the massive hangers like hillbilly's visiting New York, but unfortunatly, the three rubes wandered a little off course and into the U.S. Customs incoming passenger area (they get a little picky about unauthorized personnel in their area) and were lucky to receive a dressing down and a kick in our collective backsides, escaping with an echoing, "get those idiots out of here!". My blood ran cold when I thought about the call U.S. Customs could have made to the Superintendent on our first day 'on the job'....beginning with "we have the three stooges in Federal lockup!" The dean would not have been happy to have his first three trainees booted out on day one of this noble experiment.

The course was very interesting. It covered the exciting history of Pan Am from its first overseas flight from Key West to Havana, to conquering the Pacific, the Atlantic, South America and around the world. Heady stuff! There was a heavy dose of how to calculate the weight and balance of an aircraft, which was required on every flight departure. Other tid-bits of the training included the geography of the Pan Am routes, particularly as pertained to Central and South America and going into the job requirements in the field. All in all, the three months were well spent, although we were keen to actually put our new found knowledge to work.

The good news came on the wings of our graduation from the ground school in the form of a plum assignment. Reeder Chaney, one of the executives in the Superintendent's office was programmed to spend a couple of weeks in the Republic of Panama checking the weight and balance operation, with a side trip for a week to

Medellin, Colombia to check out our affiliate, COPA airlines. The good news part was that I was selected to accompany him. Finally some action!

We arrived in Panama and checked into the posh El Panama Hotel and had a great couple of weeks working with the Tocumen Airport Pan Am Operations staff. For our third week we jumped a COPA DC-3 and had a harrowing trip thru the mountains to the lovely city of Medellin. I had a wonderful experience except for my lack of understandable Spanish prohibiting any meaningful conversation with a beautiful hotel elevator operator (giving me extra incentive to bear down in my upcoming Spanish classes at the 'U'). The end of the fall semester found me back at school with renewed commitment and looking forward to my next assignment.

Although I was in my mid-twenties, I still enjoyed the Spring semester at school.... dating and all the usual undergraduate activities however, I was more interested in completing my school semester and returning work with Pan Am. When I was informed that my summer semester would be spent back at Tocumen Airport in Panama, I gave a whoop of joy! I had barely scratched the surface in discovering all the interesting facets of this lovely country during my visit with Reeder in late January.

This station required a Station Manager and four Duty (assistant) Station Managers to operate a busy 24 hours a day schedule. Panama was the cross-roads from California thru all the Central American countries enroute to South America; flights from Florida and Panagra (Pan American-Grace Shipping) flights from Chile, along the west coast of South America enroute to New York.

It was a homecoming of sorts. I received a warm welcome from some of the airport personnel I had met while on temporary assignment with Reeder a semester ago. Asking around for suitable accommodations, I was steered to Pension Mexico in Panama City, as a well located, inexpensive lodging near the Pan Am employee bus route. The owner/operators spoke a little English and managed a friendly, clean and spacious guest house. Any meals that I might require wound up as 'bacon and eggs' since that's the only culinary delights that both of us understood, but since I ate a meal or two daily at work (the airport restaurant had a dandy Panamanian 50 cent special for employees) eggs worked for me. One of my favorite dining experiences at the airport was surplus first class meals taken off the Panagra flight from Lima, Peru. There must have been a master chef in their flight kitchen as the chops, steaks and lobster presentations were mouth-watering, even when re-heated in our commissary at 2:00 AM.

The Station Manager, Findley Howard, called me in and welcomed me back with, "good to see you again, Charlie. We applied to use you as a temporary relief Station Manager to cover George Hambleton, who is going to San Salvador to manage the station while the manager takes some time off. We realize you're a student trainee, but we only have a couple of weeks to check you out before we 'throw you to the wolves' and let you run your own shift!" This announcement precipitated sweat popping up along my upper lip.... anticipating the difficulty of running my own shift in one of the company's most active stations. I thought...run, Charlie run! At this point one of my eyes developed a tic as if internally protesting this mad plan. I took a gulp and mumbled the usual nonsense about 'doing my best for the team' and I may even have mentioned 'winning one for the Gripper!' Just to nail it down, I added a 'you can count on me!' for good measure. Nauseous stuff! Nobody said I couldn't suck up with the best.

It seems that I was to replace George Hambleton (a graduate of Princeton, no less and whose father was reported to have been an early Pan American Director) who later became Pan Am's first Station Manager in Moscow. It was once reported that George had a problem with movie actress Terry Moore's Panamanian husband's lack of enthusiasm when George wore her fancy pajamas to a Halloween party. No mention was made on how George came by the pajamas!

I paired up with Assistant Manager Bob Walker, an ex-navy carrier pilot who had a pronounced limp (probably from crash landing on a postage stamp in a rough sea). We were on the 11 pm to 8 am night shift, which wasn't too busy handling the occasional late flights along with the scheduled Panagra coming in from Peru. Bob was a good teacher and seemed to enjoy company during the long nights and under his tutelage I gained some confidence as the week passed. Another plus was Bob's automobile which made it a convenient transport back to the Pension Mexico.

Completing the shift on the first morning, Bob asked me if I needed a ride home, but warned that he usually stopped for a few beers at his favorite joint in the city. I confessed that my daily schedule didn't include drinking beer at nine in the morning. He reasoned that we worked all night, so nine AM was like five in the afternoon and the sun would have been over the 'yardarm' by now! His logic overwhelmed me and I found that drinking beer in a scrungy dump featuring dirt floors and a scratching chicken at nine AM, seemed perfectly normal after a couple of days. It seemed easy to adapt while swilling beer!

When I started my own shift as a 25 year old college student supervising career Panamanian staff... I did something that probably went a long way to insure a successful assignment in Panama... I got friendly with Jose Delgado, who functioned as Chief of Operations and another stalwart heading up the Traffic Department. I asked them to help keep me from making novice mistakes, since we all understood I was a college trainee on my first down-line assignment. This worked extremely well and Jose would saddle up to me in the managers office and casually say, "Charlie, if I were you I would do so and so," and walk away. The old adage seems to apply, 'a word to the wise is sufficient!' and another potential career endangering disaster was avoided.

During the few weeks I had the day shift, I usually drove back to the city after work with Carson Davis, the Chief Mechanic, and a few other mechanic types in his assigned company station wagon. I appreciated the lift and enjoyed the camaraderie, particularly when thirst would overcome us and we would pull the station wagon into the parking lot at the 'Casa de Amor,' sit around one of tables and order a bottle of rum with coke setups. We would sip rum and talk over the riggers of the day at the airport. Initially, I was surprised that we were using a well know house of ill repute as a cocktail bar and other than ogling some of the talent (a term loosely applied) we would finish the bottle in an hour or so, and leave with our virginity in tact.

Another surprise awaited me when I received word to present myself to Findley Howard in his office... immediately! As I entered I saw Carson and a few others of our afternoon tea club standing at attention, while the red faced manager sputtered, "have you guys lost your minds?" Spittle was spraying like an aerosol bomb!

Neither Carson nor I got the drift of this verbal attack. We figured that we either bungled an aircraft repair or sent one to the wrong destination (more on this later). But, alas, it was even more serious that that! He had worked up to a full shout when he got to the punch line with, "for God's sake! When you're going in a whore house, park the damn Pan Am station wagon in the back of the joint and not in front where every passing car on the highway can see the big, blue Pan Am ball logo on the side.....The next time this happens you guys will be hoofing it down the road!" Sheepishly, we accepted the logic (that's why Findley got the big bucks) and on subsequent visits we took special care to hide the vehicle in the far rear, even if it took longer to stagger to.

Carson and his wife Peg had a plush apartment near my lodgings, where I was often invited to dinner and more importantly to use their washer and dryer for my bi-weekly laundry. As an extra plus, they had a lovely young daughter who was a delightful date and as much as I wanted to 'put the moves' on her, I am proud to report that other than an 'accidental' feel, she remained unsoiled as a special tribute of respect.

One night on the ramp, I took one of the bicycles we used for transportation to the cargo hanger around 300 yards away to evaluate the next cargo load and to take a peek at a caged (thankfully) Jaguar, reported to be the most evil looking big cat you will ever see. Merrily peddling along, whistling a happy tune and emulating my youth when I rode a lot without using hands on the handle bars. Suddenly, I hit something on the dark ramp-way like a fully extended fire hose, flipping the bike and the happy whistler ass over teacup onto the tarmac. To my horror, I wound up with a battered bike tangled up with a very large and very angry (probably a local python) snake thrashing around. The cold blooded snake had probably crawled out of the surrounding sawgrass to warm up on the tarmac and in the near darkness we did not see each other. I managed to disentangle myself from bike and snake and no doubt set an outdoor sprint record toward the lighted hanger. Still shaking, I marshaled a few of the cargo guys and drove a tug back to retrieve the bike. The headlights revealed the snake had gone, but some good natured (?) ribbing indicated the staff wrote this episode off to a clumsy Gringo that had just fallen off his bike. Incidentally, after all this… I did see the Jaguar and it WAS one mean looking cat!

The summer was going fast, when on a day off I was offered the opportunity to join one of our mechanics on a COPA DC-3 trip over the isthmus to the Caribbean side to perform maintenance on our Aerofare Station. The procedure required that we take a five gallon can of gas and a charged truck battery, along with any tools, filters, oil and such as the Aerofare job may require. We landed in an abandoned WWII U.S. Army Air Force base along the coast and taxied to a deserted Ops area. We poured the gas in the tank of an equally abandoned, rust encrusted troop carrier truck, hooked up the battery and cranked it up to a sputtering, hole in the muffler roar. Following a dirt road a couple of miles through the jungle, we came to a rickety dock on the sea. In due course, a 25' outboard powered cruiser pulled up with Henry, the Aerofare Station Manager at the controls along with two San Blas Indian helpers.

A gregarious Henry introduced himself and gave me a quick rundown, "its about a twenty minute run to our station located in an old army outpost in one of the San Blas Islands. Pam Am had to set up the Aerofare (aircraft guiding system) when we started service into Panama from Miami, because no other agency would or could provide the facility. I live in one of the old barracks and with the help of Pedro and Job," he continued, pointing to the helpers, "we keep the station operating 24 hours a day."

As we cruised through the islands, I remarked, "I have never heard of the San Blas Islands, but they look a little like the Florida Keys."

"Quite a few Indians are living on these islands and in really squalid and primitive conditions," he responded. It wasn't until many years later, with improved access, that tour groups discovered the islands and helped them to become a popular tourist destination.

Advised that maintenance on the diesels powering the electrical system would take at least 6 or 7 hours, Henry asked me if I would like to go fishing. I jumped at the opportunity and was soon ensconced on the cruiser, complete with an Indian captain cum guide. Trolling a yellow jig we hooked a fish on almost every pass between two small islands. It was a blast hauling in five pound Yellowtail Snapper, but after a dozen were flopping around the boat, the captain stopped over a beautiful, shallow reef, hopped over the side and proceeded to spear half a dozen Spiny Lobster (Crawfish) for the pot.

After a wonderful lunch of really fresh seafood, Henry said, "Charlie, if you want to take my shotgun and walk down by the river chances are that you will be able to shoot a few pigeons and doves for my freezer," as he handed me a 410 shotgun. Now a 410 is the smallest caliber of shotguns in general use....mainly used for small game, birds and firing a shell barely larger than a pencil.

My personal shotgun was a 12 gauge which seemed like a cannon compared to the 410, but I figured what the hell, you don't need a bazooka to pop a dove.

A short stroll took me by flocks of doves sitting on tension cables supporting the huge Aerofare antenna and presented no problem in shooting a few for Henry's freezer. After knocking down a couple dozen doves, I soon tired of this non-sport, but continued walking along the river bank until I discovered fresh, BIG cat tracks in the damp mud. This development stopped me in my tracks while my mind flashed back to that vicious looking Jaguar I saw in the cargo area. Standing there in close proximity to a really powerful and probably nasty tempered predator with a popgun in shaky hands, I decided it was like bear hunting with a switch and threw caution to the wind with another mad dash to the safety of the station. Panting from the exertion, I suggested that Pedro pick up the fallen doves since I had no plans to do any more exploring without a well armed squad of Marines.

I enjoyed living in Panama and visiting the many picturesque and historical sites the country was famous for. One of the most popular was the ruins of Old Panama, sacked by Sir Henry Morgan in 1600. The stone walls that delinated the settlement were still standing allowing the present day viewer to imagine what it was like at the time of the sacking. In another splendid outing, we motored to Davide, in the mountains, where we viewed gold frogs and a strain of square trees, which I was amazed to see actually existed. A 'must see' of course, was a trip to the Panama Canal, the Mira Flores Locks and Lake Gatun.

On a more serious note, the Pan American City Office in Panama City was bombed on two occasions while I worked in Panama, fortunately resulting in no injuries. A 'return the Panama Canal to Panama!' group claimed responsibility and ultimately helped shape U.S. thinking, resulting in President Jimmy Carter's decision to relinquish control to Panama.

Devoting a day to visit the city of Colon on the Caribbean side of the Isthmus where the entrance to the Canal starts, I borrowed one of the company's station wagons and proceeded to race thru a 'speed trap' on the main highway. A second or two later, I heard the screaming of a motorcycle cop's siren and the dreaded flashing red lights. Crap! Pulling over the officer told me I was going 60 in a 35 miles an hour zone and asked me for my license. He carefully looked it over, and then slipped it into his shirt pocket saying, "Senior, you will have to go to the police station in Colon this afternoon and pay a fine to retrieve your license!"

After a filling lunch of beans, rice, pork and plantains in a hole in the wall mom and pop restaurant in down town Colon, I took a spin around the area and presented myself to the police station, cum court house, to wait for the judge to show up from his siesta and get to my case. Sitting on a very hard bench with other potential felons, waiting for the wheels of justice to grind down, was not what I had in mind for the day. Being a foreigner and speaking only a smattering of Spanish at the time, I was quite apprehensive, and was startled when a weasel faced character slid in next to me and in English said, "Senior, perhaps you might like to settle this situation like gentlemen instead of waiting for the judge to arrive?"

I wasn't sure about the 'gentlemen' part, but I surely wanted to haul my sore ass out of Colon with my license snuggled back in my wallet. "Yes. I would very much like to (I wanted to be careful of phrasing here) to 'pre-pay' my fine and get back to Panama City without further delay! How much is the fine?" I asked, playing along with this rip-off.

The Weasel, with a quick glance around replied, "Only twenty dollars, Senior!"

As I slipped the twenty into his hand, he reached over and dropped the license in my shirt pocket and in a flash scurried away, wishing the 'senior' a nice day. Later, back at the airport, I was telling the story to a few of my more experienced co-workers, one of which said, with a laugh, "you have to fold a twenty in your licenses and the next time you get stopped for a traffic violation the money will disappear, but you will not have to waste time going to a phony court." Good advice is welcome wherever you find it, even if a little late.

During my assignment in the Republic of Panama, I met a charming Canadian young lady who had somehow found her way to lodge at my pension for a week or so while waiting for a ship to Australia for the 1956 Olympics. This worked out well for a horny young fellow who had only been able to pick-off a stewardess now and then on a hit or miss basis. On our first date, we went to dinner and dancing at a popular joint called 'Pete's Catalina' on the waterfront. It was a huge, open windowed restaurant and gin mill that served great fresh seafood and featured a hot Latin band blasting away to a frenzied throng of sweaty dancers. The Cha Cha seemed to be the popular poison with a 'dancing until you drop!' philosophy that sent exhausted dancers to their tables long before a particular tune ended.

Wrapping up the evening with 'one for the road,' we got back to the Pan Am wagon where I answered the call from a frisky libido, while planting a passionate smooch on my companion. To my delight, she responded with enthusiasm, obviously spurred on by my fatal charm....or perhaps by the booze we had been sampling for the last several hours....choose one of the above!

After this first episode in the wagon, our activities did not include the missionary position. Apparently, my lady friend had the belief that making love standing up kept one from getting pregnant, a dangerous theory 50 years ago in the English community. I hope her theory held up by the time she got to Australia.

Just before I rotated back to Miami to tackle my next semester at school, I threw a 'thank you' dinner party at the Gamboa Country Club in the Canal Zone, operated by the sister and brother-in-law of the Pan American Director for Panama. The golf and country club was built primarily for the use of U.S. personnel working in the Zone and hence was very inexpensive, Thanking my friends and co-workers with drinks and dinner in small recognition for all their kindness and help during my assignment was the least I could do. On a happy note....after multiple cocktails and lots of Chinese food for nine guests the total bill came to something like twenty dollars. It seems like twenty was he magic number in Panama in those days!

After settling down to another bout of school where I picked up last semesters pieces of an algebra disaster....it seems like I didn't have one clue of what algebra was actually about, so I skipped the last half of the course and reported early to my afternoon part time job as a bookkeeper for a large concrete supplier. As an amusing side note: I worked beside the head bookkeeper whose resume' contained a reference to his hobby of 'collecting Oriental Art' all on the grand salary of $65.00 a week. Although my grades were even dazzling me (if one could ignore the algebra)....there was only marginal interest in this school thing at my age and I was a happy camper when Pan Am called for another round of training.

My next assignment was at the Miami International Airport, then located in Miami Springs at 36th Street, the scene of the infamous 'Customs fiasco' a couple of years before when the rookies wandered into the restricted area. I was actually keen to take on another foreign assignment, but realized that working as an assistant manager in the company's busiest airport had a lot of upside. After six weeks I was intrigued when orders came down to proceed to Port au Prince, Haiti to connect to the flight to Guadeloupe in the French West Indies. Our French manager was going on vacation for a few months and I was going to get the opportunity to operate my own station.

Arriving in Port au Prince, I cleared customs and immigration and went to find the Station Manager as he was dispatching my arrival flight. Heckathorne was a very gregarious guy and after taking a massive ring of keys off his belt, he unlocked the office door and ushered me in. I asked if he had had a problem with robbery around the airport and he answered with, "no, but I have had more than one bomb threat!" Talk about an attention grabber!

Heckathorn unlocked one of his desk drawers and pulled out a huge hand gun (horse pistol?) and shoved it into his belt as he asked, "do you want to ride into town with me and take a look around while I pick up a few things? You have a lot of time before your flight to Guadeloupe."

Venturing another question, "what's going on in Haiti that we need to carry a gun?"

"Last week when one of our head office managers came down from Miami, the local bad buys tried to turn the station wagon over and scared the hell out of him. I thought that this might discourage that kind of foolishness if it happens again," he answered, patting the pistol for emphasis.

My companion was right that on almost every corner there were groups of men mulling around....angry eyes following the slow progess of our vehicle as we rolled down the main street of the capital. We finally stopped at a record store and again at a meat market, appearing in no hurry or concern for the rabble that were, at this point, content to keep a safe distance. Much to my relief, no aggression was forthcoming and as time neared for Pan Am Flight 432 (the island hopper) to whisk me away, we returned to the airport. Thankfully, the wagon was not turned over nor was the office bombed in our absence.... at least not that day.

A few years later, I heard rumors that Heckathron was suspected of being a CIA Agent, having been assigned first to Guatemala City during the height of the communist take over in 1952, and then again to Haiti in the current troubled years. A few years went by when we heard other rumors that he had been transferred to some country in Africa and died there from a heart attack....a theory widely debunked by the Pan Am crowd in favor of a more dramat*i*c departure via assassination.

When I arrived at the Pointe a Pietre Airport in the capital city of Guadeloupe, I met with what few employees we had, most of who, thankfully, spoke English. I was then taken to the city to meet with the owner of a private travel agency that operated our city office, in lieu of using Pan Am personnel. I solicited suggestions on suitable accommodations and came up with a lovely spot featuring a great French restaurant complete with a dozen quaint individual cottages located on a bluff overlooking the Caribbean Sea. The place was called 'La Pergola' which should have rhymed with a home away from home, which it certainly became. The cuisine was outstanding and the staff very friendly, which was amazing since they were French citizens with a reputation for being difficult.

Working at the airport was pretty cushy, since we had only one 'scat' flight a day, which remained on the ground for only ten minutes. I had to get used to a really short ground time requiring two of the four piston engines on the DC-6B to remain running while we rushed the few passengers destined for the island off and the departing ones on, bags off and bags on, close the door....start the other two engines and wave good bye as the aircraft taxied onto the runaway and away. Whew! After a quick return to the Operations Office to send the departure message to Miami Control, the work day was pretty much over. By that time ... we figured the flight was controlled by the next destination and not likely to return to Guadeloupe in the event of a maintenance problem. You can see why this kind of service was referred to as 'scat'. The whole daily operation only took a couple of hours before aircraft arrival and a half hour after, before I could make a dash back to La Pergola to sun by the pool, sip a beverage and contemplate the extensive (and exquisite) dinner menu. Not a bad job for a student!

My relaxed demeanor was shaken one day when our daily flight developed an engine failure and came in with it feathered (always bad news) and was grounded for replacement. Imagine the enormous complexity and myriad of problems, when an aircraft full of passengers' enroute to somewhere else is all of a sudden stuck in what was a small city on an island with scant accommodations. Replacing the engine was another can of worms… with the closest replacement engine and mechanic change crew a thousand miles away in Miami.

After the diagnosis was sent to Miami Headquarters, we had the challenging task of trying to find rooms for the passengers and crew. Luck allowed us to place all the passengers, to the last room, in the only suitable commercial hotel. The crew of six men and women were left to camp out in my cottage and one more available at the Pergola for the few days it would take to round up a crew of mechanics, load a new engine on a cargo plane, fly down to Guadeloupe and then change the engine. I spent the entire time at the airport sleeping when I could on the office sofa, handling the arrival of the cargo plane, organizing the departure of the delayed passengers on the next day's flight and constantly keeping the French airport authorities and Pan Am Control advised of developments. The crew apparently enjoyed the stay, utilizing the beach, pool and fine cuisine and as a result the Captain wrote a glowing letter of commendation to my boss, the Superintendent of Stations, on how well I had handled the situation….certainly a big plus for my budding career. I was relieved, however, when the new engine was in place, the crew and mechanics gone and I could settle, blissfully, back into my old slovenly ways.

One evening while eating my way through five courses of delicious French cuisine at the La Pergola, I heard American voices at a table behind me. On closer inspection, I recognized the singer/actress Lena Horne and her husband, band leader Lenny Hayton. I waved a 'hello' and after dessert, they invited me over to their table to get acquainted, have a brandy and enjoy a little home country talk along with some fascinating 'show biz' antidotes. They were quite charming. As I recall, Lena could speak French, having lived in France earlier in her career and kindly helped me to order menu items that the waiters understood, resulting in the delivery of dishes that I actually ordered! Imagine that!

Languages were not my strong suit, but I did learn to say a few words, other than 'bier' in French, such as 'ice cream' and 'little bridge' (the former I used a lot and the latter only once, stretching a point as there was no bridge in sight at the time, 'petite or grand') Obviously, I did not distinguish myself with linguistic acumen and in addition managed to embarrass myself when I pulled a nifty French phrase a friend once gave that I thought meant something like 'it's a pleasure to meet you' and actually meant 'would you sleep with me?' The City Office owner claimed he was flattered if somewhat reluctant ....at least I got a laugh out of the faux pas, and fortunately not a sleeping companion. I later heard this practical joke was often perpertrated on gullible rubes… and I guess I qualified!

In the few days Lena and Lenny remained at the resort, we continued to have late drinks and welcome conversation, and for a few years Lena and I exchanged the odd activity updates and holiday cards. I was sad to note her recent passing.

The French owner of our City Ticket Office also owned a sugar cane operation they used to support the manufacture of a fine tea colored rum made on their seaside property. One day I was invited to spend the afternoon at their private beach, have lunch and tour the rum factory, with a carte blanche to sample as much of the product as prudent. They really knew how to extend a Caribbean welcome…. offering their beautiful daughter as my companion, a picnic basket with a superb French (of course) wine and finishing late on a glorious afternoon with a couple of their fine rum and cokes…its hard to beat island hospitality.

I felt like a yo-yo, spinning back and forth between school and a job I really loved with Pan Am, but I seemed to thrive on it. When I was going to school at the 'U', I enjoyed partying and dating a variety of young ladies….one of which was the 'Roach." She was a petite redhead with a cute little body, intelligent and a lot of fun. I never found out where she picked up such an unflattering nickname, but everyone called her the 'Roach'.... mostly with affection. It wasn't only her trim shape I admired, but in the garage of the house she shared with her grandparents, resided a creampuff of a 1935 Auburn convertible automobile, garnering at least part of my interest. I tried to buy it, but the grandfather had a fantasy that he was going to tune it up, buy a touring cap and gloves and motor off into the sunset, to spend his rapidly declining years visiting 'this great country!' I hope he followed his dream and is still out there on the highways of America like a modern day Flying Dutchman.

One night, the Roach and I were playing around in the back seat of my Ford, when she whispered in my ear that, "I can do things to you that will curl your toes!" Needless to say, my encouragement was quickly forthcoming and this mystery was soon solved with a seemly endless bag of tricks! If my toes did not curl....it was close! When she returned to her home in Tampa, I must admit I missed the 'Roach!'

My last undergraduate posting was for the winter of 1957. When I arrived in Nassau, in the nearby Bahama Islands, I went on duty as one of two Assistant Managers. The other manager was an older gentleman, Mr. Curry, who was a 'Conchie Joe (named after an edible shellfish and pronounced 'conkie'), a local name for a white Bahamian. Our Director/Station Manager was Mr. Morley, a former English school teacher. The story circulated that Mr. Morley tragically shot one of his sons with the blast of his shotgun in a White Crown Pigeon shooting accident on the Island of Andros a few years before. A remaining son, who kindly took me spear fishing in the bay off Nassau, is now a prominent Real Estate Broker in the Bahamas.

Pan Am's City Office was located on the bay near the present bridge to Paradise Island (then Huntington Hartford's Hog Cay), a convenient location when sea planes were the only air service available. The pink airport terminal office was at Oakes Field, close to downtown Nassau and exuded colonial architecture and charm in its last year before moving miles away to its present location at Windsor Field.

I was pre-booked into a boarding house that provided room and meals, but after a few days, valuing my privacy, I rented my own apartment a block off Shirley Street, close to the famous 'Steps' and an easy walk to the bright lights of Bay Street. All the tourist hot spots were there, like Blackbeard's, Junkanoo Club, and Dirty Dicks, along with a movie theater, shops and restaurants.

I developed a routine that included arriving at my apartment in the early evening after dispatching our last flight of the day, a DC-7B to New York. Our aircraft caterer usually had a leftover first class incoming meal earmarked for me to take home and pop into the oven (the handy microwave was not yet in use), for a quick, delicious meal while I showered and dressed for a night on the town. Eat....dress and head for Bay Street and a night on the town. In those days, upscale tourism was flourishing and almost any area of New Providence Island was safe for the visitor, including one of my favorites, 'The Cat and the Fiddle,' a semi-open aired club with a big dance floor and a hot island band.

Spear fishing was one of my most enjoyable activates on the occasional free day. A few of us would rent a skiff and motor out of Nassau Harbor to places like Sandy Cay, a picture post card small island, fringed with white, sandy beaches and scattered with stately coconut trees. The Cay (pronounced 'key' in the Bahamas) was the ideal spot to relax in the shade and enjoy lunch, before returning to the hunt for Snapper, Grouper, and Spiny Lobster. Since spear guns were illegal in the Bahamas, I had to get used to using an Hawaiian sling, a hand grip piece of bamboo, which propelled a 6' to 10' steel shaft, using rubber tubing for power. I could hit the odd moving fish, but never developed the skills the local lads had, hitting fast moving targets from long distances with deadly accuracy. I was, however, awarded the unflattering nickname of the 'Sniper' earned by my long, inaccurate shots that bounced harmlessly off the reef making a 'ping' noise, usually followed by me begging one of the local boys to deep dive to recover my spear.

At Operations one day, I fielded a call from our New York Customer Service, advising that they were sending Mrs. Sak's (perhaps of the department store fame?) mink stole down on the next flight. Apparently, she had enjoyed the hospitality of the Pan Am VIP room and boarded the flight to Nassau sans the stole. I met her as she disembarked the flight, a little dazzled by her beauty, and delivered the message with the assurance that I would personally deliver the stole the following evening after the flight's arrival.

With the stole firmly in hand, I called her and offered to drop it off at the British Colonial Hotel's front desk. She countered with an invitation to join her and her ski instructor companion for dinner that evening at a nearby restaurant. During a very pleasant meal, her ski instructor (presumably not in Nassau to teach snow skiing!) excused himself for a pit stop. She leaned over and said, "I am going to Barbados next week for a house party....would you care to accompany me? My friend has to return to Colorado."

Surprised, flattered and sorely tempted, I confessed, "I would love to, but I can't get a vacation in the middle of the high season!" I didn't have the nerve to tell her I was still a lowly student, but in a rare bout of good sense, and dripping mental tears, respectfully declined.

Behind the traffic counter one afternoon I met and chatted with Benny Goodman, the famous bandleader and clarinetist, checking in for our New York flight. Another afternoon I made a quick $25 pushing a baggage cart across the tarmac as an extra (apparently I wasn't ready yet for prime time) in a low budget movie that was being shot in Nassau. It featured a Christine somebody, easily recognizable for a bunch of 'B' movies. My mind wandered.... as I looked around for thongs of adoring fans fighting for my autograph, but sadly...

found no one remotely interested to turn down with a haughty, "sorry, no autographs today!"

One day the airport employees were tittering with news that zillionaire, Howard Hughes, had flown one of Trans World Airways Super Constellations into Nassau and parked it for a week (why not… he owned the company). He then reserved the entire second floor of the Nassau Emerald Beach Hotel on Cable Beach for his entourage… I guess if you're going…go first class!

As the assignment drew to an end, I met with one of my local acquaintants at the Junkanoo Club one evening, who invited me and a visiting friend to join him in touring some of the 'over the hill' watering holes around the island. He drove a 1951 Chevy hardtop that whisked us from club to club, sampling the local spirits with some abandon. Around five in the morning while traveling down Bay Street, the driver decided it was time for a little snooze and proceeded to pass out at the wheel. Occupying the passenger seat gave me a bird's eye view of the rapidly approaching corner of a substantial building now blocking our way. To my credit, I had enough reflexes remaining to give a hardy, and I thought a quite descriptive "look out!"

Aroused from his slumber, he swung the wheel to avoid the building and crashed, instead, into a steel light pole (minding its own business at the edge of the street) bending it some six feet horizontally before coming to rest as a hood ornament on the Chevy. As a result of the impact, my forehead smashed a hole in the windscreen (also know in the United States as a 'windshield'), opening a large half-moon cut above my left eye. My friend from Miami was launched, stunned, to the floor from his back seat perch, while the driver was slumped, unconsciously over the wheel. Unbelievably, I did not lose consciousness and retained the presence of mind to shake the driver awake and suggest he might consider losing the half empty bottle of scotch before, rather after, the arrival of the police.

When I arrived at the Princess Margaret Hospital, a nurse met me in the emergency room and painstakingly tweezered out the many bits and pieces of shattered glass from the wound. An English doctor finally appeared and applied a butterfly tape over the shredded flesh, gave me a tetanus shot and sent me on my way. On the front page of next day's Guardian Newspaper, there appeared a very graphic photograph of the ill fated Chevy with a caption reading, 'Escaping Death!' Accompanying the picture was a brief article recounting how 'Charlie Pflueger was spared in a near deadly automobile crash.' I was later advised that the driver of the Chevy was disappointed that I had not offered to help pay for repairs (I would have thought that you would have to jack it up and drive a new car underneath the wreckage). My response was that my suggestion to make the booze bottle disappear and my declaration that the driver was sober as a judge, was a sufficient donation.

When my Mother picked me up at the Miami Airport and noted the big, white tape job on my forehead, you would not want to be within hearing range. It's a good thing to keep in mind that mothers get a little uptight when their children tempt fate, run amuck and do stupid things!

The Graduate - Jamaica Bound

I waited until a month before graduation (to make damn sure) before I called the Pan Am Office to advise that a diploma looked like a reasonable bet and was checking to see if I had been penciled in for full time employment. My heart sank when the Personal Manager suggested that I should have called sooner... then elation followed when he said that they had an Assistant Station Manager's job for me in Montego Bay, Jamaica. He advised that I should get down to the office pronto to fill out the employment forms and the request for a Jamaican work permit. It seemed that all that paid fun I had as a co-op student was actually going to pay off with a real job. Miracles never cease!

Graduation day finally came. I slipped into my black cap and gown and with my Mother, Father and Grandparents in attendance, marched down the isle to proudly accept my Bachelor of Business Administration from the University of Miami. I think my family gave a collective sigh of relief that at the ripe old age of 27, I finally graduated (there had been some talk of having to 'blow up the school' to get me out). Five days after this monumental event, I boarded Pan Am Flight 432 and flew away to my new life.

Milo Alexander, the Station Manager, a handsome, crew-cut man of some five years my senior, met me upon arrival and after a quick tour of Operations, drove to my temporary lodgings. I was stunned by the hillside tropical beauty of the Hacton House, where the sea view bar and dining patio were under a huge, sweeping oak tree (the honeymoon suite was actually in the upper branches but did not seem to shake this monster tree when in use). The picturesque wooden cottages, with quaint front porches, were scattered around the hillside. A redheaded, English Mage Taylor was the charming owner/manager while son, Pat was the Operations Manager for Pan Am. I immediately felt at home.

Milo and I worked quite happily for the next year and a half, even with a seven day a week work schedule. When I started there was no need for a night shift as all our flights were during the day. Where this plan went awry was affiliate, Avianca (Colombian National Airlines, touted to be the oldest airlines in the Western Hemisphere started in 1919) had a late afternoon arrival from New York in its route to Bogotá, and vice versa, via Montego Bay, and Kingston. At the time, Avianca was in the last year of operating the three tailed piston-engine Super Constellation, before leasing Pan Am jet aircraft. The aged Super Connie's Wright engines were starting to create maintenance problems along with wind blown spotting of all my white uniform shirts from the oil dripping engines. Maintenance delays out of New York were becoming routine, causing the flights to arrive later at night on a regular basis. Normally, I would come to work at 8:00AM expecting to get off later in the afternoon, and having to hang around the airport to handle the late flight made for very long days. Milo and I finally decided that I would come in late in the afternoon to cover anticipated delays. This was an improvement, allowing time to handle any personal business and get some beach time. I remember one lovely sunny morning paddling around on my float in crystal clear water at Doctor's Cave Beach, thinking 'I've got it made!' A very exhilarating ... if fleeting... feeling!

At 2:00 AM one winter morning, the Avianca flight finally arrived and as we watched the passengers sleepily deplane, a titter of excitement rippled through the support staff as movie star Errol Flynn wobbled down the stairs. Avianca's First Class Service, out of

New York, was well known as being exceptional and particularly generous when it came to keeping the booze flowing during the four hour flight to MoBay. With Errol was his current, well documented girl friend, Beverly Adland, dazzling in a white dress and showing no sign of the trip fatigue, nor the late hour. In the intransit area I introduced myself and exchanged a few pleasantries before the flight was called. After a short flight to Kingston, a limo ride took Errol and friend to the Titchfield Hotel (a famous landmark from the turn of the 20th Century) he had purchased some time before and where his yacht 'Zaca' was moored. It was exciting to meet one of the biggest movie stars from the 1930's and 40's... Robin Hood, Captain Blood and a world class playboy, all rolled into one.

While earning a living was time consuming (to be a full time Bon Vivant was far beyond my financial capabilities) the job provided the means to enjoy the exceptional social life offered on the north coast of Jamaica in the popular winter season. Being young, decent looking, energetic and unattached, provided the opportunity. Almost nightly formal dinner parties at wealthy expatriate homes brought numerous 'extra man at dinner' invitations, requiring a carefully pressed tux or a crisp, white dinner jacket. I took to these 'black tie' affairs like a bee to honey and got the biggest kick out of standing around making inane conversation with beautiful women in long, expensive gowns and carefully coffered hair, sipping champagne and trying to figure how to get them home and into bed.

One of my most important contacts was an older, socially well placed English woman, Celia Byass. A widow whose husband Rupert was the second son of an English Peer and one of the heirs to a continental liquor company. Rupert and Celia were reported to have partied and gambled away over half a million pounds in the mid-thirties... enjoying Monte Carlo and other upscale watering holes, when the English pound was worth $5.00 U.S. and the world was in a depression. Later, having depleted the fortune, they retired to Montego Bay, where Rupert died and Celia, now almost penniless, went to work in a duty free shop. Oddly, now being a working lady did little to diminish her considerable social clout (herself coming from the upper class having grown up with an uncle who was Minister of Air during the WWI period). I met Celia at one of Stanley Vaughn's fun parties, where we played charades and other parlor games, while sucking down enough scotches that everything was funny. Although Celia was 62, some 32 years my senior, we enjoyed each others company and decided to share a house rental in Redding, a few miles out of Montego Bay. This move helped both of us with reduced rent and utilities, and in addition, Celia also managed the staff of a cook, maid and yard boy. In one six month stretch, her demands for perfection from the reigning cook required their replacement at least monthly, as her arrogance and expectations either drove them to verbal assault (and on one occasion, physical assault) or resignation with references as to where she could stick the position. On the other hand... when we dined, it was with grace and style.

Another more valuable perk for me was the social aspect; for example, Celia asked me to escort her to dinner at the nearby winter enclave of the Duke of Marlborough. His lovely, hilltop home overlooking the lights of Montego Bay glittering in the distance was spectacular.

Charlie at the Duke of
Marlborough's Dinner Party,
Montego Bay, Jamaica 1962

Charles Pflueger

Expecting a full blown party, I was amazed to sit down for dinner with the Duke (call me 'Bertie'), three lovely, young ladies, Celia and myself. Having the opportunity to chat unabatedly with 'Bertie' about the history of Blenheim Place, while sipping a drink from Coat of Arms crystal glasses, was surreal to stay the least. A few months later, Celia and I were invited for another slightly larger dinner party at the Dukes, perhaps proving that the first night wasn't a fluke. Sampling the heady delights of the top drawer of the international jet set was, indeed mind boggling!

Another night we went to a dinner party at Tryall Golf and Country Club at the seaside villa of Joe Thomas, a Wall Street Stock Broker, and his lovely wife Poppy. Beside Celia and me, the guests for the evening were Douglas Fairbanks, Jr. and his family. It was fascinating to hear this famous movie actor chatting about the making of various films, including one of my favorites, the 1939 'Gunga Din'. The allure of never knowing whom you might meet in Jamaica in the winter high season was addictive.

At the world class 'Round Hill Hotel' we dined at an outdoor dinner party of a dozen people, hosted by the legendary Jamaican hotelier, Frank Pringle and his ex- model wife. At the table was Alan J. Lerner of 'My Fair Lady' fame and his French attorney wife, and sitting next to me was the famous conductor Leonard Burnstein, who was mesmerizing with a vivid description of his recent South American tour. For a shameless name dropper, this was mind blowing future cocktail party fodder.

A few blocks from our cottage, Francois and Anna (Ance) Dupree, owned a considerable property, consisting of a mansion complete with a huge swimming pool, pool house, garage for half a dozen cars and various outbuildings. Francois was a man in his mid-seventies (1888-1966) who owned the well know Parisian hotels... the George V, the Plaza Anthnee, and the Ritz in Canada., and was at one time accused of German collaboration in WWII. Early each evening, he would dine with Ance, his beautiful 48 year old

Hungarian wife, after which he would retire for a good nights sleep. Not so Ance! She would retire to the pool house where her Greek friend would be waiting for a few hours of adult activities, before returning to Francois and the Greek to his quarters in a down town hotel. Quite a satisfactory arrangement apparently, before some malady befell the Greek at the last minute and his presence was suddenly and sorely missed by Ance (apparently his special talents were not to be easily replaced at short notice).

Ance, bemoaning her situation to friend Celia shortly after her arrival on the island for an extended season, struck a sympatric cord which Celia scurried to help fill. Celia, flowing with generosity, suggested that her house mate might be reasonably capable, if not an ideal substitute for the absent lover (Celia knew that I had little compunction to whiling away a few hours now and then in the company of a beautiful woman).

Knowing that I was a questionable stand-in for a professional European companion, and that there was no 'workmen's compensation,' I did give it my best shot. Three or four nights a week I would slip into the pool house while Ance had dinner from 7 to 9 PM with Francois. With her husband in bed, Ance would retire to the pool house for a couple of amorous hours doing the best we could to forget the Greek. Later when the Dupree's were returning to France, Celia said that a financial stipend might be forthcoming as a reward for services rendered, however, I declined the suggestion... not wanting to lose my amateur status.

It's not exactly true that all I did was work and go to parties... no indeed... I scheduled all the fishing I could! The Snook fishing at the Great River was particularly interesting. Wading down a fast and shallow river with deep, scattered, crystal pools hiding two or three pound Snook that would flash out and hit your fly like a miniature freight train, was a very sporting proposition. Fishing our way down to the deeper mouth of the river required a change of tactics to spinning rods with deep running plugs to entice fish that on occasion ran over twenty pounds. Another productive spot was the Martha Brae River near Falmouth, where we walked up a path along the river away from the main road bridge, hooking decent sized Snook in slow running but deeper water. In a mile or so at the end of the path, we would reach a 5' waterfall where the fish lurked, pounding the bait that drifted by. This kind of fishing provided plenty of mental relaxation, exercise, not to mention a tasty dinner at the end of the day.

Deep sea was my favorite kind of fishing, and Jamaica's north coast had an abundance of it, including the much sought after Blue Marlin. As chance would have it, I leased a seaside villa next to the Montego Bay Yacht Club from photographer Jerry Murison, who was

off to a six months tour of Europe, exposing (not the raincoat kind) myself to a myriad of offshore angling opportunities. The most sought after species, by far, was the Blue Marlin (MoBay record at the time was 496 lbs hooked at he edge of the harbor), that appeared in vast numbers from Port Antonio, the original tournament venue, to Montego Bay, also prolific, if a johnny-come-lately on the tournament scene.

Blue Marlin Montego Bay,
Jamaica 1960

1960 I was fortunate enough to win a trophy for the largest Blue Marlin caught from an outboard powered boat, weighting in at a small (for Marlin) 110 pounds. On a side note, the fish was foul hooked in the 'V' of the tail after a missed strike on the ballyhoo bait. It screamed line off my 10/0 reel, diving some 600 feet. After a twenty minute tug-of-war, I managed to reel the fish to the boat, tail first, drowned from water passing the wrong way over the gills. There wasn't much competition for the small boat prize, since there was only one other outboard powered boat in the tournament. It was a hollowed out cottonwood tree, sporting outriggers and a ten horsepower outboard. There is nothing more stimulating than high caliber competition.

A Canadian friend, who was the chief accountant for the airport restaurant and flight catering service, had a 16' skiff with a 40 hp Johnson outboard engine that we used on a regular basis to troll for Marlin. Using a 6' tree limb for an outrigger and a couple of smallish 6/0 Penn reels full of 50 lb test line, we spent many happy afternoons trolling a two or three pound Jack or Longjaw (large needlefish) around the blue water, only minutes out of our dock at Reading.

One such afternoon, we were trolling some ten miles offshore, chasing a school of small Tuna, and lost track of time in the slashing frenzy of 8 to 10 lb fish, trying to be the first to grab our small, yellow jigs. The Captain, finally noticing a rapidly sinking sun, and with more than enough fish in the box, called out, "pull in your lines.... it's getting late and we're quite away off shore with a rising wind!"

Henry Hostelley, a Pan Am Assistant Manager, and a bear of a man protested, "Hold on! I just got another strike" a pause, then ... "no, it's gone. Let's go home!"

At that moment, the Captain threw the outboard's gear in neutral allowing Henry's line to sink in the water as he prepared to bring it in. As Henry started to reel, the rod tip was slammed down on the gunnels and the reel's drag started to scream. The monofilament line hissed through the water like a knife, indicating something on the line a lot bigger than the small Tuna we had been catching.

My jaw dropped in my lap, when a 7' Blue Marlin made its first leap. It's not unexpected to find a 'Blue' in a school of small feeding Tuna or Bonita, since they are some of their favorite preys. What was unusual, however, was the fish hitting a tiny three inch jig. Henry carefully fought the fish as the sun continued to fall, growing more fatigued, in part from to his inability to don the rod support harness due to his size.

Finally with the sun down and a rough ocean spray crashing over our heads, Henry brought the fish to the side of the boat. With T-shirt off and wrapped around my hand to reduce the abrasion of a rough bill, I crouched near him in the dusk and prepared to 'bill' (grab the Marlin's bill). After a miss where the bill should be, I slid my hand down the leader-wire and secured a firm hold on a stub of a bill, holding its head steady in the pounding sea. The Captain, keeping the boat steady, had the 'mongol' (a Jamaican term for a short baseball type of club made out of the dense Lignum Vitae tree) ready to kill the fish with a jolting blow to its head (and hopefully not mine, in this fading light and rough sea) to avoid dragging a live... mad as hell....7' fish into at 16' skiff. This part was a little tricky and a dangerous maneuver that went off as scheduled, and the Marlin was finally in the boat!

By this time, it was almost completely dark, ten miles off the coast, with no flashlight, in a pounding sea and a howling wind, as we pointed the bow toward the twinkling lights of Montego Bay. As we neared the harbor we met the search party from the Yacht Club that had been hastily mobilized from the odd drunks hanging around the Club's bar and Skittle table (God love'em). Once on the lighted dock, we discovered the probable cause for such a large fish hitting a tiny lure... the Marlin had broken off its three and a half foot bill at one point in its life and was forced to feed using only a third of the normal bill, resulting in trying to kill smaller fish than tackling its usual much bigger prey. A hell'va exciting afternoon and mystery solved!

Non-fishing readers can relax; I only have one other Jamaican fishing experience that stands out. Billy Moreland, a local Pan Am mechanic friend and I decided to build a 12' pram type skiff from a Popular Mechanics Magazine plan. An unused area of the maintenance building was commandeered and with the help of marine plywood and fiberglass, it soon was finished. I bought a used ten horsepower Evinrude engine from one of our Pan Am pilots for $100, which he delivered on Flight 432 from Miami, and easily bolted to the transom. Finally completed, we slid the boat onto the back of a pickup truck and with a couple of porters, launched it off the beach near Royal Caribbean Hotel. Billy and I brought a rod and reel with us and rigged a Longjaw for bait... no use, we figured, missing out on a little fishing during this inaugural run, since the blue water was only a quarter mile offshore.

I laid the rod and reel in the bottom of the pram and flipped the drag lever to allow free spool in the unlikely event of a strike. Billy was operating the engine, while I basked in a beautiful, sunny afternoon watching the bait skipping along in our wake and marveling at the seaworthiness and sense of accomplishment of what we had crafted. Realistically, we expected no epic sea battle like the 'Old Man and the Sea'; just a easy test run to get the kinks out, when a dorsal fin appeared behind the bait followed an instant later by the slashing bill of a huge Blue Marlin. The bill viciously slammed into the Longjaw, knocking the line from the clothespin secured to a small rigger. I yelled at Billy to put the engine in neutral to allow the bait to sink in the water as if killed by the bill strike!

As the bait settled, the Marlin snatched it in its mouth and made a sizzling run, burning a hundred yards of line off the reel in the bat of an eye. The rod was now in my shaking hands and in the excitement of the moment, I realized that we were in a tiny, homemade skiff with a small engine facing a huge fish. It was lucky

I was seated as I don't think I could stand to do battle with knees knocking, even as adrenalin flooded though my body.

When the Marlin stopped its run to swallow its kill, I shouted, "ok, Billy... gun it!" He shifted the gear to 'forward' and gave the throttle full power to give me all the thrust it could muster (which was pitifully little in this situation), as I jerked the rod back with all my strength, slamming the hook into the corner of the Marlin's jaw. As the hook penetrated, the big fish surged skyward, exposing over half of its huge body, while violently shaking its head in an attempt to dislodge the bait. With mixed emotion, I watched as the gyrations tore the hook lose, tossing the mangled Longjaw 20 yards into the sea, as the Marlin disappeared into the foaming water. My immediate reaction was a relieved 'phew!' Then disappointment in missing the thrill of fighting and attempting to boat a Blue Marlin in the 250 to 300 lb ranges from a Mickey Mouse rig. On the flip side, however, it could have been a disaster in the making if that monster had decided to charge the boat!

It was convenient living for a time next to the Yacht Club, where fishing invitations were easy to come by. On a few occasions I enjoyed fishing with author James Jones, who revealed he did his best writing while imbibing alcoholic beverages in considerable amounts. He was temporarily living in Montego Bay working on his novel 'Go to the Widow Maker', which was finally published in 1967. I enjoyed reading some of James' blockbuster novels such as 'From Here to Eternity' and 'The Thin Red Line'. He was a very interesting fishing companion, and I was saddened to hear of his death in 1977.

Going South

In 1959 I received a transfer notice to report to Miquetia, Venezuela, the airport on the coast that serves the capital city, Caracas. I was not overwhelmed at the thought of leaving Montego Bay, where I had settled in nicely. Whining a little, I reluctantly packed up what I needed and gave or sold the rest, including my 1951 English Ford that I had purchased for 75 Pounds. It was named the 'Blue Bird' by the previous owner and to recoup my investment (and have a little fun) I printed 100 tickets costing One Pound each (a Pound at the time was worth $2.80 U.S.) and raffled the car off. The lucky winner was the Pan Am secretary who gave it a good home with her and her boyfriend, and provided many more years of service.

Since my flight to Venezuela would take me through Trinidad, Miami Headquarters instructed me to spend a week there at the Pan Am Piarco Guest House at the airport. It was an opportunity to work with the Pan Am Director and observe the Port of Spain operation. I had the chance to accompany the Director to the local Rotary Club meeting where I gave a short talk on Pan Am's training program. The high point of the trip however, was seeing Rita Hayworth, Robert Mitchum and Jack Lemon, over nighting at the Guest House, waiting for a morning flight. I understood that they had been working on the movie 'Fire Down Below', and were relaxing in the small bar and listening to steel drum musicians (steel drums were made from used oil drums and originated in Trinidad during WWII).

Once in Venezuela, I rented a room at a small hotel near the seaport town of La Guira, having the convenience of being located on the route of the company pickup shuttle to the airport at Miquetia, a few miles to the north. I was somewhat stunned by the high prices for goods and services, but calmed down when advised my salary had doubled from Jamaica.

I joined Walt Ames from California as Duty Station Managers under Station Manager Jim Kervin, a prison camp survivor, having bailed out of his shot-up bomber over Germany. I usually took the 3:00 PM to 11:00 PM shift (or until the last flight). Since Walt was married with children and I was single and hated to get up at 3:30 in the morning for the 5:00AM day shift, I opted for nights. Living in Venezuela was a poor substitute for my previous station, not only from the social aspect, but in addition, we felt the local people were anti-foreigner and particularly anti-American.

One day on the ramp, Walt was carrying the flight document briefcase for a departing flight and unthinking took a short cut thru the ranks of an assembly of Airport Authority soldiers standing at attention. The Commandant, outraged at this perceived insult, pulled his ceremonial sword from the scabbard and chased a desperately feeling Walt, running for his life to avoid the thrusting blade from penetrating his posterior. Fortunately, Walt was fleet of foot and made it to the aircraft unscathed, slamming the door behind him to thwart retribution. The aircraft was only delayed ten minutes for all to cool down!

Another time our Operations crew failed to read a message from Miami Control changing the route of a incoming flight from California / Central America and send it to Miami in place of a turnaround that would normally go back to California (you got that?). The object of this departure from the norm was to send the California aircraft to Miami to our main overhaul base for a required major inspection. Unfortunately, no one, including Walt the shift's Duty Station Manager, discovered the message authorizing the route switch and the aircraft was dispatched as usual. The Scheduling people were not too amused when the wrong aircraft arrived back in California, requiring it to be ferried (without passengers) across the country before the aircraft could be put back in passenger service. Once again Jim Kervin was called on the carpet, this time to Miami Headquarters to explain the screw-up and to save Walt's job. I felt that I had dodged a bullet when I was off that night, since I usually let the Operations boys sort out those types of messages and giving the situation, would have probably made the same mistake.

Aviation in South America was far removed from the new wave of international jet travel that the North America to Europe routes were having with the introduction of Boeing's 707-121 pure jet aircraft around 1958. The New York to London Pan Am jet was all the rage and usually booked to capacity (In 1958 I took the last piston engine flight out of Boston to London. Jet service started the next day). Again Pan American World Airways was the leader in transatlantic flight. The old phase 'Pan American, first across the Pacific, first across the Atlantic and first around the world' had new meaning. Feeling left out in South America, we were soon to be back in the aviation loop when training began for the handling of the first jet service from New York to South America. New mechanical support equipment and technical manuals started to arrive in Miquetia, along with training personnel. Exciting times were on the way!

Our Operations section had the responsibility of preparing the required weight and balance documents and that proved somewhat daunting with last minute calculations that could substantially affect the projected lift. Simply put, for every knot of headwind, we were allowed to add 450 kilos (2.2 lbs per kilo) of load and for ever degree drop in ramp temperature from the basic temperature we could add another 400 kilos until we reached a maximum amount allowable. This became tricky if the flight was late in the afternoon when temperatures usually dropped, picking up extra allowable weight while on the flip side, it was usually accompanied by a drop in wind velocity thereby negating extra load. Throw in the requirement of having to dip-stick the fuel tanks to measure the actual weight of the jet fuel within an hour of departure (when you are dealing with many thousands of pounds of fuel, a few dismal points can add to serious variations depending on the atmospheric conditions), and you have a mad, last minute scramble in Operations.

As I was considered the most accomplished weight and balance man, it fell to me to handle the inaugural flights documentation, causing some sleepless nights. When the big day came, it was like a fire drill, as we prepared to dispatch the first commercial jet aircraft to hit South American soil. The Pan Am Chief Pilot at the controls coolly advised, "Charlie, relax or you'll have a heart attack! We'll get this bird off the ground!"

My mind was swirling with 'did I do this?" and 'did I do that?' as I finished the calculations and sprinted to an already loaded and ready to go aircraft. As soon as the briefcase was in the hands of the Captain, I took the ramp Jeep and raced to the end of the runway with my Super-Eight movie camera to record the first jet take off from the South American Continent. My heart was pounding in my chest, as I stood off the end of the runway at the edge of a cliff (in Miquetia when you get a few hundred feet beyond the end of the runway there is a serious drop to the sea below... at that point the aircraft is flying, one way or the other) shooting film directly into the oncoming aircraft. The 707-121 poured billows of black smoke from its thunderously roaring engines as they burned cooling water along with the fuel... hitting V-1....then V-2 (the speed at which you had to pull the yoke and put it up)... then the teeth rattling overhead airborne launch! A wildly exciting, pulse hammering and unforgettable afternoon, to say the least.

Pan Am operated the jet schedule from Miquetia (Caracas) to Ascension, Paraguay, with stops in the Guiana's. Direct flights to the Argentine capital were, at that time, restricted until Aerolinas Argentinas was able to initiate their own jet service.

It was some time before we could run an all jet South American service for our regularly scheduled flights. One problem route, touted to be the longest, non-stop overland route in the world, Miquetia to Rio, was operated with our top of the line piston engine aircraft, the Douglas DC-7B. This flight of 2,500 miles over largely uncharted territory, even required a navigator (long range electronic communications devices had not yet been perfected to penetrate the vast Amazon region) who would stand on a step-stool and use a sextet to shoot the stars through an overhead Plexiglas bubble. The route was also marginal from the standpoint of useable payload due to heavy fuel demands, not only for the flight from 'A' to destination 'B', but regulations demanded extra fuel in the event of inclement weather or other factors that might cause the flight to divert to an alternate airport 'C', in this case, usually San Paulo.

On extremely long flights, the Flight Engineer would climb on the wing and supervise the critical fueling process as indicated on the weight and balance by Operations. After pumping the pre-ordered requirements, the Flight Engineer would advise the gas man to "add another 50 gallons in each tank, for my children!" There's nothing like a little extra safety factor when flying over the world's largest rainforest at night. If dicey weather was predicted en route or at Rio, the Co-pilot might saddle up and quietly order another 50 gallons per tank (presumably for his wife or girlfriend). One night I confronted the Captain with, "your crew has gone bonkers! The Flight Engineer put on an extra 200 gallons, and damn if the Co-pilot didn't come along five minute later and tell refueling to put on another 200 gallons! This puts us way over weight limit. You are not going to get this thing airborne tied to the Graf Zeppelin!"

"Give it a rest, Charlie! There is some serious weather enroute we may have to get around. You worry about dispatching the flight... I'll worry about getting the wheels up!" he growled. I don't know if he actually needed all that extra fuel to vector around heavy weather, but thank God, he did get the wheels up and did land safely in Rio.

On my late shift one night, the Operations Manager advised that we had another problem with the Rio flight, resulting in a substantial overweight situation. We had a full passenger load, cargo and mail, which is problem enough, but the joker in the pack was the inclement weather moving not only into Rio but also to Sao Paulo, the alternate field. The next available alternate was a lot farther than Sao Paulo, requiring considerably more extra fuel.

I thought for a minute before giving Enrique my game plan, "lets put in all the required fuel... tell the crew to be frugal with their children and mother's share... then we'll follow up by off loading all the cargo necessary to come within the weight limits." Not Solomon, perhaps, but sound, company policy, so I continued with, "if that doesn't get us there... off load the mail!"

A short time later Enrique caught up with me on the ramp with the dreaded report that the cargo was off and so was all the mail and we were still way over weight. The crew did their usual 'dipsy-doo' with the fuel, flatly refusing to take a teacup less. Taking passengers off was not a viable option, particularly in view of the Ford Motor Company convention in Rio, a destination for most of our passengers. I scourged the passenger list looking for any sublos (company employees on a pass) to haul off...coming up with a few that I reluctantly removed .Drat... not nearly enough weight!

With the departure time at hand and an elusive solution, I finally had an epiphany! Gathering my ramp baggage personnel around me I told them to remove as much passenger baggage as Operations tells us we need to get within take off limits, but when the carts are loaded, pull them away to the dark side of the ramp into the hanger... If the boarding passengers see their luggage being off loaded there is going to be a 'knock down and drag out' (I wasted this metaphor, since most of these guys only understood basic English). They did, however, understand enough to slip away into the darkness with roughly half of the baggage, finally getting a 'thumbs up' from Operations.

With this bit of subterfuge in place, the flight was boarded and dispatched without further incident. This was not to say that all hell didn't break lose when the flight arrived in Rio and the hapless passengers were greeted with the unwelcome news that "'some of your bags were left in Caracas and will arrive on tomorrows flight!" The Rio Station was not too happy with us when it took another three flights to get all the bags down and by then it seemed that we faced enough threatened lawsuits to keep a gaggle of attorneys busy for a decade.

Our City Reservations Office in Caracas pulled a dandy caper when they moved the reservation record control from one floor to another and in the process lost the Caracas to New York reservation sheet for the evening's flight. The sheets we received at the airport Traffic Managers Office had little resemblance to passengers actually confirmed. We soon discovered a less than agreeable (a fiasco, in fact) check-in procedure had already taken place we had to take off at least a dozen confirmed New York travelers. As a side note: when Venezuelans traveled they had all their relatives down to Aunt Minnie going to the airport with them for a protracted farewell, filling the check-in area and the upstairs open aired 'waving gallery'. While this provides a pleasant and inexpensive outing for friends and relatives, it sometimes creates an unruly crowd, ready to evolve into a mob scene when a departure is handled in less than a professional manner.

This was one of those times when the word filtered down in a hurry that the despicable Gringo airline was kicking their countrymen, friends and relatives off their confirmed flight to New York… unfortunately true, but at this point unavoidable. Shouting the foulest slogans and cursing the traffic staff, who valiantly tried to weed out those going and those staying, the unruly crowd turned into a howling mob. We were the Monster and all these Villagers needed were some burning torches and we were in real trouble.

I didn't need a degree in riots to see where this was going, but I did know we needed some back-up and fast! When I telephoned the Jefatura of the airport, he surprised me by readily agreeing to send the airport security over immediately (I guess he heard the roar in the next building). I received another surprise when the police actually arrived and attempted to quell the riot.

With the threat of a cracked head, the crowd was starting to fade away. Now is the time, I thought, to call the flight, load and dispatch this bird, lock up the joint and get the hell out of here. With my hand on the P.A. system mike and clearing my throat for the departure announcement, my Traffic manager rushed in yelling for me to hold it, "we have a hombre at the counter that says if he doesn't get on the plane....the flights not going!"

"Who the hell is this guy and can he stop the flight?" I groaned, snatching a quick glance.

"Si Senior, he is the Minister of Transportation!" he replied, wide-eyed.

This revelation pretty well put paid to my 'lets get the plane out and leave town' plan. It was one thing to off load the average loyal customer, but entirely another to deny passage to the Minister of Transportation, in his own country.

Thinking fast, I called the Chief Mechanic and asked him if he had an extra row of 3 economy seats he could use to replace the row of 2 first class seats, thereby gaining the one extra seat (if not as comfortable and certain to piss off the other two first class passengers in that row) we needed to accommodate the Minister. Over-riding the Chief's objection of this unauthorized seat change, we made the switch and thankfully dispatched the flight. With the help of the Jefatura of Police, we managed to get the stranded passengers safely off to a nearby hotel to await the next days flight. I later calmed down, had a couple of beers in a local bistro and shelved my plan to blowup the Reservations Department.

One of my many airport memorys is not for the faint of heart or animal lovers! For many months a pack of homeless dogs greeted the arriving passengers as they disembarked the aircraft. The dogs seemed to know a free meal when they sniffed one. They would congregate at the foot of the exit steps in anticipation of a free hand-out of half eaten meals and assorted tasty garbage from the cleanup crews. Deplaning passengers were obviously intimidated... walking through a pack of mulling dogs of unknown disposition on their way to Immigration and Customs.

When passenger complaints reached the 'can't ignore anymore' level, our office called the airport authority and added our voice to the growing concern of various other airline operators. This extra twig on the camel's back seemed to set the wheels in motion and the authorities moved against the 'hounds!'

If we were under the illusion that the Humaine Society, arm in arm with the SPCA, would drive up and gently remove the dogs to new, loving homes, that theory was quickly and violently dispelled. We were sadly and horrifically enlightened, when the 'goon squad' ripped into the pack (s). There was no care taken that the deplaning passengers were spared the onslaught, some visually blanching at the sight of dogs being hit with clubs, roped and strangled, and I understand later poisoned to liquidate any wily escapees. It was reported that more than 40 canines perished in the purge. We all felt badly that our complaint helped lead to this fiasco, but reason dictated that something had to be done, although a tad more sensibility would have been appreciated.

Another pest problem we had to deal with was the pack of large rats that a enjoyed a comfortable rat hotel under our walkway from Operations to the ramp, that had more holes than a Swiss cheese. To constantly run into these brazen creatures, was becoming less than amusing. One wag suggested that a bushel of snakes would do the trick! We tried a couple of regular rat traps and only caught a few of the dumb ones. Poison seemed worth a try until we reasoned that a bunch of dead rats decaying far under the concrete walkway was a questionable solution. Finally, after much agonizing and gnashing of teeth, we did the obvious and called in an exterminator who solved the problem with live wire traps using peanut butter. The clever ones that avoided the traps were poisoned with a water seeking concoction that got them out of the holes. At least we had avoided the snakes!

I regretfully traveled very little while in Venezuela, and wasn't aware at the time, that some of the world's finest Marlin fishing was right at my door in Macuto. I did take a sightseeing flight one day to see Angel Falls, the tallest falls in the world, located in the mountains south of Caracas. American pilot Jimmy Angel crashed his plane on the mountain in 1937 and survived the impact to walk out to the Orinoco River and back to civilization. Speaking of the Orinoco River, it was a source of yellow diamonds and gold. I bought three gold Indian head coins minted from Orinoco river gold, but never mustered up enough funds for the diamonds.

On occasion, I took the cable car from Miquetia to the top of Humboldt Mountain (named after the discoverer of the Humboldt current in the Pacific) located between the coast and the capital city, to enjoy the cooler mountain temperature and the alpine vistas. I would stay a night at the first class Humboldt Hotel, trying my hand at their ice skating rink, enjoying excellent food and change of pace mountain views.

I had few opportunities to enjoy the company of the fairer sex, so when I heard that a lovely, Cuban stewardess friend from Miami was coming through my station on the Rio flight, I was elated. This night I was particularly horny and aided by a sufficient layover time was determined to convince Olga to come with me to the Pan Am conference room for a little hanky-panky. She was reluctant at first, citing the possibility of the flight departing without her, "if that flight goes without me, I'll lose my job!" she whined.

In my present needy condition, I would have none of that and with a touch of ego (and drama), I played my ace, "Olga, it can't depart until I take the briefcase out and dispatch the flight!" This logic and maybe the excitement of it all, won the day. We slipped away and made love on the huge conference table. The story ended well, with her making the flight with time to spare, thanks to my swift release of an urgent need. A few days later, during our weekly management meeting, it was hard (no pun intended) to suppress a grin as my mind replayed the conference room's 'extra' session of the week.

Late one night, while I was checking the cabin on our Rio to New York flight, I saw this lovely blonde woman relaxing in the First Class section. She was stretching her legs in the aisle and as I stepped around them, I recognized her as actress Kim Novak. We chatted for a few minutes about the opening of her new movie in Rio, and since I rarely saw celebrities in Caracas, I lapped up this opportunity.

After almost two years in the Caracas with no transfer to a more appealing station in the works, I decided to pack it in and try to get a position back in Montego Bay, where the lifestyle was more suited to my imagined persona. As a single man, pounding it out in the metaphorical trenches of one of Pan Am's most active stations, it was becoming tiresome. When it became apparent that I was more interested in an active social life than a solid aviation career, I decided to call it quits and sent my resignation to the Superintendent of Stations in Miami, with my deep regrets.

There was a little stir, since I had been with the company for some time and had friends in virtually every country in the Latin American Division. The company responded with regrets of their own and a request to remain on duty until relieved by the replacement manager, Lou Reshanplat, a fellow trainee graduate from the University of Miami. As it turned out, it took Lou three months to untangle himself from his current assignment and allow me to get on with my life.

When Findley Howard found out that I had resigned and was leaving Caracas, he invited me to return to Miami via Panama, where we spent a great 'final farewell' week, He suggested that he had expected me to be promoted soon and gave me hell for not contacting him before resigning. As for Lou, he more than adequately replaced me and went on to a brilliant career with Pan Am, rising to Director in Japan and Brazil. He was a talented guy that had the misfortune to die young from a cancer that started in his leg.

Moving On

Returning to my parent's house in Miami after living on my own for so many years was not the ideal situation. Beaching it and doing some fishing wasn't enough to keep me happy while waiting for an employment situation to pop up in Jamaica. I had kept in touch with my girlfriend Joan Fraser, the Pan Am Traffic Manager in MoBay and she had her contacts in the airline business on the alert. In the meantime, I decided to build a duplex apartment on a lot I had purchased while in Venezuela, located near the Miami International Airport. I found an interesting set of stock plans in a local architect's office and enlisted the help of an old childhood friend, Roscoe Needham, now a building contractor, to lend a hand. Roscoe did the layout and supplied some of the labor from his job for extra late afternoon carpenters. Surprisingly, the local Sun Bank had no problem giving me a construction loan, although I was currently unemployed.

While building the duplex, I kept my fingers crossed for a break on the job scene. I knew it would take a major company with specific managerial needs and with no Jamaican candidates available, to make a return possible. Since Joan and I were emotionally involved, I figured she had a vested interest in exploring any opportunity that might come along.

It was like winning the lottery the day Joan called me in Miami and gushed, "I think you have a chance at the Colombian Airlines Manager's job in Montego Bay, but I suggest you hurry down and meet with Colin!"

This bombshell was both euphoric and perplexing since the current Avianca manager was old friend, Sam Fairchild, an Ivy League 'Eastern Establishment' type guy with a lovely family. I knew him to be wealthy, firmly established, and had a fabulous home on a high hill overlooking the Great River. In any event, I immediately booked a flight to Jamaica for the following day.

Arriving at Palisades Airport, I met with Colin Hay, the Avianca Regional Manager, who I had known before, and in ten minutes was hired to replace Sam when he left to manage the Tryall Country Club. Colin suggested that I could start in 60 days, which should give him time for the change of managers and to apply for a Jamaican work permit. I spent a few days in MoBay visiting old friends and particularly Joan who had made the new job possible. We were both giddy that I was returning and that we had 60 days for me to finish my Miami duplex (my Mother and Stepfather Jack moved into one side and sold our old house near the Orange Bowl). In addition, Joan and I planned to go ahead and take advantage of my last Pan Am free sublo pass and work in a trip to Europe, since vacation time would be scarce for the foreseeable future.

I had stayed in touch with Walt and Pat Ames, from my Caracas days and when I asked them if they would like to join Joan and me on a month's trip bumming around the Continent, they enthusiastically responded. The plan developed that Joan and I would visit London first, and then meet Walt and Pat in Paris. While Joan and I were in England, we took a side trip to visit her brother Guillermo (Bill) Fraser, who was Chief of Surgery at the hospital in Poole, on the southeast coast of England. Bill had graduated from the renowned medical school at Edinburgh, Scotland and was living in Pool with his English nurse wife Ann, son Garth and daughter Sharon. I enjoyed spending a few days with Bill and family, but decided to return to London to continue sightseeing and take in a show in the London West End theater district, while Joan continued her family visit for awhile longer.

I booked a room at the well located Marble Arch Hotel and asked at the desk what was the most popular show in town, "My Fair Lady, is a smash hit playing at the historic Durey Lane Theater," was the reply. I found my way to the theater thinking I would buy a ticket and still have plenty of time to enjoy a pub dinner before opening curtain. When arriving at the box office window, I confidently asked the clerk for one ticket in the orchestra section. The clerk replied, "for which performance, sir?"

Taken back by the reply and figuring that this guy was an idiot, I stammered, "why for tonight, of course!" The clerk gave a little laugh (perhaps to cover a sneer for this rube or on a kinder note, to show some sympathy for a pathetically naive foreigner), and patiently explained that My Fair Lady was sold out for the next eighteen months, but he had an available seat at that time. I blanched at this discovery which made me look like the idiot (apparently, not a difficult task) and it certainly put a crimp in my dinner and theater plans.

I gave him my best smile and weaseled, "I have no idea when I will be back in London, so that option is out! I really would like to see the show tonight!" I think I threw in an extra little pathetic snivel.

He took a deep breath, struggling for divine patience in dealing with this ignorant lout and said, "if you will kindly stand at the closed window on the side of this ticket box, behind that lady," pointing to a matronly woman staring at a closed office window," there may be an opportunity to purchase ticket for tonight's performance, since there should be at least a few cancellations. The window opens at 7:30. Good luck!"

As this was a positive step and injected an element of hope, I dutifully cued up behind the lady who turned out to be a fellow American on holiday from her teaching assignment at one of our German military bases. We passed a reasonably pleasant hour chatting when the window finally opened and the first available cancellations were announced, "Two seats, third row center!"

These were great seats, close enough to the stage without actually having a part in the musical, and I would have taken one even if it was on the roof. The lady from Germany excitedly shouted, "I'll take one!" while I yelled over her shoulder for the second ticket, probably damaging her ear drum in the process. I shelled out a Guinea (one Pound and one Shilling or $2.94 U.S.) for the ticket and took this fantastic seat to enjoy what was one of the most magical theatric presentations of my life. Rex Harrison and Julie Andrews had already moved on to Broadway, but one of the hits of the show, Stanley Holloway as Lisa Doolittle's father was still wowing audiences.

A day later Joan arrived from Poole and we were off to exciting Paris to meet the Ames and plunged into the usual and almost mandatory tourist venues. We saw the Louve', Napoleon's Tomb, the Arch of Triumph, and culminated with Joan and I holding hands on the second platform of the Eiffel Tower (I was too chicken to go to the top level) at night, with a cool breeze blowing through her hair and gazing at the famous 'City of Lights' (did I mention it was 'April' in Paris?). You tell me... could it get any better than this? Visiting Paris was a lot easier since Joan had studied French at the University of Toronto and could understand the language.....a big plus!

Since all of us were flying on free company tickets, it was mandatory for gentlemen to wear a coat and tie, and we were lucky enough to be upgraded to First Class on the big, Pan Am jet as we departed Paris. While flying toward Rome, the flight service offered a white glove, table top breakfast, starting with champagne to clear the palate and delicious eggs benedict. The morning was crystal clear, providing magnificent snowcapped views of the Alps, framed by a strikingly blue sky.... talk about your friendly skies!

Arriving in the 'Eternal City', Walt, Pat, Joan and I made haste to visit the usual spots, such as the Coliseum, sharing surprise at the walls standing on the arena floor which once housed the gladiators, animals, props and other items needed for the 'games'. The Apian Way still showed the ruts of Legion chariot wheels on cobble stone roads, while climbing underground into the Catacombs sent shivers down my spine when viewing stacked bones of ancient Romans, residing over the millenniums.

The Trevi Fountain took a back seat to the marvel of watching hordes of tourists turning their backs and throwing coins over their heads into the fountain. I guess it was a case of 'monkey see... monkey do' when we took our turn, insuring that one day we would return to Rome (I guess it must have worked, as I have been there four times).

The visit to St Peter's was the most interesting, not only for its architecture but also its priceless art. We lingered around the bronze statue of St. Peter, watching pilgrims stroking its sandaled foot worn smooth by 500 years of admiring hands. The main attraction however, was Michelangelo's Sistine Chapel fresco covering the entire ceiling, where a slow day allowed us to linger on benches and contemplate the intricacies of his paintings. I have to confess, I did not remember studying this famous work of art or even hearing about it until we arrived in Rome. Did I skip my Art History class that day at the 'U'?

Staying on schedule, we rented a new 1960 Fiat four door, which was less spacious than a Volkswagen (or perhaps a shoe box) and somehow loaded the four of us and all our bags into and on top of this wretched vehicle and less than grandly, motored south to Naples.

In Naples, we lost little time in visiting the ruins of Pompeii that offered a time capsule of life a few thousand years ago. I was amused when our guide separated the men from the women and children and whispered to follow him to a locked closet containing some pornography of the day in the form of a cartoon figure wielding a super-sized penis. It was not too titillating by today's standards (or lack thereof), but probably very racy stuff in those days. The guide topped this off with a tour of a house of ill repute, featuring beds carved from solid rock, hopefully used with soft mats.

Ferry boats to the fabled 'Isle of Capri' ran often across the Bay of Naples. I think my companions tried to ditch me to get away from my constant interpretation of one of my favorite songs which I thought was apropos.... 'Twas on the Isle of Capri that I found her....under the shade of an old walnut tree'... I sang it over and over until there was almost mutiny aboard the good ship 'Capri'! They did eventually get me quieted down with a couple of hands of cards, until Walt felt obligated to 'feed the fish' his lunch, although we had not left the Bay of Naples. Some sailor.

Capri was very hilly with great vistas and loaded with huge lemon trees, quaint cobble stoned streets, sidewalk restaurants, and horse drawn carriages. Our hotel was comfortable but cold. It seems like the local hoteliers turn the heat off on the first day of Spring, no matter what the weather is like. A good local wine at fifty cents a bottle, however, helped to take the chill off. We toured the island in a carriage, including a ride to the boat docks where tours of the famous 'Blue Grotto' were launched. Unfortunately, high winds drove the pounding surf dangerously high making an entrance inside the grotto impossible. After a night of superb local cuisine at one of the sidewalk restaurants, complete with strolling violins, we prepared to return to Rome and on to our next destination.

Barcelona, a lovely Mediterranean city with Moorish influence was certainly worth the visit. After a city tour, we rushed to the bull ring and purchased 'Sombra' (shady side) tickets for the next Corrida. In deference to Hemmingway, I wore an ascot and carried a leather goatskin bota (bag) full of cheap, red wine, but drew the line at wearing a neckerchief and beret. In the ensuing excitement, I sprayed red wine all over the front of my shirt trying to hit my mouth, confirming a sneaking suspicion that a little more practice with the bota might be in order.

As this was our first bull fight we didn't know how to rate it, but the crowd did not seem too enthused by the performances. We understood from the surrounding aficionados that the bulls were too large....somewhere in the 550 to 600 kilo range.... causing them to lose their agility and frequently fall to their knees when attempting a sharp turn. After a long afternoon of derisive hooting from the incensed crowd, we finally made our way out and found a picturesque cubbyhole bistro featuring snails (locally called 'Caracoles') smothered in wine sauce....a gourmet's delight for my first but not last escargot.

Dining in Barcelona turned out to be a delight. We discovered 'Renos' a four star restaurant that adhered to the old adage that 'when in Barcelona, do as the Barceloians do'... which was to eat late. One night we were finishing an excellent 'flan' dessert at 1:00 AM and when we left the restaurant it was still over half full of patrons. When you're young you can get away with eating late and going to bed. If done in later years, it might be considered suicide by heartburn!

When we pushed on to our next destination, we discovered that Lisbon had seven hills matching those of Rome, and we walked most of them. Occasionally, at the end of a street a huge elevator would lift pedestrian traffic up or down a level to continue the passage. Lots of bright colored mosaic sidewalks added a quaint Mediterranean flavor to the old city. It was interesting to note that many world discoveries were launched from this small country some five hundred years ago.

Enjoying a few glasses of wine one evening in a bistro near our hotel, a woman stood against the wall under a spotlight and with the accompliment of a guitar player, belted out a 'Fado'. It was strangely entertaining to see the performer sing a sad song of unrequited love... tears streaming down her face....no body movement....soul in torment...pleading for release from this torture! Watching this late in the evening with a little booze under the belt and not withstanding a lack of knowledge of Portugese, one might even manage to squeeze a tear or two, or maybe a little sob, for his own 'lost love'. This was good stuff and reminded me of a few 'she done me wrong' country music bars I used to frequent in Georgia.

Our last stop was Madrid, the Spanish capital, where we checked into the famous Palace Hotel built in 1919 and expensively refurbished, with a closet as large as a standard hotel room of today. Thanks to a very strong dollar and a poor Spanish economy, the room rate was absurdly inexpensive at $8.00 a night..... double occupancy. We knew that this was a deluxe operation when we went into the restaurant for lunch and a cart of raw steaks and chops was wheeled out for our inspection and selection. I was really wowed, when I ordered a bottle of domestic beer that came in a iced, silver champagne bucket....a class act, indeed!

Having been assured that the disappointment we suffered at the poor showing at the Barcelona bull fight would not be repeated at the Plaza del Torres in Madrid, we booked our 'Sombra' tickets and prepared to take another crack at bull fighting as a spectator sport in this world famous venue. It was obvious from first glimpse, that these bulls were less ponderous and murderously agile fighting bulls that challenged some of the most famous matadors in the world. It was the Golden Age of bull fighters, featuring world class matadors such as Manolete' and El Cordobes.

After practicing with the bota in Barcelona, the spurting wine targeted in pretty well and only a few drops hit my shirt, as the first bull charged into the arena. The matador minced around for a few minutes before it all fell apart and he wound up on the horns of one mad bull. After a good shaking, the bull flipped the matador in a heap in the dust, and was rushed off, I presume, to surgery. The next matador was tossed into the air like coin, apparently dislocating a vertebra. To his credit, with sword in hand and revenge in his heart, he chased the enraged bull around the ring while dragging one leg. After a few more passes, he finally delivered a lethal, over the horns, thrust to the heart, amid a thunderous applause from appreciative aficionados. For his courage and tenacity, the matador was awarded an ear. This was heady stuff for a young American who liked to read Henningway!

Looking for less heart pounding activities, we booked a days bus tour to 'El Escorial' in the Valley of the Fallen (El Valle de los Caidos), where a Benedictine chapel has been built inside a salt mountain to provide a final resting place for the remains of those who lost their lives in the mid- 1930's Spanish Civil War. Another 'must see' was a visit to the notorious El Rasto flea market to buy a few souvenirs, with the caveat to keep your hand firmly on your wallet, or some one else would! I purchased a large bull fighting painting for my Grandfather, which proudly hung in his home for many years until his death at the age of 93.

Working down our list, we saved the visit to Del Prado, one of the world's most famous museums, established in 1819, containing a treasure trove of priceless art reflecting a prosperous country, rich with spoils from conquests in the New World. The museum features master painters such as El Greco, Peter Paul Rubins, Titian, Velazquez and Goya to name a few, that flocked to the wealthy Spanish capital, leaving a multitude of world renowned art for coming generations.

Finally, it was time to wrap up the best trip of my life and head back across the Atlantic. As we made our farewells with Walt and Pat, it would have been hard to imagine that it would take forty years for a reunion that would take place in Ft. Lauderdale in the new Millennium, after Walt had suffered multiple strokes, which had obviously diminished his quality of life.

Back to the Future

Returning from Europe to Miami, I hastily wound up my business, including leaving the finishing touches on the duplex to my parents, bid a fond farewell to my pals and gals, and once again headed south. It was back to Jamaica and hopefully a bright future!

I happily took over my duties as Avianca Manager – Montego Bay, a position that soon afforded years of fantastic living in one of the world's most popular winter jet set enclaves. For a young man of modest means, it was an amazing opportunity to immerse myself (if only on the periphery) in the lifestyle of the rich and famous, (I figured I was shallow enough to handle it) having had only a small sample in my previous Jamaican Pan Am assignment. Since I only had one round trip flight (Saturday up and Sunday back) a week to New York and back to Bogotá', it left plenty of time to bring the 'extra man at dinner' concept to new highs (or lows, as the case may be). In other words, I had plenty of free time to explore hedonistic pursuits, as opportunities were presented.

I took over a professionally decorated office cum-VIP room upstairs over the Pan Am offices and overlooking the airport ramp and runway. Expensive living room furniture and an elaborate, well stocked wet bar made entertaining boarding and intransit dignitaries a delight. The ritual of a small, Sunday evening cocktail party with friends to celebrate the end of a two day work week and cheering the takeoff of the Avianca flight (thank God it got off the ground) with a dry martini, was a cherished weekly event. Princess Liechtenstein of the European Municipality of the same name, an acquaintance from one of the parties, dropped into my office one day to say goodbye and give me her partially read copy of 'The High and the Mighty,' a gripping story of an impending airline disaster, telling me, "its not suitable to read while flying!"

Pan Am personnel provided the ground support, under contract to Avianca, along with aircraft and flight crews in the early stages of the jet age, making their prop Super Constellations obsolete. My familiarization with the Pan Am procedures and my close association with Randy Johnson, the Pan Am General Manager, allowed me to take over the personnel and run the operation for the Avianca flights. Within a year or so Avianca had delivery of their own new jets and had trained their Colombian crews.

The social life was soon going full blast, particularly as winter approached, when the people that had real money returned to the north coast of Jamaica to resume residency. Having very little to occupy their time, pre-occupation with gala parties assumed an important role in the expat's daily island life. This nonsensical lifestyle suited me just fine and I was always ready for a party and dinner, minding my manners and taking care not to slop food down the front of my tuxedo.

Some of the most elegant dinner parties not mentioned previously, were hosted by the well known English bookmaker, Billy Hill of 'Hills Pools' whose gambling parlors seemed to cover the U.K. Billy was obviously a very wealthy man and enjoyed the comforts of his estate high on a hill top overlooking Montego Bay, next door to the Duke of Marlborough. Black tie was a standard requirement, as was the mind bogging buffet display of fine cuisine and exotic champagne and wine. On one occasion while chatting with the host, I marveled at how much I enjoyed the huge, lush strawberries dominating the fruit presentation, since I had been unable to find them at the supermarket. He smiled and enlightened me with, "Dear boy! Just dispatch a taxi to Mandeville in the mountains and you can get all you want!" Good, but impractical advice! Now that's attention to detail!

IT WAS ALMOST continuous dancing at the Casa Blanca Hotel on Saturday night last as the winter season in Montego Bay was opened officially with a grand ball organized by the Montego Bay Hotel Association. Here are seen partners dancing away merrily to the strains of Eric Grant and his Casa Montego orchestra.

Charlie and friend at the Casablanca Hotel,
New Years Eve 1961 Montego Bay, Jamaica

Round Hill Hotel and Resort, was one of my favorite spots for an evening's entertainment, including a couple of wonderful New Year Eves when our airline family booked a large table next to the outside dance floor, welcoming the New Year in style. One of the early supporters of Round Hill was William S. Paley, who started CBS. In the winter of 1962 I was introduced to Robin, Marquis of Taverstock, son of the Duke of Bedford, and his lovely new bride, model Henrietta Teox, model, debutant and daughter of a wealthy English banker. While they made an exceptional couple and obviously enjoyed each others company, a two month honeymoon even at Round Hill seemed a little much. When Robin mentioned to me that he was a fisherman, I invited him to join me in some river fishing for Snook and offshore for Marlin. He was a pleasant companion who shared my fondness for sun and sea. In later years the couple operated the Bedford Estates in England, where I heard that he recently passed away of a heart attack.

The Pan Am VIP room also had its share of celebrities relaxing before a flight. Randy Johnson asked me to take Debbie Reynolds, her shoe magnet husband, Harry Karl and children (the girl was Carrie Fisher later of Star War fame) for a drink before their Pan Am flight. It was an engaging afternoon, proving once again.... you never knew whom you might meet on a popular tourist island destination.

Among the big hitters was Dr. Rudolph Light, grandson of Upjohn of pharmaceutical fame and a retired Professor of Surgery at Vanderbilt University, and his wife Ann. She was the daughter of a silent movie director and an actress in her own right, but more interestingly, she was reported to be the ex-wife of one of the richest people in the world, oil man J. Paul Getty and the mother of his children.

We met at a party and developed a friendship, resulting in late afternoon invitations for martini's and conversation. When available, I would bring them a copy of the New York Times, hot off the daily flight resulting in the same day paper being delivered to their home in Jamaica....no small feat in those days. On occasion, I would join them for a candlelight dinner in the garden under starlit skies, and enjoy amusing conversation such as Dr. Light complaint about the Duke of Marlborough 'pinching my pheasants' from his neighboring estate in England. I guess it was hard for the pheasants to know to whom they were obliged to let shoot them!

The Lights were very kind to me and once offered to give me their chauffeur driven 1954 Bentley from their estate in England for the cost of shipping it out. For some reason (perhaps temporary insanity) I declined their kind offer. Later, when I told Rudy about wanting to start an egg farm on Grand Bahama Island (maybe the insanity wasn't temporary) he generously invested in the project, but that's a story for later pages.

Ann hated flying, but Rudy would take Avianca to New York as needed, first class, of course. On one trip we had actress Ginger Rogers booked on the flight Rudy was taking, so I arranged to seat him next to her. Later he told me how wonderful it was to be able to chat with her all the way to New York. Due to Ann's aversion to flying however, they would normally take the Grace Steamship Line from New York to Kingston along with their Rolls Royce. Whenever I could, I would lend a hand and fly to Kingston, overnight at the Hilton with them and drive all of us back to Montego Bay the next day.....Nothing like tooling around in a Rolls, even if it's not yours!

Since having raffled the 'Blue Bird' when I left Jamaica a few years before, I purchased a 1952 Jaguar Mark IV sedan for sporty transportation. Don't let your mind wander to a sleek Jag convertible....this baby was a monster of a four door with big wheels, two front bucket seats and a ballroom size back seat. I bought it from Allan Dawson, the Pan Am Sales Manager for 100 Pounds, and enjoyed zipping around the countryside with the sunroof open, allowing the fresh, Jamaican breeze to blow through my hair. I finally discovered that while owning a unique automobile was fun, having everybody know your whereabouts at all times was not so attractive, resulting in the purchase of a new 1960 English Ford and melting back into the crowd.

As a by-produce of living in Jamaica, I came to love the native profound sayings that cover many of life's everyday situations, such as 'Cockroach has no place in fowl fight (or fowl yard) meaning 'don't stick your nose in someone else's business'! More of these wonderfully descriptive sayings and proverbs are as follows:

'If you can't catch Sammy, you catch him shirt' ... meaning if you don't make your goal at least you'll get close.

'One, one coco fill the basket' ... meaning add a little here and there, one at a time to finally attain your goal.

'Don't trade black dog for monkey,' ... .meaning the 'grass is not always greener'

'If it's for you, it can't be un-for you' ... meaning it's preordained.

'Better belly bust than good vittle go to waste' ... don't waste food or opportunity

'Chicken merry- hawk is near' ... when things seem to go well, beware.

In 1962 I heard that some fine beachfront properties in the Cayman Islands were being purchased by Jamaicans. I didn't know whether the Jamaicans were hedging their bets buying land on a nearby island that was to remain British, or that the word was out on a future hot tourist destination, or both. Since I had a few extra dollars and thought of buying land on world class beach fronting pristine water, with the prospect of a stable government, had some appeal.

Joan and I took a few days off and with the courtesy of free passes on BWIA; we flew from Montego Bay to Georgetown, Cayman. The town was not overwhelming, but there were a few decent looking small hotels on a long, white sand beach. We booked into a room near the Yacht Club, dropped our bags and hired a taxi operated by a local woman to show us some of the available properties.

The taxi driver was also an 'Estate Agent' ... a local variety of our real estate agent, and well schooled of what was on the market. She showed us one exciting parcel, reasonably high and gently sloping to a 300' white sand beach, fronting a tropical snorkeling reef. This piece seemed to have it all, and for a reasonable price of $3,500. U.S. We told the agent we were very interested and made arrangements to meet the next morning.

That evening Joan and I dressed for dinner and started walking from the hotel to the Yacht Club. The casual stroll, in the romantic moonlight turned into an all out sprint for the safety of the club in a vain effort to escape the angry hordes of mosquitoes that were having US for dinner. Arriving at the club, winded, hot and sweaty, I said to Joan, "I think this place will never be anything except a mosquito swamp!" I had obviously never heard of spraying for mosquitoes. This over reaction (and stupidity) cost us a pile of money when the Cayman Islands became the new Caribbean hot spot and property values went through the roof. I guess we should have had dinner at the hotel.

Another high point in 1962 was hatched by Randy, the Pan Am Manager and me to break the monotony of 'every day is a perfect day in paradise.' With free airline passes clutched in our hot little hands, we decided that a couple of weeks in Europe were just what we needed to rekindle our creative juices and broaden our cultural horizons (what a load of nonsense, but it played well).

Heading first to London, we promptly got involved with some ladies of dubious character that were hustling drinks at five quid (Pounds) per hour in a club off Shaftsbury Avenue. This small detail was not revealed until it was apparent that we were getting ready to leave when the bill for 'companionship' (more likely babysitting) was presented. Our lack of enthusiasm was duly noted by the bouncer who created somewhat of a row (as they say in the mother country), which precipitated a rapid departure in a barrage of abusive language... the best of which was 'cheapskate bastards'.

Our next stop on the 'cultural tour' was a return to Paris, where we had dinner at Maxium's before attending a performance of the Barber of Seville in French, at the world famous Paris Opera House. The majestic, old opera house was certainly elegant and worth sitting through the 'Barber' just to wallow in the ambiance of the past glories and to feel like international playboys while hoisting a brandy at intermission. To show our versatility, the next night we enjoyed a performance of the 'Follies' with long legged and topless show girls (I was told that most of the showgirls with the nicest breasts and legs were actually British). This show beat the hell out of the opera!

At that time in Paris, there were a multitude of police on the streets, armed with automatic weapons, as a civil insurrection by the French colony of Algeria, whose followers developed a nasty habit of throwing bombs into crowded cafes. Only slightly nervous, and after an evening's activities, we ordered the traditional onion soup in the wee hours of the morning, under the the watchful eye of the gendarmes. We were however, prepared for a mad scamper in the event of the first sign of trouble.

One night Randy ran into some friends and gone out for the evening of 'what happened to?' leaving me to my own devices. Taking this opportunity, I hailed a taxi and went to the only place I could think of that spoke English... Harry's American Bar. This was a very well known watering hole from the 1920's, boasting a collegiate décor with Ivy League pennants covering the walls. This joint probably helped juice up Hemmingway and the 'Lost Generation' expat crowd. The atmosphere was the 'Wiffenpoof Inn' in New Haven and a far cry from downtown Paris. I spent a few pleasant hours sipping drinks and talking with my fellow countrymen, realizing how much I missed the sound of English when in a country where you don't understand much of the language.

We checked into the centrally located Krasnepolski Hotel in Amsterdam and were delighted to note that the hotel was located only a few blocks from one of the biggest red light districts in

Europe. This quaint area, locally known as 'Roseburg' (means Pink or Red in Dutch), was in an old section of town and admired for it's 14th century gothic architecture along with, of course, one of the largest collections of ladies of easy virtue in Europe.

When wandering through the crowded, narrow streets, glass panel windows allowed viewers to gaze into comfortable apartments lining both sides of the streets. Prostitutes of all ages and sizes were either waving at prospective johns or carrying on a normal 'at home' evening, but were seemingly ready to respond to a rap on the door or window from an eager swain.

I decided to take a table at a corner bistro and have a beer or two and do a little crowd watching. It wasn't but a few minutes later when a fellow from Iowa, staying at my hotel came by and I hailed him with, "doing some window shopping?"

He laughed and said he already had all the action he wanted for one evening explaining, "I found a nice looking blonde in one of the apartments who answered my 'shave and a haircut' rap. She charged me something like $5.00, took my trousers off and did a cursory wash. So far so good, I thought! Then things started to go down hill and I quickly found out that the saying 'one can't shoot pool with a rope' is true! After she did some unsuccessful coaxing, the noble experience was finally abandoned and I slinked out!"

I laughed with him and said, "She probably wasn't too unhappy at not having to be inconvenienced by the pawing of some half boozed tourist," and kiddingly suggested that he should have gotten a refund!

While in Amsterdam and since Randy and I advertised this trip to the home folks as the 'Cultural Tour,' we felt obligated to actually seek a few more cultural opportunities. This week the local opera house was performing Donizetti's L'elisir d'Amore (the Elixir of Love) in English, which we actually managed to enjoy. After the show, we had a late traditional Indonesian dinner featuring a table full of various dishes, causing a taste bud explosion and an annoying heartburn at two in the morning. In hot pursuit of culture, before we left Amsterdam we had to spend a few hours at the famous Dutch Riiks Museum. Many of the works by Rembrandt were on display and I was particularly impressed by one of his most famous paintings, the huge 'Night Watch' from 1642. Check one more 'cultural' event for the home team!

Our final stop was the lovely lakeside city of Lausanne, Switzerland, where I developed a miserable head cold and decided to finish the tour and head home to sunny Jamaica. Thus ended the (in) famous 'Cultural Tour!' Applause, please!

I arrived back in Jamaica just in time to find that local Rasafarians, dreadlocks and all, swooped out of the hills and attacked a gas station and motel with robbery and mayhem in mind. One of the Jamaican motel guests made the fatal mistake of running out of his room to see what the commotion was all about and received a few fatal machete' slashes for his trouble. This ghastly deed prompted the motel manager to telephone the police in Montego Bay, a few miles away for urgent assistance. Police headquarters, annoyed that this happened on their watch, soon dispatched a car of constabulary to the scene. As they arrived they were met with a howling, ganga (marijuana) inspired Rasta mob, mulling around a nearby cane field and brandishing wicked looking machetes. Once on the scene, the police sergeant franticly attempted to issue bullets (at that time the police did not carry loaded firearms) to the group of police, but before the pistols were ready to fire, the Rasta's fell on them with bloodcurdling screams and slashing machetes. A few of the police officers were hacked to death before the antagonists vanished into the hills.

Obviously, the country was outraged and frightened that the bloodbath would spread island wide. The local police mobilized and went in pursuit while the Prime Minister in Kingston ordered out the National Guard troops which were promptly ferried over by commandeered BWIA passenger aircraft. A few things happened in a very short time...one was a run on the services of the local barbers, perhaps going on the assumption that a bald Rasta was a live Rasta, as they tried to melt into the background. Another was a wide dragnet rounding up any and all the Rastas the police could find with a very rough delivery to the police station. I drove by the station and witnessed police officers rolling handcuffed captives from the back of high bedded trucks onto the pavement... amid screams of agony and fear. How many of the actual perps were apprehended, I never found out, but the brutal roundup sent a firm signal that the authorities were less than amused and subsequent prosecution put paid to the insurrection.

On a side note, the day following the attack and as the government mounted their response, Emil Campbell, the owner of the airport restaurant and aircraft catering, found me at my airport office and asked me to 'ride shotgun' as he prepared to drive into the nearby hills to his farm and was afraid to go without backup. Emil owned and operated a vegetable truck farm used to supply produce for his airport food catering operation and the recent attack, made this urgent tomato run very unappealing.

I did not embrace the thought of a load of tomatoes being a fair exchange for the possibility of facing a murderous Rasta ambush, but I finally agreed to give it a 'go'!. I had second thoughts when Emil opened the locked glove box and handed me an old Colt horse pistol, giving me a momentary flashback to my tour of Port Au Prince, Haiti a few years before. We rattled off the main highway onto a remote gravel road in Virgin Valley keeping my finger firmly on the trigger (if we hit a pot hole I would probably have shot out the dashboard). If I had been Custer's Indian scout, I couldn't have kept more of an eagle-eye on ever tree and bush all the way to the farm. To my immense relief, we found no Rastas in the bush and after loading many baskets of fresh, vine ripened tomatoes, we headed back to the airport without incident.

While I generally felt safe in Jamaica's north coast during the early 1960's, we did have some problems. I had become friendly with Mrs. Scott, a Ministry of Tourism greeting desk representative at the airport. She was an attractive woman of English decent, perhaps in her mid-fifties and had the gift of making arriving visitors to the island feel welcome.

Mrs. Scott lived by herself in a lovely home in a hillside subdivision near Falmouth, a dozen miles from her desk at the airport. She employed a yardman to maintain the grounds, as many local residents did at the time. These unskilled employees commanded very little wages and were well known for purloining the odd unwatched item, their indolence, lack of intelligence and snarly attitudes. Apparently, Mrs. Scott's yardman fit the mold, resulting in a constant, if not daily, scolding, adding to his surly demeanor.

One day a horrifying story circulated around the airport detailing the gruesome events that led to the dismemberment of the popular Mrs. Scott by... you guessed it!... her long time yardman. The story unfolded that she, suffering yet another atrocity by her employee, gave him a final tongue lashing, culminating with the termination of his long time employment This unleashed a built up, wild, cutlass hacking rage to the determent of Mrs. Scott and the eventual hanging of the perpetrator. A tragedy by any standards! I learned a lesson from this affair that I have carried over the last 40 years, that when living in a third world country (or anywhere else, for that matter) never berate and humiliate an individual to the point of rage as there is, in many cases, only a thin veneer of civilized conduct masking basic animal instincts.

In the winter high season, the Montego Bay Airport welcomed quite a few celebrities. One year Avianca flew Santa Clause (a Jamaican Tourist Board caper) from New York to Jamaica, stopping first in Montego Bay. Jamaican radio had heralded the arrival days before, creating a huge crowd of screaming children, licking their collective chops at the thought of Santa Clause (Father Christmas) flying in with bags of gifts for them, actually provided by various local civic organizations stashed away in the hanger for "Santa's arrival. As the Avianca Manager I basked in the limelight, as I headed the welcoming committee at the bottom of the stairs, giving Santa a hardy Spanish 'Abrazo' (enthusiastic hug) to the roaring cheers of the juvenile assembly.

A reporter from the Kingston radio station shoved a mike in my face, giving me a chance to blather on about how Santa selected Avianca Airlines (shameless, but harmless deception) to fly down from the North Pole and bring gifts for the good children of Jamaica (reports had it that not a bad kid could be found in the crowd). Santa then advised the children in Kingston that he had a wonderful flight on Avianca since he only used his sled on Christmas Eve and that he would soon be there with toys for them. Is everybody Happy? You bet! On a personal note, one of my perks was receiving admiring glances from some of the attractive mothers, who probably figured that any friend of Santa was a potential friend of theirs. Ho! Ho! Ho!

Harry Belafonte was not only a famous figure in the U.S., but he was extremely popular in Jamaica for his calypso recordings, his handsome good looks and family ties in Kingston. After a visit, Harry took our Avianca flight back to New York with an hour stop over in MoBay to fuel and board passengers for the New York leg. As the flight departed Kingston our office called and told me Harry was on the flight and to escort him and his daughter to our VIP room to receive a call and enjoy refreshments before continuing. It was soon apparent that his arrival was no secret, resulting in a mob of airport working girls, armed with advance notice from their cohorts in Kingston, lining the ramp side of the airline offices to catch a glimpse.

As Harry came down the stairs with his daughter (very likely a young Sharon Belafonte, later a beautiful and talented actress) on his shoulders, I introduced myself and warmly shook his hand. He put his arm around my shoulder, allowing me to draw closer to be heard over the ramp noise, to advise of the impending telephone call. Knowing that there was a packed house of young ladies overcome with excitement and watching our every move, I gave my best 'swallowed the canary' smile, as if amused by a personal tidbit shared by Charlie and his good friend Harry, for the benefit of the adoring crowd. My local stature jumped a notch with the airport pretties, particularly when I let slip later, that Harry and I were old friends. Apparently I have no shame when working the crowd and almost shouted out, "no autographs, please!

Arriving at the airport after lunch, I noticed quite a few men in dark suits buzzing around the ramp, obviously preparing for the arrival of some VIP. When the expected aircraft arrived, Lyndon Banes Johnson, the then Vice-President of the United States deplaned. His arrival created quite a stir, which reminded me of the time I had the opportunity to see President Eisenhower in the Republic of Panama when he arrived in the then presidential plane, the 'Columbine' (a Super Constellation piston engined aircraft in 1956), for a Central American Conference in Panama City. He was met by his four door Lincoln convertible and sped away in a blur of flashing lights and blaring sirens from dozens of escort motorcycles. While watching some of the other Central American Presidents (and a few dictators) load into heavily armored and guarded vehicles, I was struck by how unconcerned President Eisenhower seemed over his safety while waving to the crows along the road from an open car, compared with the other leaders of state.

Upon the President's departure a few days later, I started up the ladder to close the aircraft's door, when a Secret Service Agent grabbed the back of my belt and pulled be back down growling, "They'll close their own door!" No chance of a bomb being thrown into that plane!

Noel Coward was a frequent visitor to the Montego Bay Airport, meeting various ballet dancers, and assorted friends, including Sir Winston Churchill and the Queen Mother. He had a lovely home in the hills near Ocho Rios called 'Firefly', where he wintered when not working. One year, near the end of the season, one of my Jamaican friends confided in me to ask my opinion on whether he should accept Noel's offer to go with him to his Riviera home for the summer season as his aide-de-camp. Although the friend was very interested in going, he wasn't sure that he wanted the 'cat' completely out of the gay bag (or closet). I advised him to do what he wanted, since I was pretty sure that the 'cat' was firmly out of the bag and screaming at the moon. I also assured him that his real friends would understand. He did go and not only had a time of his life on the south of France, but learned to speak some French to boot. Coward died in 1973 and is buried at his beloved 'Firefly.'

Ian Fleming, author of the 'James Bond' books, also owned a home not too far from 'Firefly, in Oracabessa, Jamaica called 'Goldeneye'. He did much of his writing there, placing the plot for his book (and first motion picture), 'Dr. No,' in Jamaica.

A favorite visitor was Andre Kostalonetz, the orchestra leader and wife Lilly Pons, the opera singer. I would meet them on our flight and take them to their hotel, the Sunset Inn, where we would have a drink and share the doings of the past year. I still display the last music album he gave me, complete with a note of appreciation taped on the cover. Nice man!

Passengers checking in for flights were sometimes a rich source of amusement. On a busy afternoon flight to New York, a passenger demanded to see the manager during check-in when he was faced with a considerable excess baggage charge for a mountain of baggage. When I went to the counter, this middle aged New Yorker gave me a barrage of reasons why he should be exempt from the charge.... some of which were, "I always fly your airline," and "I play golf with your president, Juan Trippe," (Trippe was Pan Am's president not

Avianca's), or a variation "Juan's neighbor," or "lodge brother,"....you get the idea. I was overwhelmed by the audacity of this gentleman (a term loosely applied), but held fast and insisted on the charge. Having shot most of his bullets, which turned out to be blanks, he fumbled in his back pocket and pulled out his well worn wallet and for the 'piece de resistance' ... flipped it open exposing a tin looking badge and with assumed authority, shouted, "I'm a New York City Auxiliary Police Officer!"

Zounds....a real live New York Auxiliary Police Officer! Now I confess, this was one for the ages and rendered me monetarily speechless, as I unsuccessfully stifled a wild howl of laughter. Obviously, the fellow mistook me for an island yokel that just fell off of a turnip truck, but he played his final trump card with such outrageously sincere chutzpah that I did give him a discount. Maybe I did fall off the turnip truck after all, but I looked at the discount as a fair exchange for an amusing diversion on an aggravating day.

A day before our Avianca flight was due thru from Bogotá to New York; I received a call from Vice President Herbert Wild from the head office in Colombia. The just of the call was to advise that the airline's Flight Service had gone on strike and the following day's flight to New York would be serviced by a short staffed, rag tag group of paunchy middle management people. In addition, it would be much appreciated if I would work the ground operation in Montego Bay as normal and then close the cabin door from the inside and work flight service to New York ...overnight at the Lemmington Hotel and work the return flight back to Montego Bay the next day.

What a bummer, I first thought... but after a little reflection... an evening in New York had some appeal, so I mumbled some nonsense about the company coming first and it would be my pleasure to do my bit! I was getting pretty good at spouting this kind of pap.

The flight was almost full but a few of my fellow flight service and myself found time to guzzle a few small but delicious Colombian beers between racing up and down the aisle slinging trays of food and dispensing a variety of beverages. As the evening wore on we finished our service and spent the remainder of flight hanging around the dwindling beer supply, giggling and swapping airline stories. This was my only foray into the flight service bailiwick, but it certainly was an eye opener as to just how tough these folks can have it.

Back at the Montego Bay Airport actor Clifton Webb checked in after a visit with Noel Coward. I took him to the VIP room and was entertained with a witty chat from a very sophisticated, if somewhat effeminate gentleman. When discussing his movies, I asked him what his favorite roll was and after thinking for a few seconds, he named his lead role in the 'Mr. Belvedere' films, where he was a nanny to a family with undisciplined children. He quickly explained that it was not because he was particularly fond of children (far from it, it seems) but because the films were huge commercial successes that put him among the most popular actors in Hollywood.

I had heard that actor Rock Hudson was honeymooning on the north coast of Jamaica, which was quite a surprise since I understood there was a rumor that he was gay. He had apparently married his agent's secretary and was in Jamaica to celebrate the union. I did have the chance, however, to see the happy couple at the airport and marveled over his rugged good looks and masculine appearance... go figure! Later gossip columns speculated that although he was reported to be very fond of the lady, the marriage was contrived by his studio to preserve his film integrity.

Montgomery Clift was a guest at a small boutique type hotel in Ocho Rios, owned by a friend. I dropped in one night to have a drink and saw him chatting with what looked like a close male acquaintance. The owner later told me that the actor was heavily into drugs and was pretty well out of it, including one occasion having bowel control problems in the lobby of the hotel. A sad commentary on such a fine actor, who died a short time later.

Jamaica Farewell

In 1960 Bob Williamson, a younger fellow Pan Am trainee, also from the University of Miami, joined me on one of his undergraduate assignments in Venezuela. Bob was a very likable southern lad from Mobile, Alabama. He and I spent many an evening drinking a beer in local bistros and talking after the last flight on the night shift.

After Bob returned to school, I had resigned from Pan Am and joined Avianca in Jamaica, but we kept in touch so it was no great surprise when he called me in 1962 with a possible investment proposition. He said that he had read about a new development starting in a place called Freeport, Grand Bahama Island, where timber man Wallace Groves, had cut most of the saleable pine trees on the large island. He then partitioned the party in power in Nassau, the UBP, under a provision called the 'Hawksbill Agreement, to allow him to obtain a large track of the timbered land and to establish a privately owned 'free-port' area controlled by a company called the Grand Bahama Development Company. This flat land would be used to start a new city controlled by the 'Port Authority' who would issue licenses to start businesses operated by investors who would be able to bring their families and enjoy the island life.

These new immigrants to the Bahamas would not require Bahamian immigration work permits, nor be required to pay government duty on anything brought into the Freeport area. A percentage of the gross income would be the only fee required....and that to the Port Authority. This proposition had a very appealing premise. An investor could start a business, live on a tropical island, run his own operation and pay no taxes (including real estate, income or inherence). They could bring in their own furniture and automobile free of duty, as long as the items remained within the vast 'Freeport' area.

Bob called me in Jamaica, where I was still the Avianca Manager and asked if I had any interest in an available license in the new Freeport area where we could be awarded 5 acres for the construction of an egg farm? He proposed that he would go to Freeport in his own private aircraft and set up the farm if I could find the necessary funding. Crazy as it sounded, it had a strange appeal, in that it had the potential of making considerable tax free money, it was located close to my home in Miami and of course, it was on an island!

After an evening of martinis and conversation, Dr. Light offered to finance the business for half ownership, which was certainly acceptable for risk capital. Start-up funds were soon arranged and Bob was off to Grand Bahama to secure the license from the Port Authority and incorporate the business under 'Bahamas Poultry Company, Ltd'. I assured Dr. Light that if my job was terminated in view of the anticipated arrived of the long range jet aircraft; I would join Bob in the management of the new company.

As planned, Avianca did receive the new long range jets in short order, which negated the required refueling in Jamaica. That, along with increasing seat demands from Bogota' to New York, the company decided to discontinue service to Kingston and Montego Bay. The long haul revenue and reduced station costs sealed the Jamaica station's fate. The Colombian Airline offered me a management position in their New York station, which I appreciated but quickly declined and made plans to join Bob in Freeport.

As I prepared to leave Jamaica, with mixed emotions, I received a call from Paul Swetland, a wealthy Clevelander, who was introduced to me a few years before by Charlie Monroe, part owner of the

Montego Beach Hotel. Paul and I used to entertain a bevy of ladies on occasion, during Paul's winter visits. He said he just heard that Avianca was closing the Jamaica station and wanted to ask if I would be interested in flying to San Juan, Puerto Rico and board his 41' Newporter Motorsailer, for a sailing adventure to Nassau, where he planed to winter the boat. He said an extra hand would be helpful since it was only a hired French captain and himself to man the boat.

This new adventure piqued my interest. I readily agreed and planned to meet at the San Juan Yacht Club. Before I left Jamaica I had a call from a lady travel agent friend who was going to book a trip to Jamaica and thought we might get together. When I explained my pending departure to join the boat, Karen surprised me by asking if she might join us. Having a pretty girl along who was also a good cook, sounded sensible to me and when I asked Paul, he seemed to welcome a little feminine companionship for the ten day cruise.

I flew to Puerto Rico and stayed with friends of my parents, while I waited for Karen to arrive from New York before boarding the boat. Paul and the captain were waiting when we arrived, and after introductions and the storage of baggage, headed out of the harbor toward open water. With the sun shining, a cold beer in hand and a pretty girl making small talk, things looked pretty good. A light breeze whispering through the mainsail and jib, propelling us silently over smooth, azure seas, was almost a leaf out of a travel brochure. Keep this picture in mind... because it changed in a hurry into the cruise from HELL!

Once offshore, the support diesel engine developed a problem and rather than chance it, we optioned to return to the yacht club. It took a little over a week to obtain a part for the diesel from the U.S. and arrange for a local mechanic. It was a rather pleasant time, however, with afternoon drinks on the deck; almost gourmet dinners aboard and at the yacht club and an evening snuggle with Karen. The low point occurred when I threw the inter-liner of one of Paul's signature plastic glasses overboard with dregs of ice and damaged my ribs on the gunnels in a foolish attempt to snatch it back. Lingering pain was probably an indicator that I had cracked a couple ribs, which eventually healed on their own.

In due course, we repeated the departure drill and this time made it to the open sea and on our way to the southeast Bahamas. Unfortunately, it wasn't long before reality raised its ugly head and I was assigned a third of the 24 hour a day shifts... which meant that I was skippering the boat for two hours on and four hours off... day and night for the next four days, navigating head on into the teeth of a snarling January sea, propelled by a vicious cold front moving in from the north. The howling seas caused us to drop the mainsail, and engage the diesel to support the smaller jib. We pounded into the angry ocean day and night. With cooking pots and pans unable to stay on the stove, anything more than sandwiches was out of the question. Trying to sleep while wedged sideways in the forward bunk, as heavy seas pounded the hull, was not conducive to a good nights sleep... nor was peering out of the wheelhouse through a spray clouded windshield at 2:00 AM. My quality of life went to hell in a hand basket! It seemed I could stand anything except adversity.

One night, shortly after taking over the late shift, about 40 miles off the coast of Hispanola, I had goose bumps when I heard an Hawaiian band playing a popular island tune. Nice background music, I thought, but a little weird since no electrical equipment was on except for the auto pilot, and we were too far off shore for it to be coming from there. I enjoyed the music, calmed down and chalked it off to an episode of the Twilight Zone!

Karen had a painful habit of hitting her head on the hatch every time she went in or out of the wheelhouse house to or from the main cabin. You could be looking out to sea and hear a thud, accompanied by a scream of pain and rage, and knew Karen hit her head again. After a few days of frustration, she finally turned sullen and seemed to withdraw into a shell. I also seemed to be losing any sense of humor... what with the lack of sleep, no proper food, no booze and no cuddling. Unfortunately, I felt right at home with this 'ship of fools' and a little pouting felt good... when I had the time!

For amusement, I bet the Frenchman that I would catch a fish trolling across the treacherous Mona Passage... and I lost the bet! It was hard to believe that I could miss even snagging a fish in all that water, but miss I did. It wasn't until we got within a day of the Bahama Chain that I started to connect and caught a few Mahi Mahi (in Florida it's a Dolphin fish, not to be confused with a Porpoise), a few Barracuda and a couple of small Blackfin Tuna. Fresh bait was no problem with Flying Fish gliding into our sail every night, so all we had to do was pick them up out of the scuppers every morning... rig them with a colorful feathered lure and start trolling... a tasty morsel for the ocean predators.

The open ocean passage was bad, but had its moments in the afternoons watching the fishing lines for a hint of a strike, sucking on the odd brewsky and basking in the beauty of a fading sun. Once we got to the Bahamas, where we were out of the howling open ocean and night time operation of the boat, things settled down. Our first port of call was Great Inauga Island in the southeastern Bahamas, closer to Haiti than to Nassau. It was a relief to stretch out on a sunny deck that was not violently pitching, while Paul took the dingy in to clear Bahamian Customs and Immigration.

As we made our way toward our next stop at George Town, Exuma, we had the opportunity to spend a few nights anchored in picturesque bays, swim in pristine waters, and lounge on white sand beaches. A couple of scotches while relaxing on deck chairs and smelling succulent French cuisine drifting up from the galley, is what I originally had in mind. Karen even got a grip and avoided hitting her head on the hatch, which we all saw as a major accomplishment. Her whining tapered off a tad and I even had the feeling that she might be starting to enjoy herself.

Paul was hell bent to keep a scheduled arrival at George Town to meet a lady who was flying in to stay at the Club Peace and Plenty and, I trust, provide him with some TLC. This urgency prompted him to guide us through the eastern entrance of Elizabeth Harbour, in pitch dark, in a mad race to collect his anticipated prize. This was tricky stuff! I still don't know how he managed to lead us through the shallow water, dotted with huge coral heads that could rip the bottom out of the fiberglass boat! It was beyond me! I guess, if the King of England could give up the throne for the love of a woman, Paul could risk one lousy boat with a riff-raft crew.

Once we got to the Exuma Services dock and tied up to an empty slip, Paul dashed off to meet his sweetie at the Peace and Plenty. In the meantime, Karen, the captain and I had a few drinks to relax after the harrowing arrival, and made a quick dinner on the boat. Looking up at a star filled sky (with a full belly and a slight buzz), life seemed good again.

Reality once again set in the next morning, when we all went to the hotel for scheduled breakfast with Paul and his girlfriend. At breakfast, Karen met a family getting ready to fly to the States in their private plane. Somehow, she managed to hitch a ride and after a quick session of packing and with great relief, she managed to get off what she perceived her 'hell ship!' She was obviously quite pleased to put this experience behind her as she scurried away in a taxi for the airport. On a side note, I did not hear from her for a couple of years, when she called and arranged to meet me in Miami, bringing with her some very welcome pictures of our 'great sailing adventure' which had mentally mellowed over the ensuing years.

After a few days, Paul's friend left and we continued our sail to Nassau, where with some relief, I boarded a flight to Freeport, Grand Bahama and to a reunion with Bob Williamson and the Bahamas Poultry Company.

Landing at the Freeport Airport was not impressing. The buildings were at least constructed of concrete block and had the prospect of being a decent complex in the future. Bob was waiting for me in the poultry truck and after some 'glad to see ya's' he filled me in on our location a few miles east of the airport on the limerock Government road (the whole island was made of limerock).

Scanning the countryside, I came to the conclusion that this was a very scruffy island, mostly flat filled with scrub pine trees. Having not yet seen the Bell Channel waterway, or the fantastic beaches on the south side of the island, I feared that we had a real 'dog' on our hands. Bob advised that the Port Authority had takers for almost all of the available licenses and that building was rapidly proceeding on the island, creating a new city from the rock and scrub. In an effort to lift my sagging spirits, he played the trump 'fishing is terrific!' card, and I soon regained at least a little enthusiasm for the latest adventure.

The Egg and I

As I pulled into the egg farm for the first time, I couldn't help but thinking of that 1930's movie with Claudette Colburn and Fred MacMurry, called 'The Egg and I,' and thought it was fitting to call this chapter of my life after that amusing film farce. There was hope that this venture was the mother lode, but things at this point, looked pretty austere. Since there was no island power outside of the main town areas, we had to install a huge generator in a nearby shed and keep it running day and night to provide a constant supply of running water demanded by thousands of clucking hens. In addition, lights were required to burn throughout most of the hours of darkness to encourage the hens to continue eating around the clock, providing sufficient feed support for an average of five eggs a week, per bird, rolling to the lips of their wire cages. At that time White Leghorns should be productive for 15 to 18 months before they were sold for the stew pot. No running around the farm in happy retirement here.

I moved my suitcase into a concrete building containing a work area, egg storage, sleeping cubicle and bathroom. Not very deluxe, but since I just got off a boat, I wasn't used to decent or spacious accommodations in any event. As I looked around, I couldn't help but notice at least a couple of thousand chickens roosting in the surrounding pine trees and got a sinking feeling in the pit of my stomach... giving new meaning to 'chickens coming home to roost!'

I turned to Bob and asked, "I don't want to be coming on as a chicken expert on my first day... but shouldn't the chickens be in cages and not roosting in trees?"

"Glad you're here Charlie, I had to charter a plane at the last minute and bring a few thousand more laying hens over to the island from Dania, before the new law came into effect, raising the duty from 1 shilling (14 cents) to one Pound ($2.80) per bird... which was something we just couldn't afford. From now on, any birds we bring in have to be 10 days old, or less for the cheaper rate. Looks like we are going to have to raise chicks for five months before they start producing," he explained, causing an unsuppressed groan from me. "Put your bag down and lets get started putting together a few wire cages so we can get those birds out of the trees! Be thankful that the chicken houses are up."

It took almost a week to build the cages, hang them and round up the loose birds. It was soon apparent that grabbing a chicken by the leg and putting it in a bag was no easy task in broad daylight. We decided that as tired as we were from feeding, collecting, candling, packing eggs, assembling and installing cages, we had to catch the thousands of foot lose and fancy free birds at night. I was finally getting the idea that this egg farm was no 'get rich quick' scheme and it looked like the 'gravy train' was still at the station... all aboard!

At night many of the loose birds would roost on the chicken house roof rafters. This made for an easier leg grab; however the main problem was the few roosters sprinkled among the hens, complete with sharp leg spurs, which were undetectable in the dim light. It didn't take too long for us bright lads to figure out the spurs were very rough on a bare hands... and gloves were the way to go. Eventually we worked it out and saved most of the rush order birds, bringing the flock up to around ten thousand.

We soon tried of sleeping on a cot in the work area and acted swiftly when a notice appeared promoting the sale of a phased-out wooden supermarket building in the Freeport Zone. It was one of the first food stores in Freeport, and was reasonably priced with a 'U move it' caveat. Drooling over its ample size, we figured it would make a great two bedroom apartment and a large feed storage area... so without further ado, we bought it. Now it was like the 6 year old kid that picked up a 5 year old girl... 'Good God, what do I do now?'

We had to figure out how to disassemble it and put it back together again on the farm, so after a lengthy scratching of heads and chin stroking, we got a couple of circular saws along with two of our farm workers and started cutting the building in six foot sections, numbering and laying them in the feed truck. We poured a concrete slab, bolted the wall sections into place and attached the roof. 'Voila,' we quickly went from a cot in the corner to a large, airy two bedroom apartment, complete with a modern kitchen and bathroom, plus a bar well stocked with our favorite beverages. Ah Bliss! The other half of the building was more than ample to house our feed supply, along with a section dedicated to our electric feed/egg cart.

Egg sales were always at full capacity, while excess demand was handled by the importation of as many cases as we needed, shipped by our feed supplier from Dania, Florida, on weekly freighters. We were starting to supply eggs to a few of the major hotel building sites, such as the Lucayan Beach Hotel, to feed the huge construction crews. Beside the local supermarkets, another big customer was the Jack Tar Resort at West End, some twenty miles west of the farm. An interesting statistic was the bottle count along this stretch of the main road, where local drivers obviously, whiled away the time by drinking beer and anything else that would pour. Empty bottles, thrown out of car windows, littered the swale bush on both sides, for the entire length of the road. On several occasions, the delivery truck broke down along this desolate stretch allowing the opportunity to roam along the roadside while waiting rescue. For amusement, I counted the discarded bottles and while I can't remember the exact count per foot of road, I do remember thinking if I could redeem them at 5 cents each, I could retire on the Riviera.

In the early days of Freeport, with the allure of the Hawksbill Agreement opening the area to Port Authority control, business owners poured in capital, manpower and expertise. Money was eagerly injected and the Zone boomed. Our business took advantage of all the perks allowable and did quite well with the exception of having to pay duty on the egg truck and the importation of birds.

As you might imagine, most of the workers were male and women were at a premium. Fortune smiled on me however, when I met a lovely lady originally from San Francisco, who was currently managing one of the few Inns on the island, the Caravelle Club. The Inn had 20 rooms and a good restaurant and bar that Kathy managed with style and panache. She had a well appointed manager's suite on the property where I spent many blissful nights far away from the pounding chicken farm generator. I guess the downside for Kathy might have been the Bahamas Poultry truck parked all night in the parking lot... proudly displaying a huge, painted 'crowing cock' on the side panel. No doubt a fitting logo!

Life was fast moving and exciting in Freeport in the early days. The area was growing at a rapid pace, providing opportunity to meet new friends almost every day. Liquor was being bottled on the island for Gilbey's Gin, Smirnoff Vodka, J&B Scotch and other brands for Caribbean distribution. The same batches of the various spirits were also bottled under the house brand of 'Todd Hunter,' which sold in 40 oz bottles at the equivalent of $1.50 per bottle for the gin and vodka and $1.75 for the scotch. Even in 1963, this was cheap and gave birth to the local joke that when going to a house party, the host would instruct you to, "drink all the booze you want...but take it easy on the Coca-Cola!'

Dining at the farm was not elegant, as one might imagine, but we managed to eat fairly well. Six extra large eggs (before we knew anything about clogging of the arteries) hot out of the chickens, was not an unusual breakfast. Bananas and papayas growing along the water overflow ditches provided all the fresh fruit we wanted. Vegetables were available for the effort of gathering them from the vegetable farm next door and traded for a few dozen eggs now and then. Other trades included live spiny lobster (locally called 'crawfish'), and the occasional grouper or snapper... all making a tasty and nutritious dinner treat.

A case of eggs usually provided a croaker sack full of live lobsters from the owner of a grocery store at East End. When cash was required, lobsters cost the equivalent of $1.00 and conch .50 cents. Being a avid fisherman, I usually provided an ample supply of fresh fish, whether the deep sea red snapper or the mangrove snapper caught in shallow water. Oranges and grapefruit could be seasonally collected from old timbermen's houses in abandoned settlements. A few nights a week, I would have dinner at the Caravalle Club to socialize with Kathy and an evening now and then... wolfing down good family style dinners at Mack's Restaurant, an inexpensive eatery in an old, wooden shack of a building. All considered, if we weren't eating exactly 'high on the hog,' at least we were eating fresh and wholesome food somewhere on the hog.

Grand Bahama Island, one of the largest and more northern islands in the archipelago, had been relieved of its vast pine forests, shipping uncounted logs on barges from the remote north side of the island. Log and earthen ramps were constructed out into the shallow water to allow barge loading access. These deteriorating ramps provided shelter for swarms of snapper and invited frequent inspection by roaming bonefish, jacks, small sharks and such. One of my favorite fishing spots I was able to access by driving through one of the old settlements on a winding logger's road terminating at the sea. From the parking area I would walk along the beach casting jigs at a variety of fish cruising in the shallow, crystal water. On one occasion, I had been battling one fish after another for over an hour in the blazing summer sun, resulting in a profusion of perspiration … draining body fluids. Feeling a little dehydrated, I reached for my water canteen to discover I had left it back in the van. At this point, I should have immediately returned to the vehicle, but as fishermen know, when the fish are biting its difficult not to hang in there for 'just one more.' With a brilliant sun drawing the moisture out of my body, I plodded on until I felt faint. Reason finally prevailed and I thought that if I passed out on the beach in this boiling sun, I wasn't going to be rescued any time soon, and would be in serious trouble. Finally I put the rod down and jumped into the sea to cool off before staggering back to the van, making a mental note to always take a canteen of water.

Financially, the farm was marginly holding its own, but the cost of shipping feed was causing some concern. The biggest problem however, was the recent law increasing the duty on the importation of replacement birds (we were subject to duty since we were selling eggs our of the Freeport Zone). Although chicks required less air transportation costs, the raising of young, fragile birds for a period of five months was fraught with a multitude of problems, such as air freight packing losses, scantily trained helpers, a variety of illnesses, extra labor costs and longer term return of investment capital, made this situation a weighty one. Bob and I felt that this change in customs duty was instigated by a Member of Parliament who had a chicken business at one the other islands and was quite possibly hoping to run us out.

In April 1964 we were invited to the opening of the Lucayan Beach Hotel and Casino. It was the first major hotel and casino to open in the Freeport area. Big time tourism had finally come to Grand Bahama Island.

It was apparent that we would need an additional and considerable cash investment to continue to keep abreast of the rapidly expanding market. Dr. Light, I think would have continued to invest in the project, but after talking to his banker in Nassau, he decided against it. Bob and I never completely understood the rationale, except we thought the banker had local loyalties, which probably included our removal from the poultry business to eventually allow a Bahamian company to move into a booming Freeport. In any event, we came to the conclusion that it was time to cash out of the egg business and move on.

Without the infusion of capital, we soon sold the business and the Port Authority license to our feed supplier in Dania. Wrapping things up, we made a deal with the local nursery to purchase our vast mounds of chicken manure piled up under the cages for use in a high grade fertilizer. The catch in this deal was that we had to deliver it to the nursery in our truck. A quick check of the potential income dictated that 'shoveling shit against the wind' was more than an old saying... it was an idea whose time had come! After a full day shoveling, we completed the task and pocketed a fast (if laborious) $1,500 each to take along with our share of the sale.

So ended the 'Chicken and Egg' man's grand adventure!

A Little Traveling Music

A few months before Bob and I wrapped up the egg farm, I had the opportunity to show Jane, a visiting friend, around Grand Bahama, while renewing the close relationship we developed during her frequent holidays to Jamaica. Paul Swetland introduced me to the auburn haired divorcee, who was just starting to enjoy life again after a 12 year bummer of a marriage. Jane was a very attractive and well built lady of thirty-six, whose charm and physical attributes were enhanced by a divorce settlement involving half of a large number of oil wells in Texas and New Mexico.

Jane asked me about future plans after the sale of the egg farm and listened intently as I outlined my proposed month's vacation to Europe. I further explained that I had a last free pass from my previous airline job and reasoned that to waste it would certainly be a sin. Jane's eyes lit up when she told me she had never traveled on the continent and volunteered to join me, if I could put up with her. Since I wasn't keen on traveling alone, I jumped at the opportunity and soon hatched a plan to meet at the Place Hotel, on the lake, in Lucerne, Switzerland at a selected future date. Back in Texas, Jane booked a European tour she had designed to terminate in Lucerne where we would meet and continue touring... I love it when a plan comes together!

I flew to London five days early to spend some time with an old girlfriend from Jamaica now living and working in the U.K. While there I called my cousin John Pflueger, a geological physicist from Princeton, who was in charge of an oil operation in the Near East and based in London. He was married to a lady also from Texas and kept an apartment in Knightsbridge. The four of us spent a few pleasant evenings at dinner and the theater before I had to proceed to Switzerland.

Having made no advance reservations, I was not surprised to windup in a Second Class compartment on a train out of Waterloo Station. Changing trains in Calais, I was assigned to share a compartment with what looked like the entire French Army for our journey across France. Now traveling all night with the troops in a small compartment (overflowing into the aisles) was one thing.....but sitting there breathing clouds of noxiously harsh French cigarette smoke was entirely another! When we arrived at the Lucerne Station, I felt par-broiled, trailing a stream of stale smoke all the way to the hotel.

Jane, true to her word, met me on the appointed date in the hotel bar for drinks and dinner. Overwhelmed with my charm and sophistication.... at least I was overwhelmed and wore my ascot to prove it.... Jane listened, starry-eyed as I outlined a proposed schedule for the next thirty days. In May's 1964 Europe, before the tourist heavy summer high season, it was not critical to pre-book every move, so deciding to leave for Barcelona, Spain the following day presented no anxiety and the flight was booked.

The U.S. Dollar was still very strong in those days, while prices were reasonable and had not increased much from my last few visits. I started to explain to Jane, that while I had sufficient funds to hold up my end of moderate travel expenses, deluxe accommodations might be over doing it a tad! Jane interrupted to relieve any monetary concerns by saying that while she appreciated my commitment, she wanted to experience a first class trip and insisted on paying for everything. I took a 'gulp' of air, as she continued by bringing out of her handbag, a packet of $100. American Express Travelers checks along with a letter of credit from her Houston bank manager, guaranteeing available funds of up to $25,000. At that point, disappointing Jane was not in my vocabulary....first class the lady wants....first class she gets! To sample the delights of Europe with a lovely companion was worth at least one rub on Aladdin's Lamp and with a song in my heart and to our mutual delight, I agreed to the arrangement. Don't think 'Gigolo'....think more... 'Personalized Tour Guide'!

In line with her first class mandate, we checked into the penthouse suite of the Phoenix Hotel in Barcelona that boasted a fabulous view of this popular Spanish city. If this back and forth to Europe like a yo-yo sounds repetitious, this was a very exciting period of my life and I feel an obligation to report it as it happened; please bear with me.

Jane and I took in a bull fight, which as it turned out, she loathed it as much as I enjoyed it, but she did confess it was worth the effort to be able to add it to her list of things never to do again! I think I lost some points with her when I cheered along with the rest of the crazy aficionados in rewarding one particularly talented and gory Matador an ear and a tail.

Our next stop took us to Palma de Majorca, one of the three Spanish Islands off the coast of Spain, where we were lucky enough to book the penthouse suite in a sister Phoenix Hotel. A rental car made it easy to tour the hilly island, soaking up the classic architecture, stopping in small towns for lunch and catching a swim at secluded beaches. In the evenings after happy hour, we sampled the island cuisine around Palma, including one memorable restaurant full of bullfighting memorabilia.... huge promotional posters, saddles, lances, rusting swords and a disgusting display of dismembered dried ears and tails awarded to some victorious Matadors decades before. The establishment provided sumptuous meals with a glass of fine house wine, for the princely sum of $1.50 each... Seems like when you have money in your pocket and the price is of no consequence... everything is inexpensive!

By the time we arrived at the good old Palace Hotel in Madrid, booked a suite and settled in, it was time to explore a myriad of sightseeing opportunities. Jane had heard of the Del Prado Museum and naturally wanted to make it our first stop. Since I had been there before, I had a pretty good idea of where the most famous paintings were located, but after hours of seeing huge paintings of nobles with goatees and frilly collars, I had pretty much had it and jumped for joy when the closing buzzer sounded and security guards started ushering us out.

Jane was bubbling over with all the priceless art she had seen. I played along as a 'Patron of the Arts' and shamelessly uttered nonsense like, "sorry its closing time....I wanted to revisit the Titian exhibition for a little more study." when in actual fact, I'd rather jump into a pen of Rottweilers! What a 'rotter' to give this sincere lady all that BS ('bogus sincerity'...got you on that one), but it sounded good at the time and I did actually know a little about the museum.

That night I took her to El Botin, the 14th Century eatery specializing in a whole roasted suckling pig, cooked to a crisp golden brown skin covering the fork cutting roast pork. A fawning Maitre'd (who probably mistook us for people of importance), seated us in the main, upstairs dining room. As we sipped our Sangrias, Jane tapped my hand and whispered, "Who is that man staring at us, he looks familiar?" My gaze followed her discretely pointing finger to a table on the other side of the room and to my surprise, landed on a famous movie actor.

"That's Peter Sellers! He played in the 'Pink Panther' and a lot of other comedies, although I have no clue why he seems to be staring! Maybe he thinks he knows us." Or, I thought, maybe he just wants to ogle a lovely woman... meticulously dressed...mink stole draped... and diamond earrings sparkling. Finally, with both of us staring back, Peter gave us a little 'hello' nod and smile and returned to the conversation with his dining companions. You'll be pleased to note, I graciously returned the nod.

After a memorable dinner, we were in time for the last show at the 'Toledo,' a basement night club featuring stunning walls of Spanish tile and Arab influenced décor, dedicated to the ancient art of the Flamenco dance. Seated close to the stage, we were enthusiastically entertained by the dance troop.... stomping their hearts out. Noting the frenzied effort of the dancers, we looked around and saw the beautiful Italian movie actress Sophia Loren at the next table, who was, no doubt, the inspiration for this sensational performance. All considered, it was a very exciting day!

On our last evening in Madrid, we had an unfortunate accident, which put a damper on the trip. Coming out of the Palace Hotel, one of Jane's high heel shoes jammed into the cuff of my trouser leg, causing a nasty fall and opening a inch gash on the eyebrow line over her right eye. She was stunned and with blood copiously flowing down her face we had doorman urgently call a medical clinic around the corner from the hotel and helped get us there. I spoke enough Spanish to work along with the doctor who mopped up the blood and stitched the wound. He tried to give Jane a tetanus shot, but she would have none of that. It did work out well in the end, however, and she reported no long term effects.

Our final stop was a return to where I started a month before.... London, my favorite city! We took rooms in the controversial London Hilton… not only the first high rise hotel allowed in the city, but located across the street from Hyde Park and overlooking Buckingham Palace. This created some consternation with the local citizens, who apparently objected to the perceived notion that tourists would sit at their windows all day, trying to get a peek into the back yard of their Queen's residence… Gads! It had only been open for five weeks and the management was still trying to convince the authorities to change the archaic liquor laws and amend them to permit this deluxe hotel to allow its bars and lounges to operate on international standards and not restricted to archaoic pub hours. This took some time, but eventually the hotel was granted extended operational hours as befitting a world class hotel.

Business Beckons

Back in Miami after the wonderful trip to Europe, I took stock of my situation and while not completely impecunious, my 'stash of cash' was dwindling at an alarming rate. I moved into one side of my two bedroom duplex.... allowing decent, and inexpensive accommodations. While comfortable, I had this strange urge (strange for me)....it was time to get a....hold your breath....JOB! There I said the 'J' word! The money was obviously important, but feeling useless day after day was also a powerful incentive.

When visiting Miami while living in Jamaica, I used to be invited to house parties with some of the Coral Gables Sears store personnel, including the assistant to the Personnel Manager, Anita Higgley. Since I had worked a few months in the Men's Department selling shirts over the holidays during my senior year at the 'U,' I had considered a proposal from the then Personnel Manager, to join the Sears' Management Trainee Program, offered to college graduates and selected department managers. I did appreciate the offer, but in the final analysis, the excitement, perceived glamour, exotic locations, and invested employment with Pan Am, caused me to decline and proceed with the airline job as planned.

During our next Saturday night house party, I questioned Anita about the prospect of checking out the trainee program. Maybe it was the scotch, but she seemed very enthusiastic and said she could arrange an interview with the store's Personnel Manager to discuss this possibility.

The Sears Roebuck Training Program the Personnel Manager offered was an eight month on the job training in the various departments of the store, such as personnel, customer service, receiving, security, purchasing, merchandising, and floor sales. Every Saturday the trainees were assigned to the sales floor in various departments, learning the 'art' of the sale from clerks who made retail selling a full time career.

While working in the Customer Service Department, I met Jean Steder, a divorced mother of three, who was working part time and assigned to bring the new trainee up to speed. As the Sears motto was 'Satisfaction Guaranteed or Your Money Back!' this department was an important training segment, since, in theory, it was the cornerstone of the company's business principles, not to mention its huge creditability in the market place, resulting in Sears becoming the world's largest retailer.

One outrageous example was a seven year old mattress that was refunded due to 'excessive wear!' The customer uttered the magic words...."I am not satisfied!" and since the customer is the only person who can decide satisfaction, the company replaced the well used mattress with a brand new one. Talk about a stacked deck!

If a customer was refused a refund or adjustment by the first line of defense, the department manager, the next stop was the Customer Service Manager, who would, in all probability, satisfy the customer. He knew that if he didn't, the Store Manager will be contacted next, and nine times out of ten, he will make the adjustment, come hell or high water, since realizing that a determined customer will follow the chain of command to its next stop at the Regional Vice President in Atlanta. The Regional VP will no doubt, want to know why the Store Manager was unable to satisfy a customer.... not a sound career move, to say the least! I enjoyed working in the Customer Service Department and wound up seeing Jean socially.

My favorite Saturday sales floor department was Hardware.... plenty of action, selling merchandise I understood.... grabbing money and ringing up sales was a fun game for me. Trying to accumulate a higher sales take for the day put a little competition in the equation. Being fast on the cash register, my day's sales volume was often up there with the professional floor sales staff. Every now and then however, I would happen on a bigger ticket sale, say a lawnmower, and instead of ringing it to my number; I would ring it on one of the full time clerk's number, allowing them to collect a commission on the sale. This action was appreciated by the full time staff and tempered any animosity toward the 'damn trainees' diluting commissions. What the hell! Trainees did not get commissions on sales, so it did not matter financially, to spread it around a little... we all had families to support.

On a real hospitality side note.... soon after being hired, an attractive lady in her mid forties and manager of the tobacco counter suggested we get together for a drink after work. That drink turned into dinner and a romp in her bed, and as much as I tried to arrange an encore, it was a 'one time, Charlie!' This was not a big ego booster and it began to nibble at my confidence, until one of my management friends explained that she looked on it as her duty to welcome new management additions (presumably.... not an officially sponsored company program) with a rousing lay, after which, they were on their own. I guess it takes all kinds, but I thank her for her kind welcome.

Three months into the training program, I was called into the office and after a chat with the Personnel Manager, was offered the job of managing the Boy's Clothing Department. Although, I wasn't in any hurry to give up on the training program, this sounded like something I could handle, so off I went to sell boys clothing....the little darlings. This was obviously, quite a change for the 'chicken and egg' man!

The Boy's Department was a challenge from the standpoint of the previous manager's lack of success, allowing a last place profit finish in the region's Boyswear Departments. I was kindly advised, off the record, by the Sales Manager, that if during my first month or two I found any items in inventory that had been around for awhile and lacked customer appeal, write them way down or completely off, even if you go over your markdown budget, and get rid of a stagnant budget drain. The obvious inference was that when the department profit and loss under my management, for the first month or two, was reviewed any losses would not be held against me as would be the case later. On the other hand, the write-offs would free up future merchandise purchase allotments, hopefully allowing the department to bring in additional new and more saleable items and increasing profits.

Asking the advice of my assistant manager on what 'dogs' might be slumbering upstairs in the stockroom that could no longer 'run with the hounds,' she selected four or five items of considerable value. One of the selected write-offs that had resided for a couple of years in storage was two huge boxes of local high school logo wind breaker jackets. The department had either gone overboard in their purchasing or the wind breaker promotion turned out to be a dud... or maybe both.

With the write-off accomplished, I now faced the problem of physically dumping the jackets, while deriving some value. After some thought, I decided to go with a special sale to give a 'free' jacket with every 'back to school' purchase of $25 or more. From the crowds, one might think we were giving away diamond rings! Lots of grabbing, shouting and the lovely sound of a dinging cash register, was proof of the value of a 'freebie' to the general public. We had turned an un-salable item into a huge marketing attraction, while freeing up valuable inventory dollars.

One day when ordering merchandise for the next month's business, I came upon an offer from one of our better shirt suppliers.

They offered a new style collarless, pullover shirt called a 'Henley,' in assorted, vivid colors. Since the shirts in the display pictures looked new and interesting, I ordered a modest 60 dozen in assorted colors, to brighten up one of the display cases. When the order arrived, I had the sales ladies present them in one of the most noticeable locations, creating an attention grabbing display with their bright colors and unique style. To my amazement (although I later acted as if I had a direct pipeline to the consumer's heart) the shirts leaped off the shelves and we were sold out in a matter of a few days....a brilliant conversion of 'opportunity meeting inspiration arriving at dumb luck!'

My sales ladies were not shy in suggesting that where ever I had bought the shirts, I had better order a 'bunch' more, in a hurry and not wait for next month's normal ordering cycle. The Henley's' were the hottest sellers in Boyswear. I raced upstairs to my cubbyhole office and with shaky hand, scribbled out a massive order and sent it out, on the spot, marked for immediately delivery.

For the next ten days I second guessed my impulsive action and would really have wrung my hands and gnashed my teeth, if not for the constant customer requests asking when the next shipment would arrive. When the big day came, I was at the receiving ramp shouting encouragement to 'get my stuff off the truck!'

We quickly emptied three full display cases and filled the space with a dazzling arrangement of the colorful Henley's. The response was unprecedented! Department sales soared with the new shirts bringing in the crowd. Critiquing our success, the early recognition and gut-wrenching decision to let it all hang out and load up on the item, was the key to this marketing event, making our Boyswear Department stand out in the region.

While this was only one item, our sales force tried to keep up to date floor records of customer inquiries and requests in order that we could anticipate early trends with ultimately future customer demands.

Working in one of the Sears 'A' stores (largest category), was not all work.... no indeed! There was a lot of camaraderie, particularly when we participated in skits during the hour before the doors opened to the public on Monday mornings. Management and employees would meet to discuss the weekly challenges, sales promotions and items of interest, with the once a month entertainment program.

Quite often, I would be selected to plan and execute one of these skits. On one occasion I donned a bed sheet, while false beard and lip synced to the Bill Cosby record, 'The World's Oldest Man.' One of my best efforts was, however, a skit where my fellow cohorts and I put on Mickey Mouse hats and sang the MM song, with doctored words to the effect that the top store managers were 'Mickey Mousers.' When I started the performance with...."I'm Sammie" for the Store Manager Sam Miller, it brought the house down. The managers laughed along with the rest of the ensemble and seemed to take it well....so I guess it was a coincidence that I was soon transferred. So much for my comedic talent.

Having spent eight months shaping up Boyswear, Anita called me to the office once again to inform me that there was a job opening in the Hollywood Store as Customer Service Manager. It was suggested that this was a step into upper store management, so with a quick 'goodbye,' I reluctantly accepted and reported to Hollywood.

Since the new I-95 super highway had recently opened and most of the heavy rush hour traffic ran counter to my apartment near the Miami International Airport, I decided to remain in Miami and drive the 22 miles each way. This decision kept me from having to move and pay rent in Hollywood, but a little stressful and time consuming. In any event, I emerged myself in my new assignment.... for better or for worse!

I took over a Customer Service Department that was barely functioning with its many facets of responsibility, such as customer complaints, layaways, gift wrap, parts ordering, service calls and

more. Now get this... there were 17 full time employees.... gulp....
all women! As you surmised, I love women, but can you imagine all
these gals in one department splitting into cliques and spending at
least some of each day in catty (don't blame me....I just call'em like
I see'em) conversations. For openers, I had to try to forge a 'lets all
do our job and try to get along with each other' mentality. After all
that squabbling... I felt that occasional whining and moaning was at
least barely acceptable and with this behind us, we could concentrate
on the snarling and complaining customers. If I heard 'I wouldn't
have your job for anything!' I heard it a thousand times. Suicide only
popped into my head a couple of times a day.

My first December was a dozy, with calls from various
departments to solve unusual return items or complaints on quality,
sprinkled with customers reporting rude sales clerks....on and on ad
nauseum. In competition with this, a line of largely obnoxious and
complaining customers waited outside my office to take a crack at
me. The cues got so long that I gave some thought to installing a
'take a number' dispenser! With Christmas Carols pounding away
on the public address system, I spent many hours behind my desk,
like a surreal Santa Clause, listening to the demands of spoiled
children, while I puffed one cigarette after another, attempting to
dispense the wisdom of Solomon over a thread pull on a blouse, or
defending a gallon of paint that was not quite filled to the top of
the can. On a side note.... one gentleman actually tried to sue us for
cheating on the volume listed on the can, but failed to find support
when we hired an independent tester that measured the amount and
found it to be exactly one U.S. gallon as indicated.

The Customer Service Office was a nightmare! Gift wrap was
jammed with shoppers in a hurry! Others were waiting in front of
the parts identifying machine to order a washer part or thousands
of other parts, from the hundreds of items sold at Sears. More
mob scenes waiting to use the layaway service, while desperate
homeowners were trying to schedule a repairman's visit. Add the
noise of the PA system blasting out a constantly dinging bell calling

various members of management to phone the operator for one 'urgent' message or another....all over the previously mentioned carols, masses of humanity pushing and shoving to scoop up the best bargains....really made for a trying holiday season.

Fortunately, the flip side of this coin delivered plenty of good times....like strolling around the store in a nice suit, chatting with the employees, mostly pretty, young women, and feeling like an important executive.. Some of these encounters resulted in after work dates and provided a very satisfying social life. As a member of the management team, one could expect a harassment suit in the blink of an eye in today's world....but thankfully, it was in the mid-60's and did not present a problem. In addition, I did not come on too strong when chatting up the ladies, only flashes of my oozing charm and 'homme fatal' personality.

One very attractive 23 year old divorced sales clerk was assigned to me for administration of her semi-annual employee review. Having been tipped off by her department manager that she was not only very good in her job, but she was also sexually active (remember, 'forewarned is forearmed'). In the middle of the interview, I unleashed my boyish charm, culminating in a sensuous kiss, which was received with enthusiasm and not a dreaded scream for help that would, no doubt, result in my being drummed out of the corps one step ahead of a tar and feather committee.

From the interview (yes! I gave her a great review) onward, Linda and I hit it off and got together a couple of times a week, some of which transpired after hours, on my lockup nights, in the store furniture department. A little un-nerving at first, but all in all... very exciting, if boarding on lunacy!

A delightful eighteen year old, with blonde hair and a nice body worked part time in one of the departments while attending junior college. She was fresh, bubbly and contrary to her wholesome appearance, very sensuous. We dated on and off and remained friends for years. Our appetites knew little bounds, and took a breather only when she went away to the university. I thought of Bobbie often, but the differences in age of eighteen years was a little on the far side of compatibility in day to day living and in a final analysis....a deal breaker. Precious memories, indeed.

At the Hollywood Store, the Monday morning skits and morale building meetings continued with unlimited energy. Pranks also cropped up on occasion, such as the time the Sales Manager and I were on the Saturday night shift and while thumbing through a pictorial calendar featuring Chimpanzees in various occupational and business dress.... we looked at each other with a grin, and another classic prank was hatched!

Bill and I went to the empty meeting room on the second floor where we dragged in the janitorial ladder, and climbed up the 12' wall to remove a dozen framed pictures of the company management. The dignified images from the Regional Vice-President to the Store Manager and on down, were removed, leaving the names and titles in place. After some careful trimming, we inserted the Chimp pictures in the frames and re-hung them. Now, while this was a lot of work that could have, no doubt, been more productively invested, our zeal urged us on with dispatch, all the while suppressing a serious case of the giggles (I know, it's a sad sight to see two grown men giggling like school girls).

At 8:30 on the following Monday morning, the management and employees trooped into the meeting room, as usual, and took their seats, while the General Manager prepared his notes at the podium. There was a lot of the usual chit-chat between employees catching up on the weekend's activities, before the manager tapped for attention. Bill and I could barely suppress our snickers and was amazed that none of the assembly had yet raised their eyes to really look at the staff pictures. Then like a thunderbolt, as the manager started his weekly, boring pep talk, one of the group looked up and gasped... pointing over the manager's droning head! Then it 'hit the fan'... all eyes darted to the pictures, which still proudly advertised the various management positions which were now (gasp!) held by a troop of Chimps. To say the place broke up would be an understatement and when the Store Manager turned around and lifted his eyes to see what the fuss was all about, his double take sent the place into pandemonium! Its one thing to include the entire store management staff, but we thought it was a particularly ballsy move to include the Regional Manager, whom, I understand, when told of the prank, got a big laugh out of it.

The Manager's face flushed, but to his credit, he laughed along with the rest of us and even had the good grace to mumble, "Well, I guess we have been replaced by some Harvard graduates!" Bill and I even feinted outrage, but started laughing more at the reaction of the crowd, since we obviously knew what was coming. Bill and I never admitted to this dastardly deed, although it was puzzling to many, how and when this transformation could have been accomplished. The prank finally fell into legend and fortunately, into the 'unsolved mystery' file.

Bill and I, fancying ourselves as the resident pranksters, decided to pull our next operation on Smitty, manager of the Houseware Department. He was a bright, ambitious, and gregarious lad, who eventually made his mark with the company. His monthly department inspection by the Store Manager and entourage (including Bill and me) was coming up on the following Monday, and not to be taken lightly. When Smitty had gone home after work on Saturday, we slithered over to Houseware for a quick look for inspiration, along with any areas of disarray, dirt of anything a prankster could get his teeth in. Suddenly.... Eureka! We discovered that although all the display cases and shelves had been carefully dusted, a glass top, sign display shelf had been over looked and happily, laden with a heavy coating of good, old fashion, garden variety dust! After five minutes of sorting out the premise of the prank, we made a quick trip to the Garden Department, where we borrowed half a dozen small potted tomato plants, growing in plastic containers. The trap was in motion.

Although there was some risk of discovery, but we felt that in the rush of final preparations Smitty would not look up as high as the sale signs and prematurely blow the deal. Of course, we had to solicit the Store Manager to go along with us and when the Inspection group arrived, he was briefed to tell Smitty that he had some complaints that the department always needed a good clean-up. The scene went down like this....

"Mr. Smith, I have had some serious complaints that your people have never properly cleaned the department," giving a decent interpretation of barely controlled indignation..

Smitty blanched and stuttered, "No sir, that's not true! We clean and dust everyday," I watched as beads of sweat began to trickle down his face. Talk about a 'hot seat!

The manager purposely strolled to one of the display cases and with a flourish, wiped a finger across a squeaky clean lower glass self. Smitty's obvious relief was joined by what we preceived as a glimmer of returning confidence. At that, Bill and I had moved to the next case and with mock disgust, called out to the entourage of our 'discovery' of a sales sign shelf so besotted with dirt and dust that there appeared to be plants growing on it! To lend a little more 'oomph,' Bill and I both snarled out a loud 'outrageous!'

I thought Smitty was going to faint, as he pushed through the assembly of inspectors, department employees (you could tell them from the hanging heads) and hangers-on, to come to grips with this current career setback. In the meantime, the 'inspectors' were busily scribbling phony notes in the 'write-up' books, adding to the chaos and building suspense. When he got to the display case the Store Manger pointed to the forest of potted tomato plants.... handing him one for a closer inspection. With a puzzled look, Smitty struggled to figure just what the hell was going on, while the entire assembly went into convolutions! Then the light bulb came on and with a sheepish grim of relief, he put on a 'good sport' face and laughed along with the rest of us. All we needed to make the prank perfect was a TV host popping out and shouting 'Gotcha!' Congratulations… another successful effort by grown men to ward off boredom….at the expense of one poor devil or another.

With over a year as Customer Service Manager, I was called to the office and advised that the manager wanted me to switch jobs with the current Security Manager, Ron Gallant, primarily for the additional job experience. The position did have some appeal, so I opted to let Ron cope with a passel of angry and whining customers, while I chased crooks and practiced my best 'book'em Danny' voice. And so it was!

The Store Dick

I went from the 'unofficial store dick' to the actual store dick, charged with the responsibility of internal and external theft and other assorted felonies and misdemeanors.

Obviously, shoplifting was one of my major problems, so I held a store meeting and enlisted the help of the department clerks to keep an eye out for suspicious activities. This effort soon paid off with an urgent call from the women's dress department where the manager observed a customer going into one of the dressing rooms with an excess number of garments. When I arrived at the department, the manager and I looked over the swinging café doors into the multi-stalled dressing area and observed a woman standing with her back to the doors, shielding any view of her activity. To her downfall however, she forgot she was looking into a full length mirror attached to the wall, which allowed the manager and me to an unobstructed view, over the shoulder of the woman tucking various clothing items under her half slip (boosting) and letting her raised dress fall over the merchandise. This was my first 'collar' as they say on T.V. and I must admit it felt good… as the police hauled the poor wretch to jail!

A few days later I was summoned to court along with the Dress Department manager to formally charge the 'Booster'. She had retained an attorney who found the manager and me outside the court room waiting to be called. He sidled up to us and said if we did not drop the charges, he was going to sue Sear's for a bundle for false arrest. I declined his offer and told him with not a little acrimony, that his client was guilty as sin and Sears' could afford to prosecute a thief no matter what the conclusion.

The judge took our statements one at a time, resulting in his ruling for prosecution and remanded the shoplifter to 30 days in jail. On our way out, her attorney once again approached us and apologized for his aggressive demeanor, "sorry about coming on strong with the 'sue Sear's bit'! I had to try anything I could to get the charges dismissed... I didn't think she could win in court with two creditable eye witnesses."

"I understand your position, but I figured we had a better chance to get her convicted under the circumstances, than you had to get her off!" I replied, as I slipped by him and out the door, relieved to be outside on a beautiful day.

A very similar incident occurred the following week when the department handling Ladies Notions called the operation to 'bell' me. She came to meet me half way down the isle to pull me aside and explained, "I saw an older woman slip a bottle of rather expensive perfume in her bag and on another isle she tried on a silk scarf, tucked the price tag in her blouse and left the store."

"You should have called me sooner... Where is she now?" I asked making my way with the manager toward the huge glass door closest to her department, leading into the mall.

"There she is, sitting on that bench," she advised, pointing to a gray headed grandmother type comfortably ensconced, apparently without a care in the world.

As I walked toward the woman, I held my hand out as if to take the purloined articles in an effort to help her relieve the building guilt. To my utter amazement, that's exactly what happened... she reached in her bag and handed me the bottle of perfume!

Shocked, I mumbled a "thank you! Now the scarf!" She immediately un-wrapped it from her neck and with a sad smile and in a sweet voice, murmured, "Sorry, I forgot that."

I told her that the police would be coming and she would be charged with shoplifting. This announcement brought a torrent of tears as she told me she was in South Florida visiting her son, and that her husband was a retired police captain. I often wondered why she sat on the bench in plain view of the department where she pinched the items, instead of disappearing into a crowded mall and safety. My guess was that she wanted to be caught for whatever reason that made sense to a trouble mind.

The Security Manager's job was interesting and on occasion... exciting, with a hint of danger. One such case started with the Camera Department's Christmas season display of boxed movie camera sets priced at $150 each and displayed on the main isle. When I saw the display, I thought that we were asking for trouble stacking a dozen expensive items on what becomes a very crowded main isle in the madness of Christmas shoppers.

It only took a couple of days to prove my intuition right, when the department manager called me with a report of a missing camera box on the upper right hand of the top shelf. After confirming that it had definitely not been sold and was indeed stolen, I reported to the store manager that it was missing and that it may be prudent to move all the cameras into the back room which was under key, while wiring down one display set.

The manager replied, "This is a fairly big ticket item for the department and we have stocked heavily, counting on selling them out during Christmas. Its hard to sell them unless we utilize the end of a main isle display case, so just tell the department manager to write off the stolen camera, put another one out and try to keep an eye on the display!"

I did as instructed, but was very apprehensive as the crush of the crowds and the usual rush of holiday traffic problems kept me hopping. It didn't take but a day to get another call from Cameras and a re-play of the previous theft. The right top corner box had also disappeared and another $150 write-off coming up. Woe is me!

Needless to say, the store manager was less than amused, but still refused to allow me to remove the display. He did advise however, that he would not be happy to see another missing camera set. Maybe I could hire Brinks to watch the damn display!

I went back to the department and stood looking at the boxes, missing the same top right one and tried to come up with some sort of a plan, any plan, to foil this persistent thief. Finally it hit me that if I got some monofilament fishing line from sports goods and tied one end to one of the bottom carton clamps, coiling about a 20 feet of line and attaching the other end to the bait lever of a rat trap borrowed from Houseware, I would have an effective noise maker as an attention grabber. I coiled the line and leaned the cocked trap against the display case behind the upper right box, figuring the thief always picked the easiest one to grab. Once he took the box, the line would play out, un-noticed by the thief in the crush of the Christmas rush, until the rat trap exploded with a bang, thereby bringing nearby sales personnel to the capture! 'Rube Goldberg' would be proud.

The rest of the day after setting this 'hi-tech' trap, I wondered how long it would take to have some kid stick his hand behind the box and come out with a couple of broken fingers and a nice law suit? In any event, I had a meeting with the salesmen in washing machines directly across from the camera display case and briefed them on what I had set up and asked them if they heard or saw anything that I expected someone to detain the perpetrator and call me.

The next day in the rush of holiday shopping, I forgot about the trap until I heard my bell (4 single bongs) on the public address system calling me to a phone. A breathless department manager rattled off a 'come quick' and hung up. Within seconds I arrived at the department to find the doctored camera box lying on the isle floor about 20 feet from the display case.

"What happened?" I shouted at the manager!

"I was waiting on a customer when I head a loud clap over the crowd din and when I looked up I saw what looked like one of our Sear's porters stopped in the middle of the floor with a camera box in his hands and looking back at a rat trap tied to a fishing line. He said to no one in particular, 'I see you're trying to catch rats!' and then set the box down and calmly disappeared into the crowd.

I looked over at a couple of the washing machine salesmen hanging on every word and asked them, "Why didn't you stop the thief when you saw him standing there with stolen merchandise in his hands?" I was sputtering at this point and very pissed.

"It's not our job to tackle a thief who could be armed," one of the brave hearts ventured.

Thinking this over for a few seconds, I could see his point and asked them if they could at least identify the thief, figuring that although I was ahead of the game since I still had the camera, maybe there was still some benefit to reap.

"He was a slim, black man wearing what looked like a Sear's porter olive green uniform, but I don't remember seeing a company logo on his shirt," the manager replied, throwing me a bone after refusing to get involved.

The Store Manager heard about the set-up and called me in to congratulate me on saving the store another loss of an expensive item and identifying the modus operandi, i.e. using a Sear's style uniform allowing the thief to wander, unchallenged, in restricted areas, helping himself to whatever wasn't nailed down.

We sent a bulletin to the other Sear's Stores in South Florida advising their Security Managers to keep an eye out for persons wearing Sear's like uniforms in stock room areas. A happy ending to this story came when the Northside store's security nabbed the thief, thereby putting an end to his very lucrative career.

Another puzzling problem, as reported to me, advising that shirts were being stolen from the Men's Department at an alarming rate. The Manager advised that all the department's personnel were trained to watch for shoplifters and they couldn't figure out how the items were pilfered and he asked for my help.

Checking around the department, I reviewed the daily cash register tapes (over and shorts) and noticed that every few days the cash register numbering sequences missed a number or two between the night tape ending sales number and the opening sales number the next day. What happened to the missing sales slips? It looked like someone was operating the cash register during the time the store was closed and keeping the missing sales slips.

Determined to discover how this was being done, I parked my car in the Sears parking lot at 4:00 AM the next morning, taking care to park between the Sears repair trucks, turned off the alarm and slipped into the deserted store. The clean-up maintenance crew, under the supervision of our maintenance manager, was due to arrive around 4:30 AM to begin their mornings work. By 4:14 I had gone to the Shoe Department, climbed to the top of the highest shelf in the stock area and made myself as comfortable as possible, while still taking advantage of a six inch space between the top of the department façade and the ceiling, giving me an unrestricted view of most of the west side of the store. Binoculars from sporting goods, aided the surveillance of the Men's Department, along with the Candy and Nut Counter.

The laughing and joking of the crew let me know they were on the way with their cleaning equipment. The group funneled out to the various areas of the store; many of them out of visual range. The employee in charge of cleaning the section of the store I was interested in started his vacuuming behind the Candy and Nut Counter. It took him fifteen minutes to clean an area ten by twenty feet, including the ten minutes it took to eat all the candy and nuts he could shovel down his throat.

Since we only had one supervisor for the entire early clean-up crew, it was small wonder how the staff could do what they wanted to do when the supervisor was in another section of the huge store.

The vacuum cart was pulled from Candy to the Men's Department and with the vacuum whining away, the employee moved down the sweater display counter holding up appealing items for size. Finally selecting one, he then moved to the shirt counter and picked out one, after carefully checking the size. Taking his two 'purchases' to the cash register he put the merchandise in a Sears bag and rang the amount, including the sales tax. After stapling the sales check on the bag, he put the bag in the cart under the electrical cord and continued to clean the area. Then taking the cart to the rear receiving and employee entrance area, he would put the properly ticketed bag in the employee check out bins which always had forgotten, legitimate employee packages over-nighting. After taking care of his 'business' he would continue his days work schedule.

The Store Manager and I were waiting at the employee exit at 11:30 AM when he got off his early shift and stopped to request his 'purchase' from the attendant in the fenced off package area. As he was handed his package, I intercepted it and asked him what was in the bag. Looking surprised, then rattled, he stammered, 'just a few things I bought at the Men's Department! There's a sales receipt on the bag."

With the bag in one hand and pointing an accusing finger with the other, I snarled, "you stole a sweater and a shirt at 5:00 AM this morning, operating the cash register to produce this sales slip....note the time and date on the slip....and placed the bag in the employee pickup area few minutes later. Let's go to the Personnel Department and advise them that you will be leaving the company today!"

After some interrogating, he confessed to the theft and further explained that on some days if there were workers in the package pickup area he would put a receipt on the bag and slide it under the counter where his wife would pull it out sometime later in the day. When we finished our debriefing and he was leaving, he was still mumbling about how I found out about his scam.... I didn't tell him I peeked!

One pitiful episode occurred one day when a manager called me reporting that she observed a sales lady, with many years of longevity, lifting a pair of pricy designer sunglasses from the case, throw the price tag in the trash can and slipped the merchandise in to her purse. I was surprised since I knew the employee in question had recently moved to Hollywood from Tennessee and appeared to be an attractive, intelligent and hard working employee.

I held off most of the day in hopes that she would pay for the item, but this long shot did not pay off and at the end of her shift she attempted to pass through the employee exit. At that point I confronted her with, "Carol, may I inspect your purse. It was reported that a pair of deluxe sunglasses in your department was missing!" I held out the trashed price tag.... as the blood seemed to drain from her face and she begain to shake.

Of course, the code on the frame matched the one on the discarded tag and I said, "in addition to the matching tag, you were seen putting the merchandise in your purse and if you have no receipt of payment, I am charging you with the theft!" This brought a gushing of tears, realizing that her career at Sears was over and she was lucky not to be turned over to the police for prosecution... all for a pair of sunglasses she could have easily afforded.

Africa Calling!

Joan Pflueger was still the manager of Pan Am's Jamaican Reservation System based in Montego Bay, while I chased shoplifters around the Sears Hollywood Store. With vacations coming up, we decided to take advantage of her free airline tickets with a two week trip to Nairobi, Kenya in East Africa. She had never been on the continent of Africa and I had only been in North Africa, so after checking Pan Am's destinations, the old British Colony of Kenya sounded like a winner. A mental picture of me as a white hunter in a safari hat and a bush jacket cemented the deal.

A check of the passport and health entrance requirements uncovered a yellow fever inoculation requirement. I had taken one some 15 years before while in the Philippines, but one every 10 years was now required for entrance to any yellow fever zone....so I reluctantly presented myself to a Public Health facility in Miami and after some whining, got the shot a few weeks before our scheduled departure.

One evening a week later, while on the late shift at Sears, I suddenly came down with chills and a fever lasting all evening. The next morning I felt fine....no fever....but had some concern as the long trip to Africa was rapidly approaching. I made an appointment with my family doctor for a check-up which resulted in no irregularities... the trip was on!

It was a long flight to Kenya, with a fuel stop in Lagos, Nigeria, where army troops, carrying automatic weapons were all over the place as we shuffled to the intransit area. I was relieved when we took off a few hours later, well ahead of an expected rebel attack. All went well upon arrival in Nairobi, except for breaking a 40oz bottle of Dewers White Label Scotch on the terminal floor, dribbling scotch thru a straw bag all the way to the exit. This came under the heading of 'poor form' in the colonies, and gave new meaning to the phase; 'ugly American!'

Once ensconced for the night at the New Stanley Hotel ('New' was a stretch), the starting point for many safaris in the past, I rented a car and prepared to push off into the bush. We headed for a lovely, old hotel perched on the edge of the roaring, 200' cascading Thompson's Falls, in time for lunch, featuring fine dining (incongruous for the African bush), in front of a crackling fire warding off the chill of some 8,000 feet of elevation. The scene was magic until out of the blue, I started feeling the fever and chills returning. To say it was not opportune to be faced with an unknown illness miles in the African bush, would be a major understatement. I did not want to alarm Joan, but I whispered that I had a re-occurrence of fever and needed to immediately return to our barely rented cottage, where I could take aspirin and get into bed. Our native housekeeper was a gray-headed old gentleman who quickly built a cheerful fire in a huge, stone fireplace and helped tuck me into bed. With a bow, he told Joan that, "Bwana going to be alright!" At this, I couldn't a resist a smile, since I always pictured myself as a White Hunter on the African Veldt and having my bearers call me 'Bwana'....but this is not what I had in mind! It was frightening to be this far from civilization with a burning fever, an aching body and not a clue what might be the problem. As an extra kick in the rear....Joan couldn't drive!

The next morning I felt reasonably well, much to my relief, with fever, chills and aches gone, a full English breakfast under my belt and a beautiful day in progress. Joan and I felt our confidence returning and we decided to continue our trip....the next stop, the Rift Valley.

Twenty million years ago the earth's crust split apart and created a rift running over fifteen hundred miles from north to south. This valley separated Kenya from east to west and was part of the most concentrated game population in the world. In this area various game preserves were created, such as the Amboseli Park where Mt. Kilimanjaro, the highest mountain in Africa, proudly stands in the background. One of the last white settlements, Nyahururu, was established in colonial times and is home to nearby Thompson's Falls, where we spent the previous night.

Another interesting area is Hyrax Hill Prehistoric Site, where in 1926 the Leakey's discovered some of the best examples of Neolithic and Iron Age life. For bird watchers, Lake Nekuru, a soda lake, is said to provide an expansive habitat for the largest flock of Flamingos in the world, estimated at one million birds (the second largest flock is on the Bahamian Island of Inauga, off the coast of Haiti).

When we drove our rental car to a parking area that offered a spectacular Rift Valley view, we had a scary couple of minutes when a swarm of screaming natives, branishing wicked knives, appeared out of nowhere! I felt very little comfort in patting my bowie knife, strapped to my right leg, like I could slash our way out of the ambush. To our immense relief, we discovered that the perceived howling, bloodthirsty mob, was in fact a group of the local youths trying to sell us home made knives and various craft items and showed appreciation when we did (sucking up to the mob) buy a few souvenirs.

We had pre-booked a visit to the famous 'Treetops Hotel' for the following day, requiring an overnight in the settlement of Nyeri, where we were delighted to find a charming, and old safari hotel. Our suite had a large stone fireplace, antique furniture with French doors leading to a flower studded patio, offering stunning views of a snowcapped Mt.Kilimanjero...breathtaking! In the lobby and restaurant a multitude of mounted heads stared down as reminders of big game safaris' of long ago, created a movie set atmosphere. All this and three meals for the unforgettable price of $18.00 per day double. I would have loved to stay a week!

When we drove up to the Treetops parking area located some distance from the hotel. We were advised that in an effort to reduce automobile emissions that tended to repel the very quarry that the visitor had come to see, we woulod be required to walk to the hotel.. The hotel's 'white hunter' guide met us with a warm, if quiet, greeting. He said his name was Nigel and his assignment was to gather the eight guests and escort us to the hotel. Looking at the rifle over Nigel's shoulder, I asked why the rifle? I don't know why I felt the need to ask that question while standing deep in the African bush in a game viewing area.

He gave a little chuckle (probably figuring that this guy is mentally unbalanced), and replied, "its at least 500 yards from the parking lot to Treetops, and while its usually a walk in the park, on rare occasions, it can be a wild run for your life with a black rhino hot on your backside! With me and my Rigby 411 rifle, I can pretty well assure you at you will survive the journey. The Rigby was designed in England in 1911, primarily for the use in this same country and in India for large, dangerous and thick skinned big game. You can imagine the need to deliver stopping power when you are looking down the horn of a 2,000 lb locomotive, bearing down on you at 30 miles an hour The 400 grain bullet, fired at 2,300' per second, is usually enough to stop a rhino in its tracks, if properly placed!" I refrained from asking another stupid question.... like what would happen if the bullet was not properly placed, and fell back on an old joke....that in the final analysis, Joan and I would only have to run faster than one other couple ....as I looked around, hoping to find an older and fatter couple.

Treetops was built high in a series of huge trees overlooking a mud hole of a few acres, where wild African game, such as the elephant, lion, antelope and such, came to drink and lick the natural and resort provided salt. Rocking chairs were lined up on the viewing balcony in front of the rooms and the dining area. Stairs from the main salon led to a flat roof observation deck, with sweeping views of the surrounding bush, and harboring a pesky troop of baboons. The baboons worked over time to bum a treat or to steal a purse not constantly under close surveillance. A plaque of historical interest told the story of the death of a king and at that moment Elizabeth, standing on the observation deck, ascended to the throne of the British Empire (pending Parliaments confirmation).

As you might imagine, the 'hotel' was not spacious, so it was interesting to observe dinner being prepared and served to eight guests and a few employees, in a very small space. The sleeping rooms were just large enough to hold a double bed and a stand to hold a small suitcase, while the community bathrooms were down the hall. We had electric lights to provide illumination for game viewing and the hotel, but the generator must have been located some distance away, since no sound or fumes could be detected.

While we were there, we saw antelope, but no 'big five' animals until early evening when a pride of lion had a few licks before melting back into the bush. This created a lot of excited whispering and sharpened observation well into the night, but only a few warthogs presented themselves. Finally, with heavy eyelids, we retired with a promise from the staff that if an elephant or other game of merit should appear, we would be awakened.

Unfortunately, nothing transpired during the rest of the night and after a simple breakfast, Nigel escorted us, uneventfully, back to the car park and we proceed on our way. We agreed that while we did not see all the game we had hoped to, it was an adventure well worth the effort.

After roaming around the African countryside, including a quick visit to William Holden's East Africa Safari Club, we moved back to the New Stanley Hotel. The plan was that we rest a day and tour the city. The second day we decided to take the hours drive to visit one of the most extensive game reserves in Kenya. It was surprising to find such a large, primitive animal reserve where hordes of wild game roamed freely, so close to a major city.

Criss-crossing dirt roads provided all the access with signs along the way advising the type of animals likely to be seen in each area. There were plenty of giraffe, antelope, wildebeest, warthogs, and zebra, with pockets of lion and some elephants to be seen during the day.

In one section, recent rains had created a massive water-hole in the middle of the road and since I couldn't get around it, I gunned the English Ford and barreled ahead! Probably not one of my better ideas .The puddle was deeper than I thought. The rear wheels started to dig into the mud, but quickly lost traction and spun helplessly, throwing mud all over the now stalled car. It was a weekday and we had not seen another vehicle in the park during the few hours we had been game watching, so help was unlikely to arrive any time soon.

As I surveyed the situation, I saw a nearby sign (this mud hole must have been a regular tourist trap) with instructions to 'Stay in your vehicle. Lions in the area!' Crap! This did not encourage me to exit the vehicle. To add to the despair, Joan did not drive a stick shift, or any other kind of vehicle....which made option 'A' of me pushing the car 20' onto the dry road ahead while she gunned the engine, moot.

I scratched my head as I pondered the Laws of Physics (or maybe it was the Law of the West, since I couldn't think straight with the prospect of a lion chewing on my backside in the near future) which precluded being in two places....pushing and driving....at the same time.

Finally, I came to the conclusion that not withstanding the lion warning signs, I had to get out of the car into the mud, take my hunting knife strapped to my leg and make a run for the brush on the roadside....madly slash an armload of bush, drag it back to the mud hole, place the brush under the rear wheels and hope there is not a hungry lion in the immediate area. Once the brush was under the wheel all I had to do was leap back in the drivers seat and pray like mad that I had enough traction to drive the car out of the mud hole. Good luck, Charlie!

In a blur of motion, I leaped out of the Ford, almost slipping in the mud and bolted for the nearby bush while grappling for the knife handle....darting eyes searching for a snarling beast....ears straining for a mighty roar that would spell doom (drama at its best). Swift, wild slashing brought down a half dozen bushy limbs, which were gathered in one swoop and with a couple of bounds I was back in the mud near the rear right tire. Cramming half the foliage under the wheel, I raced around to the other side and repeated the procedure. Then with a burst of speed, I sprinted back to the driver's side and slammed the door (in the face of an imaginary snarling lion). Sweating profusely and with twitching hand, I started the engine and while holding my breath, popped the clutch. Relief flooded through my body as I felt the rear tires catch on the bush as I gunned it, fishtailing out of the mud and on to safety.

Joan, sitting quite sanguine, couldn't understand what all the fuss was about and I could barely talk to explain the pent up fear an imagery lion can cause. She responded with, "Charles, I don't see any lions!" Thank you for the observation, my dear.

After a day in the field, we returned to the hotel to notice a crowd gathered around the teletype (remember, its 1968 in Africa) machine in the lobby. Pushing my way in, it was shocking to see the news story of the assignation of Robert Kennedy, adding another sad chapter to American history.

On our Pan Am flight home we were routed along the mighty Congo River, which remained under our 707 for hour after hour, giving a real measuring stick to how long the Congo actually is. During this period, I started getting leg cramps and a slight fever and was not felling well when we entered a ferocious tropical thunderstorm an hour out of Monrovia, Liberia, where we were scheduled to land for refueling. Of all the years in the Air Force and extensive commercial airline travel, I had never seen a storm this bad! The aircraft was all over the sky! Piercing lightening bolts seemed to touch the gyrating wings, with mighty claps of thunder drowning out the sound of the pelting rain on the fuselage. Physically sick and white-knuckled (not to mentioned babbling with fright), I thought the plane would never get to Monrovia.

Once on the ground and in the intransit room of the modern airport, my nerves calmed down until the announcement to re-board to continue the flight. I thought of running off into the bush and hiding out until the flight took off rather than take another beating back in the air, but my progressing, unknown illness persuaded me that I had better get going back to the United States and seek some medical attention. Fortunately, once airborne, the storm seemed to have mostly dissipated and I finally fell into an exhausted sleep.

Crossing the Atlantic from Morocco was uneventful until we neared our destination of New York where weather conditions forced us to seek a landing at our alternative destination of Bermuda.... Much to my despair; we landed in Bermuda and waited out the New York weather for several more hours. All considered, it was a miserable flight and one I wanted to forget.

A day later, back in Miami, my doctor suggested I check into Mt. Sinai Hospital for evaluation. Not a happy homecoming, but a necessary one. After eleven days and many, many blood tests (night and day... needles... needles... needles... I was sure there was a vampire in the lab), I was released with the diagnosis of 'serum sickness' caused by a reaction to the horse serum in the yellow fever shot taken weeks before. The fluid build up in my system finally settled in my right ankle, causing serious swelling that took three months to absorb before I could return to Sears and resume chasing shoplifters.

The Old Island Itch

During the last few years while working with Sears and in keeping with my unrelenting love of islands, I purchased a home with guest cottage on what later became 'Millionaires Row' on Plantation Key on the Florida Keys. It was an acre of land on the ocean with a small inlet and dock, with a zoning of 'Motel/Fishing Camp.' My hand trembled as I plunked down 10% of the $25,000 sale price and signed a mortgage for the then astronomical sum of $22,500... Big bucks to me in those days (and not chopped liver today!).

My real estate broker in the transaction suggested that I get a Florida Real Estate License and work with him on my days off from Sears. I decided to give it a try and learn the real estate business while enjoying the Keys and my new cottage.

The arrangement went well for most of the year. I had some success in selling a waterfront lot here and there, however, the best thing I did was to buy a waterfront lot at Venetian Shores, an upscale residential development located across a deep, wide canal from the office. With unusual generosity the original developer dredged 100' wide canals to a depth of 25', allowing exceptional room for the dockage of deep draft boats. The canals led to Snake Creek, a major channel between Plantation Key and Windley Key, offering small boat ocean and Florida Bay back country access. My $10,000 lot jumped in value to $30,000 within a few months, when the Snake

Creek Bridge installed a 'draw' to allow yachts of all sizes ocean/bay access. I thought I was pretty smart buying in Venetian Shores, but in reality, I was just at the right place and the right time.

My Sears job was starting to bore me, even with the intrigue of the security position. The bottom line was that it was against my nature to be cooped up inside day after day. I soon came to the conclusion that it was time to bid farewell to the retail business and move to my house on the Keys, at least as a temporary substitute to real island living in the Bahamas or the Caribbean.

As much as I enjoyed the opportunities Sears offered, moving to the Keys was like a 'lifer' suddenly being paroled, standing outside the gate for the first time in years. Driving to the Keys was one of the most exhilarating days of my life, right up there with graduating from the 'U' and being discharged from the Air Force. In your heart you know you are only dumping one set of challenges for another, but its uplifting to start with a clean slate and have another opportunity to muck-it up!.

In sort order, I found out that as a full time diet, hanging around a less than busy real estate office becomes boring in a hurry. On an average day, Wayne the broker who lived in an apartment behind the office, would start cooking exotic dinners around two-ish in the afternoon. Along about that time, he would pour his first (but certainly not last) scotch and soda for the day. At first I declined his offer to imbibe on the grounds that I never had a drink until the proverbial 'sun was over the yardarm!' I only used alcohol for relaxation, but when faced with the lack of activity, a couple of stiff drinks early in the afternoon seemed to stimulate conversation (mostly B.S.) and help speed the day along.

I remember one afternoon going home with a snoot full; lying on the carpet in front of the television and the difficulty I had of trying to watch the landing of the first man on the moon. Needless to say, Jean was less than amused and forcefully suggested that I might consider refraining from drinking so early and limiting the drinks to one or two.

Taking this to heart and not enjoying going to bed before nine every night, I came to a rapid conclusion that I had to conform to the above suggestions and in addition, I needed to seek more stimulating employment.

About this time, as in answer to my prayers, Paul Swetland from my 'sailing from San Juan to Nassau' days called me with an interesting offer. Paul and an old school mate from Cleveland, Armand Angelone, found out that Lawrence Lewis, heir to the Henry Flagler railroad and Standard Oil fortune and the developer of the Club Peace and Plenty in George Town, Exuma, had the 32 room resort for sale and he and Armand were interested in buying it.

Paul, talking fast, said, "Charlie, are you interested in buying into the deal and managing the Club?"

"Paul, remember I was in airlines and retail....I have never managed a hotel!" I shot back, intrigued, but cautious.

Shrugging off this logic and with confidence, he returned, "anyone can run a hotel....can't be much to it!" This sounded like a Chimp could handle it.

"Where did you say this hotel is located?" I asked, with piquing interest.

"You spent a couple nights in George Town on our trip through the Bahama chain on my boat," he prompted.

"Paul, we saw so many islands… I can't remember which was which," I confessed.

"I will have a 65% ownership and Armand will have 30%. There is 5% available for you, if you want to give it a go! Tell you what, meet me in Nassau next week and we can fly down to Exuma and take a look to see if you like it," he wheedled. Since I had no plans to invest much of my savings in this shot in the dark, 5% sounded doable.

I met him in Nassau as planned and flew the 150 miles to Exuma along the 110 miles of the breathtakingly beautiful Exuma Chain of 365 islands and cays. The many shades of deep blue to turquoise water were mind boggling. Uncountable miles of world class, white powder beach rimmed each cay, providing a deserted sandy paradise to the scattered yachts anchored in a multitude of protected bays, inlets and cuts. I was half sold when we landed at the WWII 5,000' George Town Airport.

When we reached the Peace and Plenty and I took one look at the spectacular Elizabeth Harbor (some have suggested that Columbus actually landed here first and not at nearby San Salvador. Columbus observed that the 'harbor was large enough to anchor all the ships in Christendom' and Exuma certainly had that feature). Memory's of my first visit came flooding back to reinforce my hasty conclusion to sign on immediately and let the chips fall....

The current manager Georges Franks, a Frenchman who fought the Vietnamese in Indo-China, welcomed me with, "let's go for a dive!"

We were soon at the dock, boarding the hotel skiff, a 24' Aquasport outboard with a glass bottom panel, ideal for checking out the reefs without getting wet. A retractable diving platform on the side made getting in and out of the water a breeze. Ten minutes later we were diving on a nearby reef and in ten more minutes I had bagged, with an Hawaiian sling and 8' stainless steel spear, the largest spiny lobster (crawfish) I have ever taken. If my agreeing to manage the hotel was not a 100% sure thing....it was at this point!

Georges was a great guy, married to a Bahamian citizen, Kitty, with two children and an excellent hotel manager. He and Kitty were offered the hotel by Mr. Lewis at an excellent price (Paul, Armand and myself bought the Club Peace and Plenty in August 1969 for $275,000), but since he and Kitty wanted to return to Nassau for the children's education, they declined to accept Mr. Lewis' offer, opening the door for us.

Paul and I made a deal for Georges to stay on for a few days and check me out on the operation, including the transcript (before computers we used to have to keep a daily record of the various charges by hand on a daily transcript), ordering supplies, an introduction to the staff and many other details that were soon to come in handy. Within a few days, Paul and Georges left and I was immersed in ordering supplies, contacting staff on when to return, drawing up menus and a host of details forgotten with time. As the hotel was closed for the transfer of ownership, I had to handle my own meals upstairs in the manager's two bedroom apartment. Every day I took the Aquasport and dived on the fantastic coral heads sprinkled around the harbor, shooting the occasional snapper to break the monotony of lobster tails and spaghetti. I ate so many juicy lobster tails that I rarely eat one today. To add to the seafood smorgasbord, I would pick up some large conch and have Charlie our painter, crack them out and whip up a fresh conch salad or 'scorch' conch (larger pieces scored with a knife and soaked in lime juice with red peppers and onions....delicious) which is eaten without cooking. When we would go diving for the day, instead of packing a lunch, we took a large pan, goat peppers and onions, to help prepare the conch we would most certainly pickup on the turtle grass flats as a great substitute for a dry sandwich. Local lore has it that eating conch will help your love life, but I can't affirm to deny, since my love life was doing just fine in those years and has gone to pot a little, so to speak, in my seventies. Maybe I should eat more conch!

I opened Club Peace and Plenty on September 12, 1969, which kicked-off a love affair that has lasted over 40 years. In those days, our only source of regular weekly supplies was the mail boat out of Nassau, bringing food stuff, booze, furniture, the odd car, passengers and of course, the mail. The 'Grand Master' mail boat normally loaded cargo on Mondays and Tuesday mornings at Potter's Cay, near the bridge to Paradise Island in Nassau. The boat departs around 1:00 PM for an overnight trip across the 'Yellow Banks' between New Providence and the start of the Exuma Chain at Norman's Cay, along Staniel Cay, home of James Bond's 'Thunderball Cave,' and down to George Town, cutting through from the Bahama Banks to Exuma Sound (an ocean depth of some 6,000') at Ruddercut Cay. A dawn arrival at the George Town Government Dock, spurs a local reception of trucks and vans, vying for the best spot for loading and a quick get-a-way out to the various island settlements. Sleepy-eyed passengers stumble off the boat and a hundred yards to the Peace and Plenty for a pick-me-up coffee before settling into their day's activities.

In the early years managing the hotel, I either picked up the supplies placed on a pallet or two on the dock, myself or with a helper. This required some heavy lifting, chalking it off to 'exercise' and the extra assurance of a careful item check and uneventful passage from dock to storeroom. In the event of a late boat or a serious maintenance problem all bets were off and chaos reigned. A few weeks before the Christmas of 1970, the Grand Master had an extensive engine problem requiring it to go into dry dock, causing a six week stoppage of service. A mad scramble ensued! I ran around to all the local grocery stores buying a case of eggs here and a bag of rice there, hoping against hope that we would be able to feed our guests until the boat became operational again. Finally, we realized that service would not return for weeks and a few of the local markets and the Peace and Plenty banded together and chartered an aircraft out of Florida with a load of choice meat, chicken and general food stuffs. Expensive, but better than hungry guests fleeing for more bountiful locations!

For seafood, we bought what we could get from the local divers, including conch, our mainstay – grouper, snapper and the ever popular lobster. The local lads would go out for a few hours close to shore, spearfish an abundance of fish and lobster, grab a few conch and head the boat for the hotel dock to cash in the catch. Wasting little time, they would comply with local unofficial protocol and retire to our bar to relax for the rest of the afternoon… a pretty nice gig!

On a hit or miss basis, Long Island (no… not Long Island, New York!) fishermen would sail their sloops to the George Town dock and send a messenger to the hotel to advise that fish and lobster were available for purchase. Since we usually needed to top off the freezers, I would take the pickup truck over, check the price and look into the holding tank for a personal inspection. The boat's bilge contained a large live fish holding tank (drilled holes in the hull allowed fresh sea water to constantly enter) containing fifty to a hundred 12 to 15 lb grouper swimming around (obviously these were either trapped or hand lined). After ordering a couple of dozen, the mate would gaff them out one by one, hit them in the head with a mallet, weigh, gut, skin and load into our truck. From our truck to the freezer would temporarly solve the seafood requirements for the time being. Lobsters, caught with bully nets on long poles using a water glass from the surface, were brought in by the sloops and delivered, live in crocus sacks, to our back kitchen area for sorting and freezing.

Later, when diesel boats replaced the wind powered sloops, refrigeration equipment made it possible to deliver frozen sacks of fish and lobster tails directly to the scales and into the hotel freezer. Other aids to a sustainable fishery in the Bahamas (visitors expect, as part of their experience, to enjoy a selection of fresh seafood) was the adaptation of a closed season during spiny lobster spawning April 1st to August 1st, and a closed season for Grouper, heavy with eggs, in November and December each year. A size limit was placed on conch and lobster year around to protect the juveniles and laws prohibiting the use of spear guns (Hawaiian slings are used) in Bahamian waters. Laws protecting the fishery are in place and helping to insure the perpetuation of the industry, however policing some 700 miles of water is, of course, problematical.

Communications on Exuma in the late 60's were restricted to telephone service from 8:00 AM to closing at 9:00 PM, when the Batelco (Bahamas Telephone Company) operators went home. If during the night telephone contact was desired.... you could forget it! Looking on the bright side, no late calls from confused Europeans to interrupt ones beauty sleep, was not such a bad idea!

When I first sailed into Exuma with Paul Swetland in January 1963, the roads outside of the settlement of George Town were unpaved. The main limerock (called 'curry') roads followed trails developed almost 200 years ago by the various cotton plantaion owners. By the mid-60 a company from the U.K. had paved most of the main road on the island. Later, a sea of bone-rattling pot holes required the government to contract for complete re-paving in the 1990's.

I was captivated by the history surrounding George Town, the provincial capital of the Exumas, along with Great and Little Exuma. A charming settlement of some 800 people was incorporated in 1793, when the fine cotton of the Loyalists plantations were at their peak production and merchant ships carried shipload after shipload bound for the mills of Manchester. Plantations owners in North America that remained loyal to the English Crown in the Revolutionary War were declared 'persona non-grata' in the fledgling United States. Consequently, these 'Loyalists' partitioned the Crown for land grants in the southeastern Bahamas Islands of Cat Island, Exuma and Long Island, thereafter called the 'Cotton Islands', to re-establish their defunct plantations in what had recently become the United States.

One of the largest land grants was to Lord Denys Rolle, who developed vast tracks of cotton cultivation and he and other Loyalist plantation owners enjoyed some 15 years of high production of fine cotton. Sometime near the end of the Century mis-management of the soil started the downward spiral of cotton's fortune. In 1804 the English Parliament prohibited the importation of new slaves to any of their colonies… all of which added to the decline of the Bahamian plantations. In addition to their problems, a new menace arrived on the scene to plague the industry in the guise of the Chennile bug that invaded the cotton fields, infecting the plants and causing the cotton balls to turn a rusty color, ruining salability. The final blow was the emancipation of all slaves in the British Empire in 1834, with complete freedom in 1838, thereby dealing the death knell to a once proud industry. At that point, the land was rendered worthless, resulting in a mass exodus of plantation owners and allied merchants and tradesmen.

The first week I opened the hotel in September 1969, we had no guests. I had yet to realize that September was historically the weakest month of the year for tourism, partly because it's the most active hurricane month. Being concerned with lack of business did not bother me, when I took off for an hour after lunch to slather tanning oil on my body, recline comfortably on a chaise lounge by the pool, luxuriating in the warmth of the sun and congratulate myself on the cushy job I had managed to snag. This mid-day sense of well being did not last more than a couple of days before I discovered that with this job there was always something that required my attention, since in those days even as General Manager, I had to do the accounting, some front desk, all the routine maintenance, dinner maitre'd, ordering of supplies and hauling the foodstuff and liquor from the mailboat to our storage room, stocking the shelves… and most importantly… smoozing the guests.

Inter-action with the guests was not to be forgotten, including enough time in the evenings to chat with everyone at the bar. In those days, Peace and Plenty was pretty much the only game in town for entertainment, prompting us to have a band three nights a week, playing popular island songs and danceable music. It comes as no surprise, that a very popular activity was our weekly cocktail party, held on Mondays from 6:00 PM to 7:00 PM, offering complimentary drinks of choice, conch fritters, chicken wings, and grouper fingers. I always made sure I was in attendance, greeting every guest and making introductions within the group.

Wandering around our Monday and Friday night cocktail parties, meeting guests was always a pleasure for me. I would nibble on hor d'oeuvres (I almost wrote 'canapes' which is easier to spell) and make inane chit-chat with the best of them. One cocktail party guest with a loaded plate of fritters asked me if I wanted one of his.... at which I jokingly replied, "No thanks, I saw how they made them!" He was the only guest that took me seriously.... and promptly put the plate back on the table, after which it took some coaxing to get him to try again.

Another funny dining room caper happened one busy night at dinner in the high season. I was assisting the dining room hostess and greeting guests at the same time. As I was walking by the table of a lovely lady in the crowded room, she accidentally nudged an unused fork off the table....clanking on the floor at my feet. Barely losing stride, I swooped down, picked up the utensil and with a flourish... wiped it off on my jacket and replaced it next to her plate from whence it came.... and continued into the kitchen. There was a gasping of breath in the immediate vicinity from the assembly of diners, along with accompanying looks of disgust from the utensil recipient.

As I reached the safety of the kitchen I could hear murmurs of outraged indignation from the entire ensemble. Luckily it only took seconds to select a clean replacement fork, polish it with a napkin and spin back into the dining room (a gutsy move on my part) returning to the table where the offense took place. With exaggerated courtesy,

I replaced the offending fork with the clean one! Her look of disgust and outrage turned into a sheepish grin when I said, "gotcha!"

As mentioned, one of my fun goals in life, in addition to travel, was to meet interesting people. Early on I discovered it was easier to meet celebrities on a tropical resort island, than to meet them on the mainland. One of the first such visitors at the hotel was Sen. Ted Kennedy, who was vacationing aboard a yacht in Elizabeth Harbor. Apparently a storm between Nassau and Exuma prohibited his return flight until the following day, bringing Ted and his group to the Peace and Plenty pool deck that evening. Our bartender, Lermon (Doc) came up to the dining room and advised me that someone wanted to see me.

I was stunned to see the visitor, who quickly stuck out his hand and said, "I'm Ted Kennedy and I wondered if we might have dinner around the pool instead of the dining room?"

I introduced myself and assured him that although it was getting dark, we would be pleased to provide a candlelight dinner around the pool instead of the dining room for him, a very striking blonde lady and the yacht captain. They had a pleasant dinner, graciously thanking me for the accommodation and returned to their yacht.

Robert Mitchem, the movie actor, was an early guest of the hotel. He seemed like a regular guy, except for getting drunk and hitting on owner Paul Swetland's wife, Jane, who complained that he was the 'crudest bastard she had ever met.' He did get 'lucky' however, when one of our very attractive lady guests (a business machine heiress, as I recall) spent the night with Mitchem on a yacht at a nearby marina. It only seems fair that a major movie star could find a little comfort when away from home.

The main bar at the Peace and Plenty is, no doubt, one of the most well known in the Out Islands and the scene of many an escapade over the last 50-ish years. If you want to know what's going on locally (many of the world's problems are also solved in the bar later in the evening after an ample flow of booze) you head directly to the hotel's 'Slave Kitchen Bar'. This previously free standing cook house provided meals for several hundred years starting with Bowe's Tavern and Slave Auction, which we think was constructed on this site, as some of the old cut stone walls can still be found in a few of the hotel kitchen's current walls.

A Union in the Woodpile

Whistling through the Peace and Plenty one fine day in the spring of 1994, spreading P.R.'sunshine' with a glad hand, when I saw a heavyset Bahamian gentleman wearing a bright green sport coat, sitting at one of the tables. He was talking in a conspiratory way with one of our hotel employees, causing me to believe he might be an insurance salesman, or perhaps a relative in town for a family function.

Later in the day, I chanced upon the employee and with only a casual interest inquired, "Who was your friend in the green jacket you were chatting with?"

"Oh!" she said, "that wasn't a friend...that was Huey Bodie, originally from the Hermitage here on Exuma! He's head of a big union in Freeport now!" She seemed pleased to continue, "He's here to offer membership in his union to the employees of the Peace and Plenty and the Beach Inn...I'm so excited" she gushed. He says we will get a lot of extra benefits, holidays and overtime pay!" She seemed to think this was a good thing for everybody, including the company...Guess again my dear!

Have you ever had a day go downhill in a hurry? You know...like your dentist telling you that you need a root canal? Or maybe when your girlfriend says, "honey, I'm late with my period!" How about, 'congratulations, you've won the draft lottery and you're in the army now." (That one is for the older guys. Something for everybody).

Sweat popped out on my forehead and my heart pattered just a little faster. I went into the office and called the owner, Stan Benjamin in Cleveland and gave him the news that a union rep was soliciting the staff. I hoped he wouldn't 'shoot the messenger.'. I had heard of some horror stories Stan told about his battles in Solon, Ohio with the union trying to organize his machine tool company. He was a wily bird who hated the idea of a union organizing anything he owned and telling him what he could or could not do with his companies.

"Charlie, try to find out all you can about Bodie and his union!" he growled, obviously not too happy and working on a head of steam for the battle ahead, "and call the Bahamas Hotel Association and talk to their union expert for some input." As it turned out, Bodie having set up in his union in Freeport, decided in his infinite wisdom that in order to grow he needed to expand his base and thought that since he was from Exuma it made sense to pick up a little spare membership here. Did Thomas Wolfe make a mistake when he wrote that 'you can't go home again?' I surely hoped not!

The union filed with the Bahamian Government for a vote and started buttering up the employees of both of our hotels. Stan, not one to hang back when it came to a fight, came down for a general staff meeting where he emphatically explained, "We do NOT want a union in our hotels!"

One of our waitresses asked Stan, "but, why can't we have a union if we want it?"

Stan turned a little red in the face and sputtered, "Because I own the hotels and I don't want a union!" I think he realized that this answer was a little harsh and in a more conciliatory tone he added, "These are small family hotels and we treat all our employees as family. You don't need a union to take your dues money every week. What can they for you that we can't do?"

Stan managed to get his point across and murmurs of agreement permeated the hall as the meeting broke up and staff returned to work. Stan, did not just fall off a turnip truck, and figured that although they all agreed that they liked the way the hotel was being run and they had no glaring problems or issues with the owner or management, enough of them would go for the union to cause a company wide vote, monitored by the local Ministry of Labour office. While I was inexperienced with unions, Stan knew that while most of the staff would swear allegiance to Stan and the hotel, many would lie thru their teeth and when the vote came, would certainly vote for the union.

A few of the areas where union promises were loudly heard were double time holiday pay and a five day week. The Bahamian labor law at the time allowed small out island hotels to work employees six days a week and all holidays were paid at regular time, without extra compensation. I presume this was in deference to the fragile income stream in the smaller hotels (under a 100 rooms) outside of the municipal hubs of Nassau and Freeport. One of the most heinous provisions of the proposed union contract was that an employee caught stealing would receive a five day suspension then have to be reinstated.... Not a chance we would go along with this foolish! We would have to be crazy to reinstate a thief after a five day min-vacation so he or she could do it again!

It was a tense few weeks before the vote. Although I was general manager of both hotels, I was primarily working the Beach Inn staff while Stan handled the Club group. Of the seventeen employees, I figured we had a chance to get nine to hang with the company. One long time waitress (who I rescued from certain termination at the Club and gave her a job at the Beach Inn) promised loyalty forever, which lasted as long as the vote, where, you guessed it... she sold me down the river and went with the union.

Our main antagonist and union organizer at the Inn was the chef from Nassau. He was working behind my back for a few months to poison the staff with 'pie in the sky' promises. Another was the head housekeeper, also recently from Nassau but originally from Exuma. I could see the pattern here, albeit a tad late.. Our management apparently was dumb and happy, oblivious to the rot within.

The Beach Inn was slated for the vote first and after much last minute assurances, we lost to the union 13 to 1 with 3 abstaining. So much for pre-vote promises of 'we're with you, Charlie!' This was a disappointment although not completely unexpected. It was time to cut our losses.

For the last three years Stan had been subsidizing the hotels with his personal funds. The Beach Inn, opened in April of 1991, and had not yet achieved much of an occupancy rate, since most of our repeat business went to the Club, and new business was slow coming during this period. Stan and I had talked about closing the Inn for the summer and re-opening in December for the high season where the 'pickings' were easier. He had decided that he would keep the hotel open and suffer the shortfall in order to keep his staff employed. That was Stan! He looked on his employees as family and was willing to put his money where his mouth was. With this union development, Stan felt betrayed and started re-thinking his money losing efforts to maintain steady employment for what he thought was 'his people'!

Stan quickly came to the conclusion that since his efforts were not appreciated, it was time to close the smaller 16 room Beach Inn until the start of the winter high season, and only keep the 32 room Club Peace and Plenty open. We decided to close the hotel on July 14th and pay the employees their last weeks pay, any accrued vacation pay, and the required two weeks pay in lieu of notice. We would give no advanced notice to the staff. Any guests staying at the Inn or due to arrive would be moved to the Club.

On that faithful day, Mrs. Ruth Pinder, manager of the Club and chief financial officer, arrived at the Inn at 6:00AM where she and I sorted out the individual checks and made sure every balance was according to the termination policy of the Bahamian Government Labour Department. I locked the reception doors and waited for the arrival of the early staff. The tension was rapidly building as the first arrivals tried the front door and found it locked. Soon the entire early shift was mulling around the parking lot wondering what the hell was going on.

At the stroke of 7:00 AM I unlocked the front door and started calling the individuals one at a time to the little office, where I sat with a stack of pay envelopes. With a solemn demeanor (I enjoyed no satisfaction from this event) I said, "The owner and management of Peace and Plenty thanks you for your service and advises that we are closing the Beach Inn for an indeterminate period. We have been losing money this summer and the owner is not prepared to continue to do so. This is your termination check and we wish you well for the future!" To say that they were stunned would be an understatement!

As they left the building to continue mulling around in the parking lot, I could hear rage and accusations being directed at the chef, who raced to the public telephone hanging from the side of our front wall. Since an open window to my office was next to where I was sitting, I could hear the chef stuttering an anguished plea to Bodie in Freeport, for help to get his newly acquired flock back on the payroll at once. After a couple of hours, the confused and demoralized former employees had wailed enough at the union shill, and started to disburse. Promises were made that President Bodie would arrive in Exuma within the next few days and straighten out the whole mess! Good luck to him, I thought, he's going to need it!

Bodie caught a Bahamasair flight two days later, and was ridiculed by a few local wags on the aircraft with, "hey, Bodie!

Going back to Exuma to close a few more hotels?" After all the big union promises of the marvelous perks the union was going to force Mr. Benjamin to give the workers, all they wound up with was termination pay and a load of embarrassment!

When Bodie arrived in Exuma, he quickly organized a protest march by the laid off staff, along with a dozen of the current employees of the Club. A union protest song was practiced and homemade signs denouncing Stan, 'Benjamin is a Slaver' and a couple nice ones about me, such as, 'Pslueger must go'… disappointing in that the idiots misspelled my name. Seems to me, that if you are going to all the trouble to celebrate someone's villainy with signing, song and march, the least you could do would be to spell the varlets name properly.

Automotive traffic was stopped in the street in front of the Club. Marching martyrs raised their voices in musical protest to the explorters from the States, down trotting the masses (I could write this stuff myself)… waving signs itemizing the transgressions, a crowd of hecklers gathered to egg them on.. One such sign carrier was our handy man, Wade, a crippled lad we employed at the Club. He was a master of illusion with three or four hiding places where, after three or four hours at work, would disappear to sort out the rest of the day in meditation. One of his favorite spots was the ladies hair salon where he would perch himself on a high chair and chit chat with the ladies for hours.

Remember Wade was crippled from an automobile accident in his childhood, and the prospect of his being able to hide in the marching throng, even behind a sign, was remote… but he gave it a try! Unfortunately, he was the only one dragging one leg down the highway, which was some sort of a give away and obvious to all assembled, except Wade (pronounced 'Vade' in the Bahamas). I guess, since Wade was still employed at the Club, he didn't want to take a chance on being recognized, at least before the Club's vote.

In any event, the group marched and sang their way past the entrance to the Club, while I stood on the steps videoing the procession with my hand held camera. When Bodie, bringing up the rear (perhaps to keep any of his flock from bolting) approached me… I advised that he should go back to school and learn to spell! This was apparently not a popular concept and Bodie made a half hearted effort to assault me, but when I further suggested that I would bounce the video camera off his bald head if he came any closer, he backed off!. He took my advice and continued his march, whether as a result of words or more likely due to the fact that a couple police officers were also watching, I can't say, but he whirled and joined his singing choir moving toward the center of George Town. All in all, it was a lot of fun and I guess it made Bodie feel better doing something for his out of work 'almost' members.

We remained closed for the next three months, ignoring a few half hearted death threats and nasty remarks. In early October, Stan told me to re-open the Inn. He hated to have it closed, particularly since a small group was going to have to be re-accommodated at the Club the third week in October. I protested with, "Stan lets keep the Inn closed until at least the 15th of December when the winter season starts. You know we have a case in the Supreme Court and to open earlier than the busy season, may create a problem!" He overrode my concerns with, "its Ok to open the Inn in light of group business pre-booked for October." I lived to regret this decision.

Another amusing side story involved a very lovely young woman employed as a front desk clerk at the Beach Inn. Her mother worked for us and was well thought of by all, so when Doris asked Stan Benjamin if he would help her with funds for school at the College of the Bahamas in Nassau, he readily agreed. The hotel would chip in on tuition and monthly expenses and would offer her a paid position during vacations.

This arrangement worked well for awhile until Doris decided to lay out of school for a semester or two. She asked and received a full time position at the Inn at the regular going salary of the time, with the usual perks of meals, accrued vacation and the usual standard labor law requirements.

She was very attractive and intelligent, showing great promise in the hospitality industry. We were pleased to continue our financial support at the time she opted to return to her education, unfortunately, she fell prey to the union rhetoric and chose to turn her back on those who helped her and voted for the proposed union.

When ZNS, our Bahamian national television station, sent an interviewer down to document the union protest march against the Peace and Plenty, Doris was chosen by the union to tell the world that, "I've been held in slavery by the hotel!" she wailed something like, "my job amounts to a hell on earth!" Talk about a damsel in distress. Here is a lovely Bahamian girl being taken advantage of by these foreign thugs...very touching indeed. I even had tears in my eyes and would have joined a torch bearing search thru the village for these scoundrels...until I realized that Stan and I were the accused scoundrels! Take it from me... it's not much fun to be a villian!

When Doris got through bashing us, I grabbed the ZNS reporter and demanded rebuttal time. Surprised, she agreed and introduced me to the TV audience as the General Manager of the Peace and Plenty Hotels (but fortunately didn't add, 'one of the main slavers.') Pretending that I didn't hear Doris' entire interview, I asked the reporter, on camera, 'I heard Doris call us 'slavers,' but did she mention that we gave her a job at our front desk at the prevailing rate, including meals and with all the labor laws perks?"

"Well, no... She didn't mention any salary," the reporter replied, abashed.

"When she called us 'slavers' did she mention that Mr. Benjamin gave Doris a scholarship to the College of the Bahamas, including monthly spending money?" I hammered away at the sad story of woe she had fabricated.

"Is that true?" she quired with an incredulous look...probably wishing she was somewhere else.

"Some 'slavers'! Giving the 'slave' an industry salary with all the perks and paying her school to boot!" I added with a derisive snarl. At that, the reporter seemingly embarrassed and the same time distressed at losing her 'slavery in the Bahamas' story, signed off, probably lamenting the 'one that got away.'

Tribunal Retribution

Things quieted down after the march and we remained closed for the next few months. When we re-opened in October, we hired a new staff at the Beach Inn except for a few (I mean like two) loyal employees. The union drifted off into the sunset and neither hotel was unionized.

I gave little thought to the past struggles with the union and looked to a bright union-less future, until I received a summons to appear at the newly formed Bahamas Labor Tribunal. It appears that there were so many labor violation cases brought against hotels and businesses in the Bahamas that the courts were unable to cope and it was projected that it would be years before all could be heard.

The Government, realizing this, organized a specially sanctioned and approved quasi-judicial court called the 'Tribunal' to expedite these cases and clear the docket. Apparently the union busting case of Bodie's union against the Peace and Plenty was one of the early selections. Bodie had two of the employees... the union shill head housekeeper and one of the cooks, charging us with closing the Inn to avoid unionizing.

I immediately called our attorney, Allan Benjamin, Esq. (no relation to Stan), who had also received notification and was prepared to accompany me to the hearing in Nassau. Allan told me, "you have to show up but you don't need to bring an overnight bag since the case is in the Supreme Court and the Tribunal will not be able to try it on their level." This was good news, so I took my brief case and flew to Nassau on a bright Monday morning to be met at the airport by Allan and taken to the make shift court.

The Tribunal was presided over by a judge with a court stenographer. Allan whispered to me that we opened the hotel too soon making it look like it was an attempt to union bust and he thought the chance of us winning the case was slim to none. Bodie and the two plaintiffs were on the other side of the room with all eyes on Allan when he asked the Judge to approach the bench with, "your honor, I request dismissal of this tribunal on the grounds that the case is pending at the Supreme Court!" At this point, I was mentally packing my brief case for a swift departure.

The Judge did not seem amused, when he replied with a frown, "there are several parts of this suit. We will try the one not covered in the Supreme Court case." My heart sank and I un-packed my mental brief case and settled down for a day of aggravation. The good news was that there was a late flight back to Exuma.

After lunch the trial was still in full swing and my hope for a speedy departure was being dashed on the wings of legal gibberish. At four o'clock the Judge drove the final spike into my heart when he dismissed the court to re-assemble the next morning. I looked at Allan, who had to admit he had not seen it coming, but offered to drive me to the Nassau Beach Hotel where I managed to wangle a comp room from my fellow hotelier Manager Sandy Sands. I also had to go to a drug store and get a tooth brush, deodorant and some blood pressure medicine. Ok, I thought, this was doable and one more day in the same clothes wouldn't kill me.

The second day went much like the first. Allan tried to bring into the records all the Stan had done for his employees and Exuma, but the Judge cut him off. The only positive thing that happened was when the Judge asked the two ladies what kind of a boss I was, to which they answered, "Oh, Mr. Pflueger is a very nice man and a good boss!" Bodie blanched but kept his blubbery mouth shut for a change. The Judge seems to accept that and I hoped that the might soften a little and get his show on the road. I was doomed to despair when he adjourned the proceedings for the second straight day, leaving me standing in my two day old underwear.

That evening at the hotel, I took off my sadly misused underwear and shirt and took them into the shower with me. Putting them over a porch chair to dry, a freak wind blew them off the porch and into the lawn four floors below, to the amusement of strolling tourists. Fortunately, I still had my pants and sneaked past the reception and retrieved the missing, but still wet garments. The next morning, with damp clothing and black thoughts, I returned to court for what I hoped the last go around.

Allan was right, of course, and in the late afternoon the Judge gave the verdict and we lost case. We would be required to pay the two employees around $3,200 each and that was that. I was afraid that the rest of the terminated employees would line up to carry me back to the Tribunal, but this was the end of the affair. Further, I never heard any more about the case in the Supreme Court, although I think Stan and Allan settled it, much to my relief.

As we concluded this unpleasant time of my life, I did get to know Huey Bodie a little better and perhaps even appreciate his position (and humor under the gruff exterior). It was a job to be done and a living to be made. I think in the final analysis, we came to respect each other a little and when he died a few years ago at a young 58, I was a little sorry to see him go!

What the Hell Did He Ever Do?

The complete sentence was, 'What the hell did he ever do for the Bahamas?' A statement accredited to Brett King, the then Vice-President of the Bahamas Out Island Promotion Board, upon hearing that Charlie Pflueger, President of the Board, was selected by the Bahamas Hotel Association as 'Hotelier of the Year' for 1991.

Brett, owner of the Coral Sands Hotel on Harbour Island, North Eleuthera, and an ex-movie actor, was a friend of mine. We were colleagues within the hotel industry of the Bahamas, going on many promotional trips to Europe, the U.K., the Caribbean and other venues, singing the praises of 'It's Better in the Bahamas!' while representing our individual hotels. Brett was a very smart guy and at one time or another was a Captain and fighter pilot in the Army Air Corps, winning the Distinguished Flying Cross in WWII, a promising movie actor in Hollywood, a helicopter training instructor and a Bahamas hotel manager/owner.

On long evenings in foreign countries, we would sit around the bar and swap real 'war' stories while sucking up a few martinis. I particularly enjoyed listening to his adventures while living at the same Hollywood apartment complex as Clint Eastwood and other budding future movie land stars. However, the one story that has remained in my mind was of his exploits in England in the early part of the war, when he fell in love with an English girl that lived near his base. Their relationship was nipped in the bud when he was shipped to Morocco as a fighter pilot in the battle for North Africa, and then to Italy as the Allies moved onto the continent.

During this period, Brett lost contact with his English love and erroneously heard that she had been married. She, on the other hand, had heard that he had been killed in battle and mourned his loss.

Brett, in the meantime was busy flying missions in the Poe Valley, shooting up Italian trains....later an excellent source of amusement while in Italy in the 1990's attending the huge 'BIT" travel shows, where we could say funny things like, "Brett, you over here to shoot up a few more Italian trains?' This, of course, was funnier after a few drinks. Going to the well once too often in the Valley finally was his undoing and on one faithful day anti-aircraft fire shot his P-47 Thunderbolt full of holes, including a few well placed shrapnel to his groin and legs. With blood streaming everywhere and a shot-up aircraft spewing smoke, he barely made it back to crash land on the base. His serious wounds demanded a return to the United States and a lengthy hospital stay.

When the war was over, Brett wound up in Hollywood seeking an acting career. I saw one of his first films....something about Jesse James, playing on TV. Brett and I had a laugh when I kidded him about his early career acting in this 'stinker!' He later co-starred with John Garfield in a prison film, but probably his best part came in 'Flying Leathernecks' with John Wayne, where Brett played the cowardly fighter pilot that kept aborting missions with imagined engine problems.

One day, while looking through his hotel brochure, I saw a picture of Brett with Elizabeth Taylor and asked him if this was a studio publicity shot. He responded with an emphatic, "no, Elizabeth and I were quite close and are still good friends, but you know Charlie, one night when were having dinner at a fancy Hollywood restaurant, I thought that here I am dating one of the world's most famous beauties and wishing that I was with the woman I left in England during the war! It's hard to figure!"

During the last day of one of the big U.K. travel shows, World Travel Market, I was in the booth packing up my surplus sales material and preparing to take a side trip to Athens before returning to the Bahamas. Making conversation, I asked Brett, "are you returning home tomorrow or taking a little R&R side trip first?"

"The only side trip this year is to the north of England to see my wartime sweetheart. I was determined to try to find her and got lucky when an investigator located her at a nursing home. You know how much I love my wife Sharon, but I wanted to see her one more time." Later, I asked him how it had gone when he finally saw her. He said it was wonderful to relieve his youth for awhile, but I got the feeling from his conversation, that the long, lost friend was not in complete control of her faculties and that perhaps leaving ghosts of the past... remain in the past was the best solution. Brett later told me she had passed away.

In the late 1940's, his career as an actor looked very promising, but when he told me that he was instrumental in the actors union exerting pressure on the studios to pay for standby time, I thought it very likely that he might have been blackballed in retaliation for his union activities. As the screen roles dried up, he turned to his flying skills.

Brett started training helicopter pilots during the Viet Nam war before gravitating to Harbour Island and the proprietorship of the Coral Sands, after his father died. In my opinion, Brett and wife Sharon ran a wonderful hotel and were great managers.

Prime Minister, Sir Lynden Pindling, Charlie
Pflueger and Brett King of the Bahamas Out
Island Promotion Board at Luncheon Meeting

After my two terms as President of the Bahamas Out Island
Promotion Board, Brett served as President with distinction and
dedication. A few years before his death, he was one of the finalists
for the prestigious 'Hotelier of the Year' and since only former award
winners could vote, I had the opportunity to put in my two cents.
I called him and when asked who I was going to vote for, I replied,
"Brett, I would love to vote for you, but you have to tell me, WHAT
THE HELL HAVE YOU EVER DONE FOR THE BAHAMAS?"
He sputtered a little, perhaps not immediately remembering his
comment when I won the award… but I couldn't keep a straight
face and finally told him I would, most certainly, vote for him.
Unfortunately, he did not receive this well deserved award, perhaps
as a result of always calling a 'spade a spade' and not sugarcoating
any of his usually (and occasionally caustic) accurate conclusions.
Brett died a few years later and is surely missed, since men of his
caliber are rare.

I've got a Lovely Bunch of Coconuts!

Our dining room business was increasing, causing congestion in the main dining area. One evening after a few snorts of Dewars, we came up with the ideal of extending the main part of the dining room by adding another 12 feet of roof, and flooring. We felt that by adding another 12 to 16 seats we could not only increase our overall capacity, but offer our guests an outdoor dining experience.

The idea was smashing, except for having to cut down a very coddled coconut tree raised from a baby to an adolescent height of some 25'. No one wanted to be the guy that told one of the owners, Jeanne Benjamin, that we whacked her coconut tree to make room for the new porch....a bummer in the making. Finally a drunk at the bar suggested, with a snicker that, "we should keep the tree and build the deck and floor around it!" Sober, we might have also snickered our way thru that one, but a light bulb went off and we all actually liked this crazy idea. Build around the coconut tree was the cry... and we pressed forward.

It mattered not that the tree would protrude up through the floor and then through the roof, taking up valuable space on the new porch's dining area... It was in the least a conversation piece! Yeah, a real conversation piece, probably like... 'These guys are idiots.'

We called a young carpenter who said he could build the new porch with 'no problem' and we told him to go for it! The first day went well with a fairly decent job installing the support timbers and the wooden flooring....carefully building around the coconut tree. The railing also was sturdy and attractive... the final job was to build the sloping roof with rafters and cover it with heavy, treated plywood and fiberglass shingles. All seemed to be going well!

That faithful morning, I was in my office ordering our weekly food supplies for the mail boat out of Nassau, when I decided to see how the carpenter was faring with the roof. As I walked out on the new deck my eye chanced to fall on some chunks of wood on the deck near the trunk of the tree.... my heart skipped a beat and in that instant I recognized the bits and pieces to be chunks of our beautiful coconut tree. There it was.... a 40% chunk out of our pampered baby that we tailored the entire structure to save! Looking up at Richard on the ladder fitting the final few rafters, I had murder on my mind. It was all I could do to keep from dragging him off the ladder and trying to pound him to a pulp... instead, I asked him, in an even voice, "Richard, let me ask you a question....why did you chop a huge chunk out of the very tree we were going to a great deal of trouble to preserve?"

Richard mulled the question for a few seconds before replying, "Well. In fitting the roof rafters, I had to make a decision.... I had already nailed all the rafters up to the tree... nice and evenly spaced, so it looked good, you know.... every rafters was exactly 18" from the next one.... see how great it looks? Anyway, when I got to the rafter closest to the trunk of the tree I had to put the rafter off center, which would throw the looks all off.... or (here it comes, I thought... this is where I strangle him!) I had to cut a chunk out and set the rafter exactly on the 18" center like all the rest. I made the decision to it right!"

Red in the face and ready to start screaming my head off, I exercised continued control since I was afraid if I lost it I would wind up in the local jail! "Richard, you did not have to make that decision since I was only 50 feet away in the office and quite willing to discuss this with you. Did it not seem prudent to avoid hacking up a tree that you knew was important to us? Now you have a massive eye sore staring everybody in the face not to mention that when we get the first big wind it's going to snap off like a twig and crash down on the roof. Please get down, gather your tools and get the hell off the property!" He saw the need for a rapid departure and wasted no time in further discussing the aesthetics of his ill fated decision.

I was prophetic to the extent that the tree did snap off during Hurricane Lily's gusts of 130 MPH, sending the top of our beloved tree spinning on to the second story porch of room number 8 in the middle wing of the hotel. Another example of the 'best laid plans' going in the dumper!

It's a Crime!

Capital crime was not normally a problem on Exuma, except for the odd domestic crime of passion. Back in the 1980's a lovely, young English school teacher working on the island for the Ministry of Education was found strangled at her home. It was said that she had become close to one of the local swains in a relationship that had eventually gone sour. One of the prime suspects departed for Nassau shortly thereafter, but no charges were ever filed.

When a company was contracted to build the new airport, one of their chief on-site foreign managers rented an apartment near the building site. The story has it that he reportedly felt the need to date one of the local girls, which probably did little to amuse her regular boyfriend. In any event, he was awakened at 4:00 AM one morning on the receiving end of some seven rounds of 9mm slugs to the chest, effectively canceling his work permit. This and other theories were suggested but the case drifted into oblivion.

One of the Bonefish Lodge kitchen employees accepted a ride home one night by an acquaintance who delivered him to a predetermined location on the side of the dark main road to be beaten to death. This slaying was also attributed to a love triangle, but no one was actually charged with the murder.

A tough one for me was the murder of a 25 year old local woman who worked with us at the Beach Inn, where I was the resident manager along with my responsibilities as General Manager for all the Peace and Plenty Properties. She also operated a small ladies fashion shop in George Town with the financial help from her Nassau boyfriend. Apparently, some ill will (and what looked to be a jealous rage) developed when, after the store seemed to be doing well, she turned her affections to an Exuma boyfriend and the former lover reverted to investor status.

One day she stopped off in Nassau on her way to Florida to shop for new merchandise. With a promise of additional investment funds, she was lured to an apartment where she was shot multiple times and promptly departed for the big fashion store in the sky. I understand that the perpetrator was convicted and sentenced to prison.

As her boss, I was expected to attend her funeral at a very small church at the Ferry, Little Exuma. Since the church was jammed packed with mourners and very hot, I tried to linger outside and watch the proceedings through an open window, but a seat inside next to two attending reverends had been saved for me... thanks, gang!

Again, as her boss, I was required to add to the eulogy with words of praise for the departed. I gave brief remarks citing her fine work with the hotel and declaring how much we will miss her. Before I could retake my seat, a sheet of music was thrust into my hand and I found myself joining in singing a song written by her fellow employees. Warbling away, I had one hand holding the music while my other hand was clutched around the waist of an hysterical co-worker, whose legs apparently failed and we were in a 'slump... sing...drag her upright...slump... sing... drag her upright' routine... you get the picture!

Suddenly... one young woman standing next to the coffin launched herself like a moon shuttle blast... prone... into the congregation ... knocking some of the mourners willy-nilly and sending other scrambling for safety.

As we stood next to the coffin, still trying to sing, the woman I was holding up seemed to stiffen like a steel spring, poised for her attempt off the launching pad and into the ensemble. Not on my watch, sister! I hung on for dear life (I figured that going down in that bunch might be fatal) and staggered into the crowd, as my sheet of music flittered like a wounded bird, toward the ceiling.

With great relief, the service finally concluded and we proceeded to the next phase where we took the coffin to repose in the back of a pickup truck. From there, we all slowly trooped along the side of the truck in the boiling sun, down the main road to a beautiful old cemetery by a crystal sea, where she was finally allowed her final rest. A very sad ending to a beautiful and intelligent young woman.

Once back at the hotel bar, a sweat stained coat and tie off, I thought it only fitting to hoist a couple of cool ones in a farewell salute. I needed it for sure!

Most of the few crimes over my forty years in Exuma seemed to be of the jealous lover category. I never felt that there was any serious physical danger to myself or our visitors, but staying away from romantic liaisons with the local ladies, as lovely as they might be, was a good insurance policy.

Travel Show Heaven

When I turned 65 in 1996, I was still happily employed as General Manager of the Peace and Plenty Properties with a daily function as Manager of the Beach Inn. In addition to these duties, I handled the sales, marketing and advertising for the Club and the Inn. It would be an understatement to say, I enjoyed the European Travel Show trips three times a year, starting with Milan for the big four day Italian travel show. After that we moved to a week of cocktail party presentations with our Out Island Promotion Board group, in various locations such as Venice, Frankfort, Zurich, and such. On one trip to Munich, we stayed at the fabulous Rafael Hotel (one of the finest boutique hotels in Europe) where we hosted a group of German Tour Operators.

After the cocktail party and presentation, one of the hoteliers and I went around the corner to where good fortune had conveniently placed the famous, 'Hoffbrau House' with its huge picnic style tables, and 'umph pa pa' band blasting away nightly. The 2 liter steins of good German beer flowed, served by strapping women, carrying a dozen steins of beer at a time. As we worked on our second beer, the band played a lively song which asked the musical question, from hundreds of throats, of "where the f__k is Alice?" in English. My companion and I, wanting to fit in and already having a buzz from the earlier cocktail party and two liters of beer, enthusiastically waved our barely liftable steins and sang (i.e. shouted) along in the musical search for the missing Alice! We followed the beer with a plate of knockwurst, sauerkraut and mashed potatoes to finish off the evening... I am sorry to report however; we did not find 'Alice' but did have a hell'va night looking for her!

After the freelancing week on the road, we used the final leg of our Eurorail pass to carry us to our final destination of Berlin. On this trip we had a late overnight in the intermediate city of Hanover... carrying our bags, boxes and assorted junk, we piled into a couple of train station taxis, only to be whisked around the same block to our hotel... taking all of about 30 seconds, where we were offloaded on the sidewalk amid a chorus of howling laughter from the taxi drivers.

During the four days we were at the Berlin show, we decided to take the usual 'Check Point Charlie' tour of East Berlin. As it turned out, it was the exact tour I had taken with Joan and Paul in the late 1960's (and possibly the same guide) with no signs of any new buildings or progress in the interim. We had to stop at the East Berlin check point for inspection by the border guards and to pick-up our East Berlin tour guide, before we went chugging off along the famous tree lined 'Unter der Linton' Boulevard. Our first stop was the world renowned Berlin Museum of Natural History, where we strolled around for an hour or so sopping up culture. We loaded back into the buses for the short drive to the Russian Memorial Park, where we walked around looking at the plaques and statues glorifying the fallen Russian heroes of WWII ... then back on the bus, returning to West Berlin through the check point... a bare bones tour if there ever was one! No wonder the Russians lost the cold war.

About the time the Berlin Wall was torn down in 1989, I was attending another travel show in Berlin. What a great feeling it was to be able to take a taxi from my hotel directly to the Brandenburg Gate on the East side, with out mucking about for an hour or so at the check point. For some reason I had the urge to buy a souvenir at one of the many flea market tables of Russian and East Germany military memorabilia in outdoor display. A Russian officer's hat, complete with large red star, caught my eye and I had to have it. While I don't recommend it for everyday wear... it does come in handy on Halloween.

The French Travel Show was held in late September, at the horse racing track in Deauville (its now held in Paris). We usually stayed at the Normandy Hotel, a very sophisticated five star hotel in the downtown area. All of the major wholesalers and tour operators from Paris and the rest of France attend these shows, signing up hotels world-wide to feature in their catalogs and programs. One year we stayed twenty minutes out of Deauville at the charming seaside village of Honflur, complete with strolling violinists around the quayside restaurant tables. Another unforgettable destination in the area was the huge Normandy Invasion cemetery, with its acres of white crosses for the many fallen soldiers. A large WWII museum is also nearby and certainly worth seeing. We also had lunch at a quaint restaurant overlooking the daunting Omaha Beach where the Allies launched their initial invasion of Europe on June 6, 1945.

My absolute favorite and second largest tourist show destination was London's 'World Travel Market,' held in mid-November each year. This show got so huge its venue had to be moved from Earl's Court Convention Center in central London, up the Thames to the new, massive 'Excel' center... a less convenient, but much larger facility. This change of venue certainly put a crimp on the occasional sneaking out to catch a quickie afternoon matinee at West End theaters. Excel, at least has easier access to the Millennium Dome, where the major celebration was held to usher in the year 2000. Curiosity forced me to take a tour of the Dome facilities in 2002 and wasted twenty quid entrance fee, to wander around what seemed to be a big tent. Also nearby, is one of the major new additions to the London skyline... the gigantic Ferris wheel, offing fantastic views of the city.

In January, the Caribbean Hotel Association draw world-wide wholesalers for a three day travel show; either in Nassau, San Juan or Cancun (no other destinations in the Caribbean had enough hotel rooms to handle the volume of attendees). Since I explored Nassau for four months while with Pan Am, I enjoyed attending the promotion in Cancun (and the area of Quintana Roo, a Federal District of Mexico) the most. It was a treat to have the opportunity to attend the bullfights, and to visit the famous Mayan ruins, dating back to 435 AD. The Mayan ruins of Tulum was the only city built directly on the Caribbean Sea, all the rest were built inland, including well known capital city of Chichen Itza, a few hours southwest of Cancun by van.

One of the most interesting historical tid-bits was the story of the serpent of the main pyramid of 'Kulkulcan.' On March 21st and again on September 21st of each year, if you view the north side of the pyramid at 3:00 PM, sunlight and shadows give shape to the body of a descending, slithering serpent. Mayan lore describes this phenomenon as the 'Kulkulcan' God descending to earth and marked the start and the finish of the agricultural cycle. Like the TV show says... "How did they do that?"

During the last fifteen years, of doing the marketing for the Peace and Plenty, I took very few vacations that did not tie in with a promotion trip abroad. After a travel show in the attractive countries mentioned above, taking side trips to Athens,Vienna, Oslo, Belgium, Spain, Italy and such, made a lot of sense financially and time wise. To me, this was one of the biggest perks of the hotel management job.

For many years from 1988 onward, I would host a party at the Wheatshief Pub near Marybone Street in London. Pam McCarty, from Windsor, England and the Peace and Plenty's U.K. representative would rent the upstairs with pub supplied food, beer and spirits. Invitees would include past guests from the area and any prospective guests that may wish to come. For three hours, we did our best to drink as much beer, wine and gin as possible, while reliving our guest's last visit to the sunny Bahamas, what was new in Exuma and encouraging the next visit... while ignoring the chilly

English winter. It was a wonderful way to say 'thank you' to our U.K. guests, and I hope they enjoyed it as much as I did.

When the World Travel Market show was over in November 1992, Pam in Windsor, as a courtesy, invited a few of the other out island hoteliers to join us in a tour of Queen Elizabeth's Windsor Castle, the largest inhabited castle in the world. We boarded a train from London's Victoria Station bound for Windsor Station on a Friday morning November 20th, excited to explore this ancient stronghold. Around one in the afternoon, as we neared our destination, I could see a snatch of the castle through a break in the trees and couldn't believe my eyes. Billows of heavy smoke were pouring out of one of the towers. I brought my keen intellect to bear and made the brillant conclusion that where there's smoke... there's fire... sometimes I amaze myself... Windsor Castle was burning!

Charlie looking for a fiddle, while Windsor Castle burns!

When we arrived at the station there was bedlam in the streets. Fire engines clanging and hooting like a Keystone Cops film, seemingly in all directions. The other hoteliers had taken a return train to London, pretty much figuring that the jig was certainly up. There would be no tour today or any other day, for that matter, for the next few years it took to raise the funds and to complete the extensive repairs. Pam finally made it through the chaos to pick me up at the station and drive to a spot on way to her house, where we had a better view of the smoking castle and the 200 some odd fireman and 35 engines fighting the blaze. Contrary to innuendos, I did not lead a group of Bahamian hoteliers to burn down Windsor Castle. We weren't mad at it!

During the time I attended the travel shows in London, I had the pleasure of a warm friendship with Lori Burns, who was the Vero Beach (Indian River County Florida) Tourism Director, a part of the local Chamber of Commerce. She is a very talented tourism representative who took part in the Florida tourism effort in the various European travel shows. A particular favorite was the London show where the entire Florida travel contingent gathered one night to provide a gala evening for the U.K. and attending European tour operators, wholesalers and such. These evenings were carefully planned and executed, at unusual locations, with little regard to expense.

Since I was representing the Bahamas and enjoyed some of the special evenings our group sponsored... such as dinner and dance on a luxurious party boat in the Thames, I was not normally invited to any of the Florida sponsored events until Lori invited me to escort her to a party held in one of the most unlikely venues one could imagine. Get this... a dinner dance for four hundred at the British Museum of National History!

On arrival, in formal dress, we were given flutes of champagne and allowed to stroll around nearby displays before moving into the main dining area where the skeleton of a 65 million year old dinosaur hovered above the surrounding flower adorned and exquisitely set tables. The band pounded away, while the wine flowed like water and five courses of gourmet cuisine titillated the most jaded palate. When the champagne hit the bottom, I even dusted off my 'A' game dance routine and swished (well... maybe 'swished' is taking poetic license and not indicative of personal persuasion) cheek and jowl around the dance floor with my attractive companion.

When dessert came, it looked like the evening was winding down, until a loud blast of pyrotechnics snapped heads to the main staircase leading down from the second floor. On the marble staircase poured Snow White and the Seven Dwarfs and a host of other Disney characters (I then remembered Disney World was a member of the Florida tourism group) dancing and singing some of Disney's famous songs and routines. After dinner, liquors and coffee finished off the 'fairy tale' night... and we didn't lose a slipper at mid-night!.

One of the most innovative evenings was when Lori invited me to a special dinner for 19 Florida tourism advertisers in the London Daily Telegraph. It was held in another strange venue situated some 130 feet over the River Thames at Tower Bridge. I wondered how in hell they were going to pull that off, when I was pushed into a 'lift' (ok, an elevator) at the base of the west tower, which whisked us off to the enclosed connecting enclosure between the east and west towers of this 1895 landmark. Portable heaters kept the freezing weather at bay, while a delicious catered dinner was presented. I was sitting next to Seminole Tribe attorney Lee Tiger and Chief Osceola who was decked out in the colorful full regalia of a Seminole Indian chief, looking every bit the part! I had the opportunity of chatting with Lee, who said the tribe was doing well with their casinos and other business enterprises. I saw later, that they had purchased the Hard Rock properties worldwide, for almost a billion dollars... doing well, indeed!

Being able to study London and this mighty river by night was a delight, but the surprise of the affair was each attendee was presented with a copy of the London Daily Telegraph from the day of his or her birth. The presentation of the complete newspaper, rolled with a colorful ribbon, was a jaw-dropping event. Lori later told me she was asked for her and her guest's birthday a few months before invitations went out. We never found out if the papers were originals from a warehouse storage facility or were copied from a master file somewhere. The front page of the newspaper May 23, 1931, had headlines reading, "Lorry Driver Jumps into Thames to Rescue Toddler!' ... must have been a slow news day, but very thoughtful gesture by the newspaper non-the-less.

Being a party animal, I rarely missed the opportunity to attend a function and doubly so in England and the Continent. On occasion, I was invited to affairs by the likes of the 'New Yorker Magazine,' where the Peace and Plenty was an advertiser. One such invitation was for dinner at the well know 'Ivy's' restaurant at Leicester Square near Piccadilly Circus, where I had the chance to meet and talk with some of the Caribbean's leading tourism ministers and officials. Another party was in Cancun at a famous Mexican restaurant near the convention center. One could always be sure that when you were invited to a New Yorker party, it was going to be a great evening.

In 1963 I enjoyed having lunch with Jane at the posh 'Marabelles' establishment in London's exclusive Mayfair district and particularly remember seeing actress Lee Remick enjoying the cuisine a few tables away. I was surprised to receive a New Yorker dinner invitation 30 years later to return to that charming venue. It was amazing to find a restaurant that could hold a very fickle clientele for that long and fun to re-visit even though nothing in the interior looked even remotely familiar after 30 years.

Charlie and Jean Pflueger selling the Bahamas
at World Travel Show in London 1996

The Bahamasair U.K. manager invited me to 'Stringfellows,' a well known ritzy supper club in London for a blow-out; while another evening it was a exceptional dinner at a local working brewery. In Soho, we partied in an Irish Pub with plenty of drinks, hor d'oeuvres and a great Irish bitter beer. Another time we were served a complete gourmet dinner for 20 in a major London department store.... after closing hours.

Another of Lori's invitations called for drinks and dinner aboard a yacht in the Thames called the 'Barracuda.' After a couple hours of cruising, we docked at Tower Hill, next to the recently decommissioned Royal Yacht Britania, where at 9:30 we all trooped up the hill to the Tower of London where all 30 guests were permitted thru the huge gates. Sobering up while standing in a freezing wind in the courtyard, we wondered what the hell we were doing here. But all was answered when the Tower Beefeaters trooped through the door from the inter sanctum of the huge complex and with great ceremony, locked the door to the main castle. We found out that the locking of the Tower of London's gate was a nightly ceremony, un-broken for the last 700 years.. We felt privileged when advised that only a limited number of visitors per night were permitted to attend this event.

Dance...Gypsy!

On one of the Bahamas Out Island Promotion Board's annual late February trips to Milan, for the big Italian travel show, a group of participating members were touring some of the famous landmark sights.

Our group consisted of eight members, including Pam McCarthy our rep from the U.K., and me and had visited the famous Catholic Church called the 'Domo'... a masterpiece of architecture from around the 13th Century. As an after thought, our guide suggested a walk-thru of what might be the first shopping mall, conveniently located across the street from the church.

As we entered the huge, high ceiling shopping center, with its expansive pedestrian strolling areas, Pam and the rest of the group was a dozen paces in front as I lingered, taking in this magnificent sight.

Suddenly, my pathway was blocked by a teenaged girl holding an opened newspaper in front of my face, as if to call my attention to something in its sheets! The two accompanying younger girls, one on each side of the teenager, all moved together to completely block by forward progress. Remember.... this is taking place in a moderately crowded, public shopping area, with my gang marching only a few paces ahead.

In an instant the light dawned! CBS recently aired a segment of '60 Minutes', calling attention to the mounting problem of Gypsy children robbing tourists in Western Europe. Apparently, these children were moving into Italy from Hungry and other Eastern Europe countries with large Gypsy populations.

Minors were being trained to accost victims on public streets.... while one girl would hold an open newspaper to mask the attack, the other one or two girls would move into the victim and in an instant remove his wallet and other valuables. In seconds, they would vanish into the crowd before the victim realized he had been robbed. When the rare apprehension occurred, the police were unlikely to 'throw the book' at such young offenders, placing them back on the streets with only a slap on the wrist.

When the teenager held up the newspaper, my first thought was that she was trying to sell something. Their next move triggered a flash recognition of the scam, thanks to the '60 Minutes' show. In a slight variation... the younger girls on each side grabbed my jacket sleeves to hold my arms open as the teenager dropped the newspaper and groped the zippered pocket of my jacket which contained my wallet and passport.

Once the girls actually placed their hands on my jacket sleeves... I figured all bets were off and I jerked one arm free (surprisingly strong grip for a little kid) and took a round house back-handed swing at the teenager's head, which if connected, would have surely qualified her as a candidate for the emergency room at the local hospital. As I swung, I remember her eyes as big as saucers.... as if she couldn't believe one of her 'marks' would actually figure out the scam in time to violently react!

At that moment, Pam decided to turn around and see where I had gone. She later said that she couldn't believer her eyes... to see me taking a vicious swipe at a strange young girl's head. In that instant, my swing whistled in front of her nose, as she disappeared into the crowd, along with her two assistants. A second later… it was as if it never happened, except for the trampled newspaper under foot!

Quickly checking my pockets, I discovered the zipper on the jacket containing the valuables, was half un-zipped. Apparently, my exceptionally fast response (again, thanks '60 Minutes') was enough to thwart losing my stuffed wallet and passport. I did marvel, however, on her perception, identifying the pocket with the valuables (bulge?) and particularly the dexterity and quickness of the assault.

A few days later, one of our group, Bill Rossbach, Manager of a member hotel on Green Turtle Cay in Abaco, was not so lucky. Exiting a taxi in front of the convention center, a Gypsy child snatched his wallet in a flash and was lost in the crowd. Fortunately, he wasn't carrying all his cash and credit cards with him, and was not terribly hampered by the loss.

I can only remember one other situation during our many European promotion trips. Our group of five or six hoteliers boarded the subway near our Milan, Italy hotel for a short run to the fairgrounds, where the 'BIT' travel show was being held. With standing room only, one of our members felt a groping at his back wallet pocket. With a swift move he grabbed the offending hand and snarled 'pickpocket' in English at the perpetrator. This declaration created little stir in the crowded car, while the thief took advantage of a station stop to slide into the departing crush. Fortunately, we had observed the 'Beware of Pickpockets' signs in Italian and English and were supersensitive to the potential threat in crowded venues.

Lord Love the Bartenders!

We have been fortunate at the Peace and Plenty to have a local gentleman by the name of Lermon Rolle, as one of our bartenders for the last 41 years. A more gregarious and welcoming individual would be hard to find. Lermon, named by a visitor as the 'Doctor of Libations,' has a warm, friendly demeanor and has more 'friends' than shells on the beach. I have seen him remember a returning guest's choice of drink years later, treating the guest as if he was here just last week!

As general manager I received a phone call in the late 1990's from the Ministry of Tourism's office in Nassau asking if they could send an English photography team down to take some promotional photos of Lermon behind our old 'Slave Kitchen Bar', one of the most famous in the out islands. I, of course, agreed and a couple of photographers appeared within a day or two to take the pictures of the 'Doc' to be used in the U.K, on giant bill boards and posters at the train, subway and bus stations, promoting a friendly welcome from the Bahamas. Our poster boy was smart enough to wear an 'I Love Exuma' button on his shirt, which gave us additional exposure.

It took three days to complete a few pictures while the bar remained closed. The thought came to me that perhaps the lads were tippling the booze, but those thoughts were uncharitable. In any event, the photographers returned to the advertising agency in the U.K.and we all carried on as usual until I received a call from our Bahamas Out Island Promotion Board's Executive Director Maura Brasil, asking if we could spare Lermon for a week or so to join us in London during the World Travel Market promotions at our Bahamas booth? Since I was president of the BOIPB and was going to attend the show, I readily agreed and told her as long as the board covered the airfare, hotel and food expenses, I would give him a few hundred dollars (admittedly a drop in the bucket in London) to spend and his salary at the hotel while he was gone.

Lermon was delighted to go and would be joining Sawyer, a one man band entertainer from the island of Abaco, in a powerful one... two punch. Sawyer would play and sing calypso songs and Lermon would mix exotic, tropical island drinks.... all in the Bahamas booth, in front of a huge façade of the photo shot in our bar months before. This display stopped traffic with a real life bartender standing in front of a large backdrop of the same scene.

Sawyer, Charlie and Lermon at World
Travel Market in London

Sawyer and Lermon were billeted at the Park Lane, an upscale London hotel, the cost of which was to be absorbed by the BOIPB. All seemed to go well and when the show ended they flew back to the Bahamas. All ten attending hoteliers were pleased how well Lermon and Sawyer helped with our promotions at the travel show, until a month later we all received a bill of $950 each for their expenses! A quick mathematical calculation even allowed the poorest student to note that the lads blew a bundle! Outrage permeated throughout the membership, trying to figure out how the hell these two, sharing a room, could run up a $9,500 bill in 5 days (it would not be such a problem today with the sinking dollar). Eventually, the angry individual members refused to chip in, leaving the board to pony up for the entire amount.

Being curious, I asked Lermon, "Doc, tell me how you did it? How did you run up this high a bill? Did you eat all your meals at the Park Lane?" I asked.

"We tried to eat out, but didn't have enough money. Anyway the Lamb Chops were terrific and only 55 Pounds a serving, plus, of course, the soup, sides and dessert", he stuttered. "And breakfast was only 18 Pounds and lunch 32 Pounds!" He explained, drowning out my groans.

I gulped, but plunged on," My God, Doc, that's a lot of money, and the room was expensive, but that doesn't come up to $9,500!" The Doc thought for a few seconds, and then, "I don't remember what the other charges were for!"

I pressed him, trying to jog his memory, "how about any drinking in the bar of the hotel?" Doc continued to ponder and then said, "Well, maybe a drink here and there!" I could imagine Sawyer and Doc chugging down mixed drinks at ten to fifteen Pounds a pop, night after night!

I was still hard pressed to completely explain, what seemed like a hell'va lot of money for five days, and was tempted to suggest that maybe the boys had a little feminine companionship to help while away the lonely hotel hours, but since Lermon has been happily married to his Mag for many years, I did not want to go there and closed the investigation.

Around October every year, with mid November and the World Travel Market looming on the horizon, Doc asked me, "When are we going back to London?" With some sadness, I have to reply, "never Doc, never! Nobody can afford you!"

While in London for the travel show, a friend working there with a large bank took me to his posh Anglers Club for lunch, located at Groverner's Square. We sat in overstuffed, leather chairs and swirled a brandy around a balloon glass, making small chit chat on the merits of fly rod sizes and various makes of lures. When lunch was ready we joined a group of four members for some company while forking down expensive lobster salad. Ah, bliss!

Noting that I was an American and probably not up to his snooty class, one of the members asked where I was from and was a little more impressed when I replied that I lived most of the year in my seaside home on Exuma in the Bahamas, along with an occasional visit to my Ft, Lauderdale house! I guess he figured that maybe I was worth a few more minutes of his time and followed up with, "Who do you have over here with you?"

Since I brought Lermon over for the travel show, I blurted out, "MY BARTENDER!"

He sat up-right with a start and said, with what sounded like a twinge of envy. "By George! I never thought of that! I ONLY TAKE MY VALET WITH ME ON TRIPS!"

I thought that after that, no mundane explanations were necessary and I responded, like the last of the international jet set, "in my crowd, a properly constructed libation is a MUST!" My sponsor blanched, choking back what looked like the start of a heart attack!

After another brandy and a cigar we left the club, with echo's of "please return whenever you're in town", and with a dismissing wave of the hand, I promised to do just that! I figured that in the card game of life, a bartender trumped a valet!

Lermon garnered some serious notoriety, riding his 14' smile on the 40' billboards around the U.K. and Continent. But back on Exuma, he surely had me upset one afternoon when I was attending a management meeting with the bar door shut to the lounge. In the other door popped Jimmy Buffet from a yacht in the harbor and said, "Doc, where is Charlie, I'm on a yacht and will be leaving shortly and I wanted to say hello!"

Now, I was in a non-important meeting not 20 feet away, but Lermon, protector of the hotel business replied, 'he's in a meeting and can't be disturbed!".... Disappointed, Jimmy said, "Well, tell him Jimmy was here to say hello. See him another time." An hour or so later Lermon casually told me Jimmy was in to see me but he, with a proud, puffed chest, told him I was too busy. I didn't kill him, but I wanted to!

In the first few years after taking over the Peace and Plenty we had a Haitian bartender, Johnny, who had one of my partners purchase a new Mercury Cougar automobile for him at the cost of $7,500 cash, plus duty and shipping... again, a sizable sum in those days.

When I found this out, I told Armand that I suspected Johnny of pocketing a large percentage of bar sales and that how in the hell could he afford this on a bartender's salary when I couldn't on a manager's salary. Armand told me Johnny saved his money (I said I thought he saved 'our' money). In any event he got his new car and we got the shaft.

When you have an employee who wants to work 7 days a week and takes no vacations, you have to know he is working not for the hotel, but for himself! I was eventually tipped off, that in addition to the disappearance of the beverage money, Johnny was in the prostitution business, running a small stable of Haitian hookers operating out of our bar late in the evenings (one of the rooms near the bar had a infamous history) after I retired for the night.

Eventually, Stan fired Johnny for stealing when the local Women's Club had a huge benefit dance for Glen Turtle, who lost his arm in a boating accident and at the end of a jam packed evening with plenty of drinking for a good cause, the expected receipts of at least a couple thousand wound up in Johnny's tin at a greatly diminished $300, which caused such screaming that Stan finally had the support of the local ladies to be able to sack Johnny.

Johnny left the island after a stint at Two Turtles Hotel across the street and probably helped himself to their funds. He finally went to Miami and word had it that he was killed in a drug deal gone bad.

Across the Yellow Banks to Great Exuma

While running the hotel it finally dawned on me that not all fishermen were exclusively dedicated to the pursuit of bonefish on the flats. Inquiries as to the availability of a boat for off shore, blue water fishing for Dolphin (also called Dorado in Spanish and Mahi Mahi in Hawaii), Yellow Fin Tuna, Wahoo and other pelagic fish, were occurring often. In the 1970s' Exuma, there were only a few open boats operated by local fishermen that ventured off shore on calm days that might, on a hit or miss basis, take a visiting fisherman deep sea fishing. They were generally not schooled in the use of modern fishing tackle and equipment, or in new techniques. No funds were generally available to upgrade their boats, hence my hesitation, as hotel manager, to recommend their services. A sudden madness came over me and I decided to buy a charter boat.

One of our guests brought over a copy of the Miami Herald, which I devoured, including the 'Boats for Sale' listings, where I found a 31 foot Luhrs sports fisherman, with twin engines, offered at $7,500. A quick visit to my friendly bank of Nova Scotia manager, Tony Allen, secured a kind word, a slap on the back, and a check for $5,000 to go along with my $2,500 and I was off to Miami.

I called the owner of the boat in south Miami and found out that he was a National Airlines Flight Engineer currently on strike and unable to make ends meet, creating a urgent need to unload his favorite play toy (much to the obvious relief of a hand-wringing wife). Upon inspection, the boat proved to be in pristine condition with like new mahogany paneling and interiors. It had a flying bridge, a head, a forward sleeping cabin and a galley with four burner stove. I had the boat pulled at the yard and inspected the bottom.... All was well and I purchased it on the spot.

I had to fly back to Exuma the next day, but childhood friend, Charley Callahan and his son, Randy, gave me a hand and prepared the boat for the trip to the Bahamas. He topped off the inventory of tackle, including a couple of new 9/0 Penn trolling rods and reels. With very little persuasion, Charley and Randy joined Captain Clifford Dean to cross the Gulf Stream and on to New Providence Island. A week later, after attending a Bahamas Hotel Association meeting in Nassau, I boarded the newly named 'Gemini' for a couple of days trip down the Exuma Chain to our final destination of Great Exuma.

It was late in the day when I finally arrived at the dock and with the sun dipping low in the sky; we headed out of Nassau harbor and headed across the Yellow Banks towards our overnight anchorage at Noroman's Cay, at the northern end of the Exuma Chain. Norman's Cay later became the Bahamian enclave of the notorious Colombian drug king, Carlos Leiter. While Charley had loaded more than enough supplies for the trip, the thought of fresh fish for dinner was appealing, and we started looking for a patch of dark bottom, an indication of a reef, usually home to myriads of tasty grouper and snapper. A rapidly setting sun added some element of urgency, and we were soon rewarded with the discovery of a dark patch of about an acre in the surrounding azure water. Clifford dropped the anchor as I slipped on fins and adjusted my mask and snorkel. Clutching my Hawaiian sling and eight foot stainless steel spear, I tumbled off the stern of the 'Gemini'.

As I hit the water on my initial dive, clearing my vision from air bubbles, I looked down for my usual quick evaluation (with eagle eye out for a barracuda or shark) and into the inquisitive eyes of a 15 pound Nassau grouper searching for the source of the commotion. In one motion I pulled back on the rubber tubing and let the spear fly… hitting the fish in the head with enough force to drive it thru, allowing the tip to open and secure the grouper. Quickly grabbing the end of the spear, I power finned my way to the surface, handing a surprised Charley the jiggling spear. Clifford, an experienced Exumian diver, couldn't believe his eyes since I had barely been in the water long enough to get wet. This gave new meaning to 'fast food!'

Just before dark, we motored up to the Norman's Cay Club and replenished our dwindling supply of beer, before anchoring in the small bay. While we were doing this, Charley prepared the grouper for a delicious fried fish finger dinner, washed down with copious amounts of beer. A great evening ensued, with a full belly sloshing around with fish and beer eventually lead to a peaceful sleep of the' just'… or the 'just exhausted!'

The next day, we cruised down the enchanting chain of islands to Staniel Cay, about mid-way down the chain, where we explored 'Thunderball Cave' of James Bond fame, located in a small cay in the harbor. Swimming thru a small passage in the rock led to a large cavern with a soaring open, air filled ceiling. Very neat stuff!

Continuing the southward cruise, we stopped to visit Dr. Chester's residential complex on Little Derby Island. This lovely cay had breezy elevations offering fantastic vistas, and importantly, a well protected dock and warm hospitality in the form of an invitation to visit the main house.

Bryan Collins, the complex manager, an excellent Bahamian chef and an accomplished diver, took his skiff and within minutes returned to the dock with a dozen large conch. A handsome young man with tousled, sun bleached hair and a swimmers long, slim body explained that, "the channel is literally and figuratively crawling with conch, so it's only a matter of taking what you need for dinner.

There is plenty of turtle grass which usually means plenty of conch." He demonstrated the proper technique for cracking conch out of its shell by taking a well battered hatchet and chopping a half inch slit in the cone area to accommodate a knife blade to sever the tail, wrapped around the interior of the cone. At this point, he grasped the bone like foot and gave a pull, quickly withdrawing the main body of the conch (about the size of your hand) out of the shell. Once out of the shell he expertly trimmed the guts and slime and announced, "Lets all go up to the house and whip up some conch fritters and scorched conch!" Sounded good… sign me up!

Over the years, I have had a lot of scorched conch, but none better than Bryan made that day. He cut the white meat into couple of inch squares and carefully cut grooves into the squares, allowing the mixture of goat pepper, lime juice, onions and green peppers to marinate for a few minutes……while this was going on, he quickly made a batter, ground up a couple of conch, added salt and pepper, and fried a delicious batch of conch fritters, an old Bahamian favorite.. 'Eat fresh' as the commercial says! Can't beat fresh fritters while sampling one of Bryan's potent rum punches… bliss!

Sitting back in the chairs, munching fritters and sipping punches, Collins asked us if we would like him to show us Big Darby Island, a sister cay across the channel, also owned by Dr. Chester… "What's over there?" I asked.

He took another sip of his drink, clearing his throat, "as they story goes… in the early 1930's an Irishman bought Big Darby and built a castle, or what looks like a medieval castle. He moved in and started running a herd of cattle on the island; but there's more to the story, but lets go over before it gets too late!"

We took the skiff across the channel and tied to a weathered dock… an old warehouse still stood nearby. A winding rock road meandered up the steep hill to a huge three story building constructed in the image of a castle. In an outside trashed utility room, twin monster Lister generators, that once provided ample electrical power for the operation, lay rusting over the decades. Once inside the main building, there were still bits and pieces of 1930's furniture, scattered helter-skelter around the living areas, as we made our way up the stairs, culminating with a roof top observation deck, offering spectacular 360 degree views..

While showing us around the deck, Collins began relating a bizarre history of Big Darby Island, "when England was embroiled in WWII, the Irish owner, no friend of the English, conspired with German U-boats plying the waters of the Atlantic and Exuma Sound, preying on Allied Shipping."

Bryan pointed toward the south side of the island as he continued his narrative, "over there is a huge cave that served as a shelter for a herd of cattle the Irishman ran.....and as the story goes, on pre-arranged nights butchered carcasses were left on the dock for small boat pickup by U-boat crews, providing fresh beef for the sub's larder. This story was never proven, but local rumors reported seeing skinned cattle on the dock that had disappeared by the next morning... True or not, it's an exciting part of the local out island lore," he concluded.

"Sounds like a myth to me, but stranger things have happened," I injected, "but we thank you for the hospitality and appreciate the tour." We left a waving Bryan Collins on Little Darby Cay, not realizing that years later he would be working with us at the Peace and Plenty, wowing the ladies and providing wonderful day excursions to the nearby scenic islands.

The rest of the cruise to the hotel at George Town was uneventful until we arrived at the Peace and Plenty dock to be welcomed home by a joyous, mixed crowd of staff and guests. After a few days rest, we refueled and were ready to offer charter boat deep sea fishing and harbor cruises. Business turned out to be decent, but a few problems raised their ugly heads! With the cost of fuel in the islands, gas engines were on the expensive side to operate, but offered more speed to reach the fishing grounds. On the other hand, the hotel dock was no more than a few miles to where we could drop the lines in thousands of feet of water, so one tended to offset the other.

Weather turned out to be another major problem limiting the number of days when the sea was calm enough to offer a comfortable offshore trip. This was particularly true in the busy winter season, when more affluent visitors flocked to the islands for a respite from frigid northern blasts. This segment of the market had the money to indulge in the sports fishing experience where, even at that time, it could run over $500 a day. Unfortunately, at this time of the year winter cold fronts howl in from North America, creating windy conditions and high seas, challenging the dedication of the most ardent fisherman, not to mention a reluctance of the crew to get their brains battered out in a raging sea.

On the plus side, we did make a decent living for Clifford and a small return on investment from charters and the sale of fish to the hotel and other local establishments. Another perk was playing wealthy, international sports fisherman... tooling around in my yacht (stretching the illusion a tad) and sampling the amenities that the Peace and Plenty could supply, such as fine food and good drink. Oh! Looking back, one more perk to owning the boat was the fun of entertaining some of our guests with a personalized sunset harbor cruise... What a guy.

One of the more serious problems that cropped up was the need to replace the twin Chris Craft engines with new Mercruisers, due to partial salt water submersion. It seems a storm blew up one night while the Gemini was docked at the hotel and the resulting high seas tore a rudder strut lose from the fiberglass hull. The next day Clifford did not notice the problem until well underway with a load of six passengers. A disaster was averted when a rapidly flooding engine room was discovered in time to return the party back to the safety of the dock.

Replacing inboard engines in the Out Islands was no small matter. First, I found a dealer in Ft. Lauderdale that had a half a dozen discontinued new Mercruisers for sale at an unbelievable price of under $1,000 each. I eagerly purchased two, shipped them to Exuma and paid the duty. Luck was with me when Mr. Nixon and his sons pulled the Gemini next to the Government Dock and craned out the old engines. They did a fantastic job of fitting the gleaming Mercruisers into the hull... a job that couldn't have been done any better by the factory.

We were back in business! All seemed well again until one of Exuma's local marine dealers (I had previously rejected a much higher bid for engines from his dealership) suggested to Bahamas Customs that I must have provided false invoices since those engines could not have been purchased for the invoice price stated. When I heard about this, I called my dealer in Ft. Lauderdale and asked him to verify the invoice. He said, "Charlie, I can do better than that... I have four brand new ones left and can offer them to anyone out there who might want new Mercruisers at the same price... under $1,000 dollars each."

Better, indeed! That's all I needed to hear. I immediately called the Exuma dealer and asked him that since he thought the price I paid was unbelievable, how many of the remaining four engines did he want to buy at my price and I would arrange to have them shipped?

He was silent for a few seconds, mulling over this information, and then advised he didn't have a buyer at this time, but thanked me for taking the trouble to call him. Of course, that was the end of any Customs inquiry.

After a few years, Clifford came to me and advised that he had a financial backer that would offer him part ownership of the Gemini if I would agree to sell it. At this point, the bloom was off the lily and I had had my fun (and heaps of aggravation). Figuring that there was little profit to be made due to all the previously mentioned limitations, I agreed and the boat was sold.

Scotiabank was no doubt pleased to get the balance of the loan off their books along with a few years interest and my credit remained in pristine condition. My personal offshore fishing was reduced to the occasional use of the hotel's 24' Aquasport open boat, which as I look back, provided some fantastic Dolphin fishing and a platform to retrieve a half a dozen Grouper traps from 100' of water near Stocking Island.

From Club to 'Crows Nest"

Managing the Peace and Plenty was demanding but enjoyable. We had a very good local band 'Lorne Smith and the Jet Streams' playing on Monday, Wednesday and Saturday nights. We usually had a packed house dancing on the patio and jamming the bar. In the early seventies, we had the only game in town for the winter residents and tourists. The hotel had a dress code of jackets for gentlemen and no shorts or halters for the ladies, and had our share of wags coming in wearing a jacket with no shirt and short pants to test our patience.

Booze aplenty was flowing but the crowd was not usually unruly and very few altercations developed. One night while working as a cashier with the bartenders Lermon and Willie the Haitian behind the bar, we were having trouble with one of our guests, a very large and loudmouthed, drunken lout. He was overly aggressive with some of the ladies and when we asked him to tone it down he advised us to 'bugger off'. That was it for me! As he left the bar to go the rest room, I followed behind and as he passed our open office, he picked up a chair and threw it, crashing against the far wall. As he reached the threshold of the men's room, I grabbed him by the shoulder and spun him around and started to launch a haymaker, figuring I had to give it all I had as he was really big. With my fist cocked and ready swing, my arm was grabbed from behind partner by partner Armand Angelone who said, "Don't hit him! He's dead drunk!" At that point, as if on cue, the drunk had to hold onto the bath room threshold to keep from falling and finally listened when I told him to go to bed and sleep it off. After it was over, I thanked Armand since I would have probably broken my hand off on that lout's head, and it's not cool to knock your guests on their ass.

In the early 70's I tried to set up television in my second story apartment by installing a tall antenna on top of the building. It was unfortunate that the only thing I could pickup was a little public television from south Florida. From this experience, and since Exuma is 300 miles from the south Florida stations, I never thought that we would have this entertainment vehicle, but with the advent of the satellite it became feasible. Our next dilemma was to decide whether our guests, most of them here to get away from civilization, wanted TV in their rooms. We decided to install six rooms and a couple of management apartments with satellite TV and see if incoming guests requested this amenity.

During this time, we chanced to have an attractive young woman staying in one of the TV rooms who liked to sunbathe on the pool deck while her husband went fishing. Unfortunately, (or fortunately depending on how you look at it!) she apparently felt that wearing the halter part of her bathing costume (ok, bathing suit) did not allow for the distribution of a proper sun induced tan... so, off came the top displaying a lovely (judgmental) set of breasts.

As I checked the weather from my upstairs apartment, my glaze immediately went to the sunbather with delight...then consternation.... While we had no posted or written rules regarding topless sunbathing, I hoped that the few guests of the hotel were sophisticated enough to ignore the situation as I was going to do, unless I had a complaint. Having said that, I whipped out my new video camera and, peeking out of the drapes, did about five minutes of video including some nicely framed close-ups, feeling a little guilty about this sneaky act but good about documenting the human body as an art form. In the throes of this mis-guided enthusiasm, that evening around 9:30 I completely forgot about the six hotel rooms with TV and put the sunbather tape on the internal circuit. I then phoned my friend and Bonefishing Manager, Bob Hyde in the next apartment with, "turn your TV on to the movie channel and take a look!" Feeling dandy that I could do something for mankind!

Bob did as bidden and shouted into the phone, "are you out of your mind? Did you forget there are other rooms in the hotel besides mine with television?"

To say I panicked would be an understatement! Visions of a monumental law suit and being drummed off the island, danced in my swirling (and stupid) head. Not being sure exactly what room the sunbather was in, I hurried down to the office and checked the reservations board to find, to my horror, they were in one of the six TV rooms! Some slightly good news was that four of those rooms were not occupied, so the exposure (no pun intended) was limited to the victim and one other room with two balloon base technicians who were out for the evening. The next morning, after tossing and turning all night, I opened the dining room before breakfast and puttered around waiting for the sunbather and spouse to storm in.

The husband came in for breakfast early, since the pickup for a fishing trip was normally at eight o'clock. The wife was not with him and probably still in bed. I grabbed the coffee pot almost out of the hand of the waitress and wobbled to his table with a big 'good morning' smile. "How was your evening. I didn't see you all in the bar last night?" I probed, as a drop of sweat dripped off my nose.

I thought my heart would jump out of my chest when he replied, "we both had a lot of sun and went to bed early to watch a little television."

I now knew the jig was up and that his next move would probably be either to hit me or advise that his attorney would be in touch in the very near future! I steeled myself for his next remark, "but we were exhausted and fell asleep only to wake up during Johnny Carson's monolog and turn it off." Thank you, God! A new lease on life and a promise to avoid this kind on nonsense in the future! Bob, having coffee a few tables away, almost fell out of the chair laughing at what, thankfully, was our private joke.

At one time, Airways International was our only direct access to Florida before American Eagle started service in1992, (after I called the American Eagle Vice-president, Joel Chusick and begged him to come out and take a look at Exuma). Airways only operated 8 passenger Cessna 402 twin engine aircraft, but it seemed they had access to as many as they needed to handle whatever bookings came up. It was almost a two hour flight from Ft. Lauderdale and Miami, and the afternoon flight was an overnighter, using the Peace and Plenty for the single pilot crew. Most of the pilots were good, hard working guys, building hours for their shot at the right seat of a major carrier that paid a lot more money, not to mention providing a plethora of long-legged stewardesses to help while away the lonely overnights in fancy hotels in strange cities.

While flying those eight passenger Cessna's with a single pilot, I always looked the pilot over carefully, almost as if I was an MRI machine and could see any potential fatal body flaws before we took off, as if I could evaluate his competence to complete the flight before falling down dead! While in flight, I watched for any sign of the start of a fatal heart attack....calculating the time it might take for me to dash to the cockpit, pull the slumped pilot from the controls and assume command.... not bothering to wonder 'what the hell I would be doing when I got there since I couldn't fly a plane'! As you might imagine, I could barely force myself to get on any of these flights much less when the pilot was a pasty, overweight guy, dragging on a Luck Strike cigarette and stifling a cough!

Another of the bazaar incidents that kept cropping up with this airline that made me start flying into Nassau then to Miami on Bahamasair and avoiding Airways International completely, was the evening I saw one of their overnighting, young pilots having a drink at the Peace and Plenty bar. Not so unusual nor necessarily ominous one might say, since FAA regulations permit alcohol with sufficient time between drinking and flying and it was still early in the evening. He was chatting with another hotel guest and a lady who was the Member of Parliament for Exuma. All seemed well.... But not for long!

Jerry (lets call him Jerry), was not satisfied with a drink or two then to bed so he would be bright-eyed and bushy tailed to pilot his early flight to Miami.... not a chance! He proceeded to run up a booze bill of $69.... And in those days this represented a considerable number of drinks and more than enough to get you whacked out of your mind, even if some were bought for others. Unfortunately, the story only started here... Jerry, with a snoot full, was apparently offered some cocaine by one of George Town's low life's, which must have seemed like a grand idea at the time. Jerry, being a little short on cash for this unexpected windfall went looking for my apartment to borrow money to finance the cocaine purchase. Being blasted must have effected his sense of direction (not to mention 'common sense') since he got turned around and was unable to navigate the tricky access to my apartment.... luckily for Jerry, since I had a low tolerance for drugs users, rendering my 'drug loan office' closed for the night.

Not to be daunted, he somehow found out the room number of the lady (the previously mentioned distinguished Exuma Member of Parliament) he had met earlier in the evening, and proceeded, at what was now mid-night, to knock on her door. In a drunken slur, he informed her that since he couldn't find the Manager, he was asking her for a loan... As you might imagine, this went over like Casanova in a convent and triggered a bout of screaming bloody murder, bringing security out of a slumber and finally frog marching him to bed where he must have fallen into a drunken stupor. On the surface, this seemed like a questionable career move for Jerry.

While all this craziness was going on, I was snoozing the snooze of the just in my apartment, hearing nothing, while security put this idiot to bed without his cocaine.

The next morning when I came down to open the office and restaurant; I got an early blast from the MP along with a few other unhappy guests. At this point, I went looking for him with blood in my eye and found to my further outrage that the wayward pilot skipped out without paying his bar bill (food and lodging was charged to Airways International as usual). I immediately called the airport to report this and late drinking to the airport authorities and police, but he had already taken off with a load of unsuspecting passengers. I then called the airline headquarters in Ft. Lauderdale and advised them of the scenario and not only creating havoc and skipping on the huge bar bill, but the ramifications of piloting a passenger flight in defiance of FAA regulations.

I understand that armed with this information the manager of Airways was waiting when the flight landed and the pilot cleared customs. He was, of course, fired on the spot, a report filed with the FAA and an assurance that the company would make good any outstanding bills from this episode. I also understand that the FAA lifted his license, as well they should have.

Paul Swetland, majority stockholder of the hotel and I did not always see eye to eye on the operation. I had been advised years before in Montego Bay by Charlie Morrow, the owner of the Montego Beach Hotel, who was a friend of Paul's and mine, to 'never go in business with him'. I dismissed the thought at the time since there was no inkling of things to come, but this warning was coming home to roost.

While Paul and I were friends socially, I thought he had a screw loose when it came to operating the hotel. One example was we had to run his burgee (nautical flag) with a big 'S' on it up the hotel flag pole when he arrived! I guess he thought this was classy, however guests and employees thought it was crass and a wag suggested it stood for 'shithead!'

Another stunt, was one very busy Saturday night around 11:00 PM, with a crowded hotel, the band playing away, dancers on the floor and the booze flowing, Paul came into the packed bar in his bathrobe and shoutsed to me over the din, "stop the band!'

Thinking that some disaster had taken place, I made my way from behind the bar and leaned in to hear him repeat, "Stop the band!"

Fearing the worse, I shouted back, "What happened?"

With a straight face he said, "I'm trying to sleep!" At this point, I could not believe my ears and forcefully explained that we have charged admission at the door and never closed until at least 12:30 and sometimes at 1:00 AM, if the bar was really busy like tonight. If we closed at eleven there would be hell to pay, and particularly for some half-assed whim from a clueless owner. I told him I would try to shave a little off the closing time and he went off, mumbling!

His irrational actions and his lack of understanding how deeply involved I was in the actual operations of the hotel (it took 4 jobs to replace me) he decided that although I was a partner (if a minority one) he thought he could do without me. Since I had had enough of Paul, I agreed with him and left the island, returning home to Miami. Before leaving, however, I talked it over with Stan Benjamin, a guest of the hotel and a Cleveland Industrialist who was also acquainted with Paul..

Stan asked me what I was going to do and I told him of my plan to lease a piece of waterfront property a few hundred yards west of the Peace and Plenty and open a bar and restaurant called the 'Crows Nest'. I had the spot picked out and had a local partner, Cressel Morely, which made obtaining a license and work permit do-able. Stan, a wealthy guy and always interested in a challenge, agreed to take 50% and finance the deal. It took a few months to sort things out with the permits and such, but I was soon back on Exuma, staying at an old Bahamian style hilltop house a mile from the Crows Nest site, that Stan had recently purchased from the editor of a well known women's magazine.

I always wanted to open a bar and restaurant in the islands and I plunged into the project with both feet and within a couple of months we built, with the help of a local contractor and crew, a fairly large main building with sliding glass double doors opening to a hilltop view of the harbor to die for! In order to jazz up a rather simple rectangle building, we built an upper observation deck (the 'crow's nest') with spiral staircase access and covered seating for around 8 to 10 guests.

I found a bunch of empty conch shells in the sea nearby and asked one of the workmen to put a row of shells around the double entrance doors to tart it up a little. Unfortunately, I made the mistake of going off for the morning and upon returning, found half the wall in hundreds of conch shells. I guess he misunderstood my instructions although they were in English, but it did become a conversation piece and prompted passers-by to comment, "I wonder what nitwit did that?"

We opened the doors to the Crow's Nest on February 12, 1972 in the middle of an active winter season. I hired a couple of the local ladies to cook and wait tables, but couldn't seem to find an unemployed (and employable) bartender to handle those duties. Finally, since I have drunk my share of intoxicating beverages over the years, I thought I could handle the bar until I found someone to relieve me. Big mistake!

A16 The Exuma Breeze - January, 2008

H A P P Y   D A Y S   1 9 7 2

■ This photo from 1972 was taken at the Crow's Nest during the 1972 National Regatta and shows from left: Brigadier David Smith, Chief of Staff, Jamaica Defence Force and formerly of George Town, Exuma; Dame Marguerite Lady Pindling, Hon. Simeon Bowe, a former Minister of Works and formally of Moss Town, Exuma; former Prime Minister, The Rt. Hon. Lynden Pindling; Mr. Charles Pflueger, General Manager, Peace and Plenty and Mrs. Jean Benjamin, wife of Mr. Stan Benjamin the current owners of the Peace and Plenty Hotel. The hotel will celebrate its 50th Anniversary with a gala party on Thursday, January 17th, 2008. - This photo is currently on display at the Peace and Plenty Hotel, George Town.

Middle gentleman is Sir Arthur Hanna then the Deputy
Prime Minister and current his Excellency, Governor
General of the Commonwealth of the Bahamas

I opened at 11:00 AM after restocking the bar and handling the banking, and remained open until at least mid-night and many times after 2:00AM., seven days a week. Operating a very long bar, that on occasion, was full, including all the other responsibilities of management, took its toll. For the first week my legs were so sore from walking miles a day on a hard surface floor (had even with rubber mats) that I felt crippled. Being a little chubby when I started, by the 6th week of this grueling regimen, I had lost 32 pounds and looked lean and a little gaunt! Finally, I hired Albert Rolle, brother of Lermon Rolle, the Peace and Plenty longtime bartender and got some relief.

Late one evening, when I was off the island, my partner Jeanne Benjamin, Stan's lovely wife, was in the Crow's Nest keeping an eye on things and having a drink with a couple of the local fellows, when a masked gunman walked in and pointed his pistol with muffled instructions to, "line up and give me your money and jewelry!"

Lining up and facing the barrel of a gun was certainly a 'mood buster' and scared one of Jeanne's companions so badly that he shouted in a screaming stutter, "s...s...shoot! S...s...shoot! A questionable and unexpected response, to say the least.

Jeanne was so outraged, that she blurted out... "It's DON'T Shoot! You Goddamn idiot! You'll get us all killed!" She was a lady that did not suffer fools easily. Later, when she retold the story, I almost fell off the bar stool, although she assured me that it was not funny at the time, staring at an armed, masked robber that was probably on drugs. The gunman apparently was satisfied the 'idiot' actually meant 'don't shoot', collected the booty, and vanished into the night.

Doctor Taylor, our government sponsored island doctor was from Australia and a frequent guest at our long, oak bar, sampling our vodka stock with considerable enthusiasm. Doc Taylor had the ability to handle what seemed like any medical crisis whether drunk on his ass or sober (I presume in his daily clinic duties). A local lad, ignoring the fact that the street near the Crow's Nest ended in a small bluff overlooking the harbor, decided it was too much trouble to turn the wheel on his huge American sedan and plunged onto the rocky shore a dozen feet below. The ensuing crash rattled the glasses on the bar, including the Doc's third or fourth vodka, prompting all the drunks to stagger to the crash site.

Doctor Taylor was back in his element, directing the rescue effort and using the flat bed on our pickup truck to transport the victim to the clinic for his expert ministrations. With a steady hand, he patched up the driver well enough to transport him to Nassau and the Princess Margaret Hospital for follow-up.

All was not rosy for Doc! He brought a young male Bahamian 'companion' with him from Freeport to Exuma to live in his house on the hill, only 100 yards or so from the Crow's Nest. This cozy arrangement went well for awhile until one evening when the Doc was hoisting a few and chatting with me about the small number of shark attacks on local divers (most on those who refused to donate a speared grouper to the insistence of a pesky bullshark looking for lunch). Suddenly, in bounds his wide-eyed lover whirling a nasty looking machete and screaming at the top of his lungs, "You're cheating on me! I'm going to chop you in pieces!" To the Doc's credit he did not move a muscle.

Taylor seemed calm confronting this maniac, but I was not amused and quickly moved down the bar to reach around the door to the kitchen and fumble around for the smooth, cold barrel of my 12 gauge shotgun loaded with bird shot. The Bahamas Government does not encourage the importation of firearms into the country willy-nilly, but permits are given for sportsmen who shoot White Crown Pigeons, a large tasty wild bird that migrates from Hispanola and is shot in the Bahamas in the fall.

Finally getting a firm grip on the gun, I swung it up while pumping a shell of 6/0 birdshot into the firing chamber. It seems that no matter how much howling and shouting is going on, the sound of a cold steel chamber slamming home a potential lethal blast to the face, is an attention grabber! The lovers arm with machete'was still in the air when his eyes followed the sound of the loading shotgun… as he stared into that large, black hole of the barrel. As his brain processed the possibility of having his face blown off, he must have figured a little outside hanky panky for the Doc was not too bad a concept, dropped his arm and made for the door, mouthing a respectful, "Good night!"

The barflys all let out their collective breaths at one time and a nervous titter replaced the abject fear of a moment before. Some one said, "Doc, you can really pick'um!" Unflappable, he confided that this happens all the time at home and he is not dead yet, but he did admit that this was particularly poor form in a public place.

Friday nights seemed to be the unofficial fight nights since Fridays were payday and we usually had a band playing at the highest volume the speakers could go. Sprinkle a liberal supply of cheap booze and some equally cheap ladies… with perhaps a dash of testosterone and this is an almost guarantee for a bout of fisticuffs. Early in the game, I would come out from behind the bar and try to get between the combatants, however after a lesson or two dodging most, but not all of the flying blows, I decided it was the better part of valor, to scream, from comparative safety behind the oak bar, "OUT! OUT!" and let it go at that. Eventually, the scuffle would wound up in the dust of the parking lot.

There were always ladies around the bar but I was usually working and not able to avail myself of these opportunities. One night, however, after 2:00 AM I locked the door but still had a pretty good crowd hanging around swapping lies, when a very attractive lady in her mid forties started chatting me up and suggested that it might be a brilliant idea if we could take a look at the moonlit view of the harbor from the privacy of the crow's nest. Her husband was chatting away with other patrons, so we trooped up the stairs to the 'nest' and soon had her panty hose off and in her purse, and proceed to make passionate, if a little hurried, love.

Climbing back down to the party, her husband, an Air Force Colonel, saw us returning from our scenic expedition and when standing next to him he reached under her dress and found no panty hose. I thought the jig was up, but he laughed and commented that he supposed the panties were in her bag. At that point I relaxed and figured that this was not the first foible for these two, who apparently had an understanding.

An old friend, Ralph Schultz and his wife Connie from the Florida Keys stayed with me while we were building the Crow's Nest and as a retired contractor, offered immeasurable assistance. In additional to his building skills, he was a master at smoking fish and conch. One day when we were searching the island dump for a few items we might use, he came upon an old wall locker which he rapidly converted into a stand up smoker with four or five old oven racks for the food items and an area in the bottom of the locker for the smoke producing material. To create a savory smoke, we had the silver buttonwood tree, similar to the kind Ralph used on the Florida Keys, growing near the water and provided an abundance of smoke producing fuel.

We next had to catch enough fish and conch to keep a steady supply of munch- able delicacies at the bar, for a little extra revenue and to encourage our imbibing patrons to buy another round. Since we were pretty busy and had little extra time to go fishing, we purchased a couple hundred feet of Manila hemp rope and six feet of chain, ending with a stainless steel shark hook. We used a jack fish for bait and a rock for a sinker, carefully tying the free end of the rope to our seaside buttonwood tree. Our 16' skiff provided the means to drop the business end of the rig far out into the harbor in the early evening for overnight exposure... the best time to fish for sharks.

In the morning we usually could see the tree shaking violently back and forth, signaling a successful angling adventure. Pulling an angry Lemon or Blacktip Shark to shore was sometimes quite a challenge, since we have caught them over eight feet long and a couple hundred pounds. Ralph would clean the fish and cut up massive slabs of white flaky meat for an all day smoke, producing an abundance of smoked snacks for the bar at a dollar a pop! We found very little reluctance by our patrons (albeit, usually under the influence of a dollop or two of spirits) to sample our smoked shark.

We sold some of the great Jamaican rums such as Appleton, pouring from 40 oz bottles purchased from our liquor purveyor in Nassau. While living in Jamaica, I used to buy a bottle now and then in the supermarket for $1.50 a fifth and enjoy an evening's rum and coke, but in the back of my mind I always wanted to buy a keg of the stuff, partially for a conversation piece. Acting on this lunacy, I called the Appleton factory and was told that the company did not sell barrels of rum anymore and I would have to be satisfied with 40 oz cases. Having my heart set on buying a barrel, I called an old, Jamaican Pan Am friend George DeMacado, who was now high up in Jamaican tourism and explained my plight. Thanks to George, I was finally rewarded with a 55 gallon oak barrel of 95 proof tea colored rum directly from the Appleton factory at a grand total of $120.

When the barrel arrived on the boat from Florida, I finally realized that my problems just started and that it was going to be rough getting it off the boat, up to the Crow's Nest and up on the oak bar. After that, how in the hell do we tap it since this exercise was to be able to actually drink this super-grade stuff. Finally, after much hand wringing, we obtained a tap and got into it. We had an Eastern Airlines pilot staying at the hotel who had a few late afternoon belts and complained that the rum didn't have much of a 'kick' ... who later, while having dinner with his wife, had his head fall 'kerplunk' into the mashed potatoes, thereby giving silent testimony to it's 'kick' potency.

While the barreled rum provided some atmosphere and customer draw, I was searching for another drink that might prove popular, when Jeanne Benjamin came in with a can of Coco Lopez coconut cream and suggested we follow the recipe' and make a couple of Pina

Coladas. In 1972 I had not heard about this delicious creamy drink, but after putting some Appleton Rum in the blender, complete with a healthy shot of Coco Lopez, pineapple juice, chunks of pineapple and ice, we lapped up quite a few and were sold on offering it to our guests.

I ordered a case of Coco Lopez cream, a large sign advertising 'PINA COLADAS $1.50,' and a case of elegant 16 oz frosted glasses to lend a little pizzazz, and settled back for the thirsty hordes. Nothing happened! Oh, a couple here and there, accompanied by, "what are they." To say that I was disappointed would be an understatement! While pondering this dilemma, I had an unusual flash of brilliance and I actually listened to my stepfather, Jack, who suggested that the answer was in a more attention grabbing name and proposed I rename the drink something like, 'Coconut Fling!' I loved the idea and figured the 'coconut' part was descriptive and tropical... while everybody has had a 'fling' now and then... have they not?

As history recorded it... I had another sign made, extolling a special fancy drink... the 'Coconut Fling $1.50.' using the same frosted glass but with the addition of a shirt button slipped over one side of the lip, advertising to the world... .'I HAD A FLING AT THE CROW'S NEST' Of course, they got another dose of Pina Colada, this time in sheep's clothing. We also decided that keeping the ingredients secret by removing the labels from all the Coco Lopez cans before use in the bar, was a great idea. This wisdom was soon apparent, when our patrons returned to their respective hotels bars and asked for a 'Coconut Fling' to be rewarded with a blank stare and, "what's in it?" Then with a shake of the head and "I don't know!" helped us to remain the only 'Fling' provider in town for the next 18 months before a slip-up allowed a can with label in tact to be purloined, exposing the deception and ending the monopoly.

Fearless (?) diver Charlie Pflueger, right, with giant
Green Moray eel later mounted at the Crow's Nest 1972

As we operated the Crow's Nest, we continued to add to our out island atmosphere with framed area maps and lots of mounted fish, including one 6' monster, green Moray Eel I shot while spear fishing (the eel had bent a spring steel 8' spear into a pretzel). Another gimmick that just happened, was collecting currency from the Bahamas and other countries around the world to thumbtack on the wall behind the bar. Before long, we had over a thousand dollars in bills climbing up the wall toward the ceiling. For additional character, I strung a fishing net from the ceiling over the bar area, where we would shoot champagne corks (banking many shots off the ceiling) into the net, along with wine corks thrown by hand. The joint was certainly island rustic.

After a few years, family demands dictated that this kind of lifestyle was becoming less attractive, so with heavy heart, I asked Stan to buy me out since I would be returning to Florida and utilize my license in the real estate business.

I think Stan was truly sorry to see me go, but agreed to buy me out. Wife Jeanne already fancied as 'Bahama Mama' replaced me as the manager... a job in which she excelled and I think enjoyed. The Crow's Nest was closed a few years later, when operating the business became more time consuming than Jeanne could commit.

When I returned to Florida and before I felt the need to plunge into my new proposed career in real estate, I decided to buy a new Mercedes Benz diesel from a Coral Gables dealer, for pickup at their factory at Stuttgart, Germany and tour Europe for three weeks with Jean.

It was a thrill inspecting the Mercedes factory, having lunch in their cafeteria and joining a factory mechanic to go over the car with us and explain all the operational idiosyncrasies. Early in the afternoon we drove to the fuel pumps and received a complimentary tank of diesel before driving on thru Austria, Italy and across France to Rotterdam where we put the car on a boat to England.

Looking back, the tour was going without incident, until I stopped at a service station in Nice, France to refuel. As I stood there with pump hose in hand, I could see a French chap jacking his old Peugeot down after a tire repair. Not an unusual sight, by any means, until the tire hit the ground... apparently the gears were in 'neutral,' causing the vehicle to adhere to the law of gravity and began its decent on the slightly sloping concrete towards the fuel pumps! As in slow motion, I watched in horror as the driverless Peugeot gained speed in a beeline toward my shinny new Mercedes.

Only a couple possible evasive actions flashed in my head... should I brace myself between the fuel pump and the oncoming vehicle? Nah, getting crushed wasn't that appealing, even to save the Mercedes... so I chose 'Curtain Number 2' and leaped aside as the Peugeot slammed into my beautiful baby... crumpling the right rear fender. I guess the good news was that I did not wind up in the local hospital, nor did the collision start a fire and burn down the gas station. The French car owner was shaken and apologized profusely, as I shouted profanities (little help in English) and threatened police action, until I pictured a long, drawn out suit, in France, trying to sue a Frenchman driving an old, beat up Peugeot.... no thanks... think I'll take my chance with my own insurance.

After a final trip to see Shakespeare's home at Stratford on Avon, we put the car on a trans-Atlantic freighter for the trip home. Enroute the Mercedes suffered another assault when some idiot dropped what looked like a gate barrier across the hood (or 'bonnet' if you're English) putting another dent in this once proud beauty. The good news was that the insurance company fixed the hood AND the bashed in fender, and I sold the car eleven months and 11,000 miles later and made a profit of $500.

Peace and Plenty Beach Inn

In 1989 Stan Benjamin, owner of Club Peace and Plenty, originally thought it would be profitable to build 16 residential units on two lots on the beach he bought years before from artist Bill Johnson. The property located a mile west of the Club, looked to be ideal to accommodate incoming U.S. Aerostat Balloon personnel. When we were advised that an Exumian, Sam Gray, had been awarded the contract, Stan suggested that we revise our thinking and build a 16 room resort instead, to compliment our existing hotel operation. One of the justifications was that we were often running full in the peak season.... another was that we could start accepting children under six that the Club prohibited. The deciding factor, however, was the possibility of offering an 'all inclusive' resort for our fishing operation.

Stan applied for the Bahamian Government's 'Hotel Encouragement Act' to help reduce the duty costs on materials and real estate taxes. When the architectural plans were ready, we applied for the necessary building permits, but ran into opposition from Ken and Harry Nixon who operated a rental complex across the street from our site. Their position was that Mt. Pleasant was a residential area and not commercial.

Our Attorney, Allan Benjamin, flew down from Nassau to assist us at the Commissioner's court to deal with the permit. The

Nixons' defended their position, but it was pointed out that they themselves, had broken whatever perceived zoning (there is no mandated zoning on Exuma) when they offered apartments for rent in their complex..

The final blow came when our attorney advised the court that the Peace and Plenty had an agreement with the Bahamian Government by way of the Hotel Encouragement Act. Once said, the Commissioner pounded his gavel and snorted "case dismissed!" and we all filed out. With the legal hurtles behind us, we hired an Exumian contractor, (who actually only supplied the labor, while we paid the payroll and building materials) and started trenching the foundation.

A few days later, I heard some of the local citizens in our bar grousing that "Stan Benjamin was buying up the island!"

This got me going.... and I was spitting fire when I blasted away with, "Guys, are you saying that you would rather have Stan take his money and build a hotel on another island or in another country? What about the 15 to 20 local jobs that will be created to operate it? You don't need the jobs here? What about the increase in visitors who will spend their money with our island taxi drivers, tour operators, boat rentals, restaurants, guides, stores and such? If this is not enough incentive to justify encouraging Stan to invest his money on Exuma.... I have a lot more thoughts on the subject!" There was dead silence in the bar, but I knew I scored some points and quieted this nonsense.

The construction phase was not text book! It seemed to drag on forever, as we watched in anguish for a total of 23 months and at one point Stan got so frustrated he told the contractor to get his ass on the roof with the roofers and finish the job... pronto!

We opened the Beach Inn on April 17, 1990, in time to welcome a full house for Regatta. A smooth opening was not in the cards however, and we were shocked to have a young, local guest blow his brains all over one of our new rooms, supposedly playing 'Russian Roulette'… a premise not entirely accepted by the community. In any event, we had to scrub and repaint the room in addition to taking a new, if slightly abused, mattress to the dump.

Since I was General Manager of both the 32 room Club Peace and Plenty and the new 16 room Beach Inn, Stan and I decided to hire a resident manager for the Club and move me into a new cottage at the Beach Inn. The thinking was that it was less demanding to manage the smaller resort considering I also had the responsibility of handling the liaison between Peace and Plenty Properties and the Bahamas Hotel Association and the Bahamas Out island Promotion Board. In addition, I had to deal with all the off island sales promotions which required three trips a year to Europe along with all the Western Hemisphere travel shows… lots of fun but time consuming.

Stan's first hire at the Club was a manager who's cluelessness was augmented by an assortment of character flaws, such as drinking and cohabitating with the female employees, to name a few of the choice ones.

One of his favorite tricks was to wander around the tables during the dinner hours with his empty wine glass in hand, only stopping to chat with guests that sported a bottle of wine on the table. His empty glass (it didn't matter if the table wine was white or red as long as it was available) usually triggered an invitation by the guest to join them in a drink. For those diners that were too preoccupied or insensitive to the manager's needs, he would casually reach over, take the bottle and pour himself a dollop, not missing a beat of the decoy chit-chat. This activity provided hours of amusement for Bob and me when dining at the Club.

Another source of amusement was watching his mood change during the course of the day. This mood swing was in direct correlation to the amount of vodka that remained in the 40 oz bottle stashed away in his room. Bob had tipped me off that he was having the room maid check the fluid level a few times during the day, while making up his room. It was a conversation piece for Bob any myself that we enjoyed on a daily basis.

Bob was working hard on developing our bonefishing business and had some excellent contacts. One of the prominent fishing video producers was Mark Sosin, who at the time boasted a popular show on ESPN. On his first production featuring our operation, he filmed a segment where he interviewed me on the front entrance discussing hotel amenities and the world class bonefishing available on the island.

I was certainly not shy and tried never to miss an opportunity to participate in a photo shoot... figuring I owed at least that much to my imaginary fans. Unfortunately, Mark had to call me later and apologize that my much anticipated cameo appearance on his show had to be left on the editing floor. It seemed that Jerome, our hotel maintenance man was bending over behind us repairing an electrical socket during the interview, while showing a large section of the crack of his rearend... mooning the audience over a pair of droopy drawers, giving new meaning to TV 'exposure'. We all had a good laugh, although my laugh was through tears of disappointment. I told Jerome he derailed my rise to stardom! Mark later made a few more programs and I did get my cameo appearance on national syndication, although I am still waiting to be discovered.

During the weekly cocktail party on the pool patio, Bob and I were chatting with Mark, when the manager tried to weasel into the converstation, angling for an introduction which had been studiously avoided. Ignored and with obvious pique, the manager slithered into the crowd and disappeared. Some days later when the owner was visiting the hotel, Stan called a managers meeting at which the manager complained that Bob and I refused to introduce him to Mark, a guest. This, he whined, was not in the spirit of the truce Stan imposed between the manager, Bob and me. The manager forcefully demanded, "I insist on knowing why you refused to introduce us?"

Bob hedged with, "I didn't think of it!"

Red faced, the manager was not prepared to leave it at that and insisted, "it was embarrassing! You saw me standing there waiting to meet the guy, but you ignored me and I want an explanation!"

With a shrug of his shoulders, Bob replied, "Since you won't let it alone... Mark told me to 'keep that little prick away from me!" So much for Bob's interpretation of 'diplomacy.'

This was not what the manager wanted to hear and sputtered with outrage! I was edging toward the door, while Stan looked like he had been kicked in the stomach. Obviously, he suddenly realized that his instructions to me of "you and Bob have to get along with the manager, or we might have to make some changes!'" crashed and burned.

The meeting broke up and at this point I figured Bob and I would have to 'get out of Dodge' pronto. When Bob and I were outside (Stan was still in the office no doubt, listening to more whining), he said not to worry, and we would laugh this guy out of town one day. As it turned out, Bob was right... the manager's incompetence and unsavory habits proved too much for Stan and we did get the last laugh as the ex-manager left town.

The resident manager's job turned into a revolving door at the Club... with few managers staying past the first year's contract. Put all the manager's faults together and they would outnumber the Chinese Army. A few had potential, but did not want to stay long enough to learn the ropes. The conventional thinking is that the Peace and Plenty is only a 32 room resort, located on a friendly tropical island, hence should be a breeze to manage... Wrong! There is quite a learning curve in dealing with employees... theft, purchasing of foodstuffs, liquor, maintenance of facilities, guest relations, sales promotion and more. All in an out island with no official assistant. Some job!

One of our managers was a self proclaimed, ex- chef to the King of Denmark. One afternoon Stan, wanting to see if he could actually cook, instructed him to cook the evening's meal for some 50 guests. He did not seem overly enthused, and as the busy, hot night in the kitchen dragged on, he turned to a sweat soaked basket case. When he finally finished the last diner and came out of the kitchen, Stan approached him with his hand out to compliment him on his efforts in the preparation of a decent meal. Apparently, the manager, still smarting from the beating he took in the hot kitchen, was not prepared to accept the tribute and refused to shake hands. I thought that this was not a great career move to slough off the boss and was not terribly surprised when his contract wasn't renewed. Where is Chef Boy-ar-dee when you need him?

Another manager received four flat tires on her car (unfortunately, my car was nearby and I got a couple flattened for good measure). In addition, a reported five death threats (a record, we think) over her year's employment, no doubt from her fans for perceived transgressions.

Once we had a tandem management team that seemed to work on shifts... she worked all day, while he marshaled his energy in order to be able to present himself at the bar at the stroke of 6:00 PM, for an evening of swilling vodka, one after another, until closing time. Kudos... for sharing the chores.

Even our staff was embarrassed when a manager, in an obvious effort to curry favor, had one of the waitresses take a daily full breakfast tray over to the Commissioner's next door office. It became so blatant that the Commissioner, coming under local criticism, had to cancel this delectable free dining accommodation.

One of our most controversial managers spent considerable time on the computer chatting up women far and wide... the more promising ones he invited to Exuma for a complimentary stay at the hotel. These lucky ones enjoyed intimate lobster dinners and unlimited cocktails at company expense in the manager's two bedroom apartment. Eventually, a compliant filtered down to Stan outlining some sort of nude 'name that tune' musical chairs game the manager and current girlfriend tried to get going with a couple of lady guests one night in his apartment. The manager at least had the good sense to move on to a better local job, sans the fancy lobster dinners, before the axe fell.

Before we move on, I have to remark on a 15 lb Barracuda that showed up at our Monday night cocktail party at our dock bar like clockwork. One night a guest pointed to the fish lurking close to the dock, seemly looking up like it was keen to join the group now crowded around the railing... oohing and awing!

It wasn't long before a half gnawed chicken wing from a guest's hor d'euoves plate plopped into the water next to the fish. With a lightening flash the Barracuda wolfed it down, bone and all and seemed to be asking for more. It was an idea whose time had come... the air filled with flying chicken wings (no chickens attached). The 'Cuda obliged with a dazzling display of slashing teeth and disappearing tid-bits. Once the fish had its fill, it slowly cruised back into the darkening bay.

Wow! I thought... pretty cool having a live Barracuda at your cocktail party (maybe a first?) and I wondered if it would survive a stomach full of bones? I shouldn't have given it any thought! We looked like a bunch of idiots naively lined up on the railing at the following Monday night's cocktail party, as if we had sent a personal invitation to a FISH!

We were working on our second libation, when I heard a murmur and could see a few of the guests pointing into the water. "I'll be damned!" one guest blurted, "There it is! It came back!" It was like Michael Jackson dropped in for a drink. All of a sudden the air was filled with food, arching into the bay and into the jaws of the 'Cuda, who in a flurry of activity, let nothing sink more than a few inches. Apparently, chicken bones are not fatal to a large Barracuda and when it had its fill, back into the bay it went.

We were amazed to see the fish return every Monday night at cocktail hour for another couple of weeks to 'wow' our guests (and myself). Of course, one night it did not come, nor ever again could we limber up our 'chicken wing throwing arms'. We never knew if the accumulation of bones finally killed the poor guy, someone caught it or it just got bored with our cocktail parties... but it was fantastic while it lasted... the real question for me however, was... how did that fish know to show up on Monday nights? Sadly, a mystery never solved.

I often bragged that our hotels' had low incidents of missing items from guest rooms. Our maids were of the highest integrity and prided themselves on a spotless record. One day a repeat guest due to return to the States that day, complained that he had been robbed of his wallet containing some $500 in fifty dollar bills and three credit cards, drivers license and a packaged condom (there seemed to be the real pity).

As his story infolded, he had partied late the night before, paid his bar tab from the contents of his wallet, gone to his room, put his wallet on the dresser and went to bed. He was certain that after he went to sleep (passed out?), someone must have slipped in through the unlocked patio doors and stolen the wallet.

I alerted the police who checked out some of the 'usual suspects' to no avail. As he was leaving that afternoon, I assured him that I would contact him in New Jersey and mail the wallet back when we located it... as I was sure we would.

A few weeks later, one of our maids came into my office and handed me a well worn wallet. When I checked it out there was a few fifty dollar bills and all the credit cards and drivers license as advised... I looked at the smiling maid and asked her, "Where in the world did you find it? It's been missing for weeks?"

"Well sir, when I checked the table lamp from the entrance switch, the bulb blew... so I got a new one and reached into the shade to unscrew the burnt out one and felt the wallet balanced on the metal struts that hold the shade," she revealed, proud of finding the much discussed missing wallet. What a hell'va hiding place I thought, with envy.

I couldn't wait to call the guest telling him where we found it, "I told you we would find your wallet! It was where you stashed it when you staggered back to you room after your grand going home party in bar." He laughed when I told him where it was found, denied remembering anything and apologized for creating all that hub-bub. My parting shot was, "I told you we'd find it!"

It's a Spaghetti World

In 1971 while waiting for my work permit to start operating the Crow's Nest Bar and Restaurant Stan Benjamin and I set up in George Town, Joan and I decided to take the opportunity to go on vacation. We thought that since son Paul was almost ten and old enough to profit from a five weeks trip around the world, we would take him with us. He was given a mandate to keep a daily activity diary (which he still has) that would require an in-depth study of some of the world's wonders.

The cost of such a trip would normally be very expensive, but when we factored in Joan's free ($30. a ticket for tax) employee and family fare on Pan American Airways, along with 50% airline employee discounts at Pan Am's Intercontential Hotels and Hilton Hotels, world wide, the trip was proclaimed doable.

Our next hurdle was planning the itinerary. Since Joan was living in Montego Bay, Jamaica with Paul, I would fly to MoBay and we would leave from there and fly to New York. Since we were going completely around the world, we could go either eastbound or westbound from Pan Am's Main Base in New York.

With almost free airline tickets, it was exciting to study the world map and know you could go anywhere you felt like going. Finally, after considerable yakking, we decided to go toward the orient and return from Europe. We booked our tickets from New York, with the first stop slated for Fairbanks Alaska, then on to Tokyo, Hong Kong, Bangkok, New Delhi, Bruit, Lebanon, Istanbul, Turkey, London and back to New York and Montego Bay, Phew! An exhausting but pluse hammering program!

Our flight from Montego Bay to New York was on Pan Am's new 747. We were kindly upgraded to First Class and enjoyed the outstanding flight service while sampling the drink and snack bar in the aircraft's spacious upstairs lounge.

After an overnight in the airport area, we boarded our flight for the first leg.... New York to Fairbanks, Alaska. As mentioned, I just missed being stationed in Alaska in the Air Force during the Korean War and always waned to see it. We rented a car and drove around the area including a visit to the University of Alaska, a carnival attraction, and took a turn at panning gold from some of the old river alluvial deposits from 1920's mining barge efforts. We did come up with a few grams of flake gold, but I guess panning gold from 1920's spillage would be a tough way to make a living. Maybe it might be worth another look, with gold at over a thousand dollars an ounce.

After a couple days being jolted daily by static electricity from the hotel door knob (leather soled shoes schlepping across a nappy carpet and grabbing a brass door knob in the far North, was a replacement formula for Brill Cream as a hair straightener), I was ready to push on to Tokyo. At the airport I was amazed by the huge mounted Grizzly Bear lofting over the check-in area. It stood over 14' on its hind legs, with bared fangs and presenting a solid argument for skipping the nature hike without a National Guard escort.

Checking with the Pan Am desk at the Tokyo airport we lucked out with an employee discount at the fabulous and just completed New Otani Hotel in the central hotel area. It boasted a wonderful full scale Japanese Garden with meandering waterways full of colorful carp and quaint oriental style bridges and foliage. Sitting down to dinner in the very opulent dining room we studied the cosmopolitan menu. It didn't take Paul long to draw a bead on the Italian section and select Spaghetti and Meatball, distaining the more exotic offerings of a star rated restaurant. Since it was one of the less expensive dishes on the menu, my suggestion to "order something interesting such as the Squid!" carried little conviction. When Paul polished off a huge plate of the pasta, antipasto and breadsticks, I knew we were on to a good thing that was sure to save a ton of dining expense over the course of the trip. No risky local cuisine for our boy!

We spent five days in Japan, marveling over the religious shrines and Japanese architecture. On the city tour we stopped at the original cultured pearl store opened by the inventor of the procedure, Mikimoto Kokichi, (where all city tours end up, no doubt, for their cut of the tourist dollar), and spent an hour driving around the Emperor's palace (aptly named 'Kyujo' which literally and conveniently means 'Emperor's Palace'). It was built around the 1850's in a large park area in the Chiyoda area of Tokyo. During the tour, I kept looking for Mr. Moto and the Japanese motion picture sleuth's old Tokyo neighborhood from his many 1930's movies, but it's probably still on the Warner's Brothers back lot!

We also stopped to view the city from the huge Eiffel Tower replica built in 1958, featuring a stunning view of the city all the way to the snow-capped symbol of Japan, Mt. Fiji. The tower is the tallest self-supporting steel tower in the world at 333 meters and weighting 4,000 tons, while the Paris tower is 320 meters and heavier at 7,000 tons.

We dedicated one day to visit Mt. Fiji, with a fascinating stop for lunch at the famous Bonsai Tree Park, built after the 1920's devastating earthquake. The park boasted the best collection of miniature trees and landscaping in the world, located in Northeast Tokyo enroute to the mountain. I watched with interest, as a gardener carefully pruned a fully grown cherry tree that seemed less than 4' high. Astounding!

Advertised as the 'freshest sushi in the world,' we took a taxi to 'Taukyi Fish Market' for a sample. The open air facility, built in the 1500's, operated a 24 hour retail and wholesale market and offered a mind-boggling variety of fresh seafood. We were not much for raw fish, but it was good and undoubtedly fresh! We did, however, draw the line on sea urchin!

My return to Hong Kong after a 20 year hiatus was startling. The massive urban development was a thing of wonder. We checked into the centrally located Hilton Hotel and immediately booked a tour on the hydrofoil to Portuguese Macao. We had lunch at a huge hotel and gambling casino before making our way to a hilltop observatory where we could see the Red Chinese mainland (a big deal in those days).

Back in Hong Kong, I took Joan and Paul to see the Tiger Baum Gardens I had previously enjoyed visiting... with the skinny master judging the eternal resting place of the dead after a series of statues depicting the pitfalls of life. No trip to Hong Kong is complete without taking the trolley car to Victoria Peak for a fantastic view of the entire area. Another must is riding one of the Star Ferry boats across the bay of Kowloon. Star Ferry service started operation in 1898 and has been moving masses of people, cheaply, since that time, for the ten minute trip across the bay.

We avoided sampling the wares of the open air food vendors, as popular as they seemed to be with the local citizens, in deference to the avoidance of a stomach disaster. We limited our out of the hotel dining to restaurants such as the famous 'Jimmy's Kitchen,' a short walk from the hotel. Thirty years later, I recommended Jimmy's to friends that were moving to Hong Kong and found the restaurant still going strong.

Our next stop was Bangkok, Thailand and the President Hotel. Bangkok is a wonderful destination that gave us the opportunity to take a tour on riverboats to visit the numerous shrines, including the famous golden 'Sleeping Buda'. We were amazed to observe the ramshackle houses on stilts along the river with hordes of children swimming in a river so muddy that you're not sure its not solid mud. A day tour to see the elephants at a working timber sawmill and an evening enjoying a Thai dinner complete with dancers wearing traditional costumes, were the highlights. Of course, no stopover was complete with out buying a souvenir or two. I bought a delightful Thai village scene painting, which still brings me pleasure from its perch in my Bahamas house..

New Delhi was looked at with anticipation, not only for its historical significance but as the gateway to one of the Wonders of the World, the Taj Mahal, in the city of Agra, some 203 kilometers to the south. We hired an air conditioned, chauffeured car and marveled at the vast numbers of dust covered pedestrian traffic shuffling along the highway in stifling heat. Once in Agra, we were treated to the famous reflecting pond view of the Taj as we walked to the main building. The Taj was built in 17 years from 1633 using 20,000 workers, by Shahjahan (King of the World) in memory of his beloved wife Mumtaz Mahal who died at age thirty-nine in childbirth. Lunch in Agra at the local hotel was splendid, with a white gloved waiter behind every chair and all for the cost of under $2.00 per person.. Such a deal! On the way back we got a taste of the dusty hell along the roadway when our car's air conditioner broke down. We shared a collective sigh of relief walking into the lobby of the deluxe Oberoi (royal) Intercontinental Hotel and into a blast of artic air conditioning.

During a city tour, we had the chance to see the massive limestone 'Red Fort' build 1638-48 as a symbol of Mughal power and went back that night for a wonderful Light and Sound show.

We arrived at the New Delhi airport and the Pan Am Traffic Counter at 4:40 AM for our flight to Beirut, Lebanon. They told us the flight was heavily booked and it looked like we may be off loaded and required to go back to the hotel for another try the following morning. When you're all set to go, the prospect of hanging around for another day and another 2:30 AM wake up call was not too attractive. Fortunately, seats were available in First Class and we were kindly up-graded and allowed to fly.

An enroute scheduled stop in Tehran, Iran sent another spear of anxiety through us when threatened with another off-loading due to an anticipated full flight. We remained on the aircraft during the stop and had another reprieve when a group no-showed and we were once again allowed to continue. As I look back, it might have been a blessing to be off-loaded for a couple of days to see this controversial city when it was possible for Americans to visit.

Arriving in Beirut, Pearl (also called the Paris) of the Middle East and home of American University, was a charming city in 1971. The Inter-Continental Phoenica Hotel offered deluxe accommodations (later a shattered hulk in the civil war but rebuilt) for a very comfortable base of operations. Since we only had a few days in Beirut, we could only allocate one day to either visit Damascus, Syria or an all day trip to see the ancient Cedars of Lebanon, 120 km away in the western mountains (the entire country only covers 250 by 50 km). We decided on taking the bus tour to take a look at the remaining 400 Cedar trees, although touring the Syrian capital was also an attractive option.

We had lunch in the visitor complex at 2,000' of elevation, in the park created to protect and display these few remaining giant, 1500 year old trees. The original vast forest of Cedars was depleted over the years by the Phoenicians, Greeks and Egyptians, throughout the centuries for homes, temples, sarcophagas and galleys.

I barely made it back to the hotel before I had a agonizing bout of stomach virus that lasted 24 hours, caused by a lamb dinner I had in one of the local ethnic restaurants the night before. Neither Paul nor Joan had a problem, so I guess the Spaghetti Paul was wolfing down not only saved money but saved us a lot of agravation since there was only one bathroom in our suite.

Our next stop was Istanbul, Turkey, the only city spanning two continents (Europe and Asia), where we booked into our old favorite Hilton Chain Hotel overlooking the Bosphorus River. Istanbul was originally named Constantinople when it was the capital of the Roman Empire and Europe's wealthiest metropolis.

Some of the outstanding sights we saw were the Blue Mosque with its six towering minarets and 260 windows. This edifice is one of the most famous monuments in Turkey and the Islamic world. We had lunch (would you believe I was able to have a hot dog) in an outdoor restaurant, a few hundred yards from the Mosque on a lovely, sunny afternoon.

Another famous monument, the Hagri Sophia Church, was built in the 6th Century by Emperor Justinian and was one of the largest basilicas in the Christian world. Today it is one of the most magnificent museums anywhere. We were there when they were refurbishing and had scaffolding over 200' to the ceiling in its vast main hall.

Paul and I had a great photo taken posing on each side of the fabulous 'Blue Diamond' exhibit in the Topkapi Palace Museum, when we spent almost a day wondering through its vast halls. There was a popular motion picture 'Topkapi' that will always stick in my mind, reminding me of this wonderful experience.

A trip through the Grand Bazaar, covering some 58 streets and 4,000 shops, was a shopper's delight. Built in the 14th Century, it is one of the worlds (seems like most of the monuments in Istanbul is labeled with the 'world's' biggest, oldest, largest or most important tag.) largest covered markets.

Our final stop was a Bosphorus Waterway cruise featuring the famous (again another well used word) Dolmabahce Palace, the last Ottoman Sultan's residence and Istanbul's largest palace..... The Beylerbeyi, the last stop on the cruise, was the most elegant Ottoman Palace, constructed in 1861-65. At this juncture, we had the chance to walk across the bridge over the Bosphorus, separating the two continents, which provided a thrilling conclusion to a destination full of historical wonders.

It was during dinner at the Istanbul Hilton on our first night, that Paul's sophisticated palate was finally de-railed, when his 'staple of life,' spaghetti, was too liberally doused with raw garlic and he received an upset stomach for his trouble! Goodbye to Spaghetti dinners and hello to expensive international cuisine for the rest of the trip....but, in any event, he had a good run!

London was our last stop before flying back to New York and Montego Bay. My first trip to London was in 1954, while Joan spent months there with her mother in 1939, as the war in Europe started. For Paul however, it was his first of many visits to this magnificient mega-city. We cherish the many pictures of Paul as a lad on London and Tower Bridges, at St. Paul's Cathedral, West Minister Abbey, London Zoo, the Museum of Natural History, the National Gallery and Buckingham Palace. London was a fitting final stop on a once in a lifetime trip.

We were happy to have had many trips courtesy of Pan Am, before and during Paul's college years at Tulane University where he obtained a Bachelor of Science Degree (Suma Cum Laude) and remained for many more years studying for his Medical Degree and Orthopedic Surgeon designation.

Like the old saying, 'all good things come to an end!,' so did all the unlimited free travel on Pan Am, when they went out of business a day after we returned from attending the World Travel Market in London in 1991. This was obviously a big blow, but at least we were not stranded somewhere and fumbling for an airline seat.... one we would have (hold your breath) to actually pay for.

The Land Baron

After I sold my share of the Crow's Nest in Exuma to Stan Benjamin and his wife Jeanne, and upon my return from a vacation in Europe late '73 I enrolled at Bert Rodgers School of Real Estate in Miami in order to take the Florida Broker's Exam.

When walking out of the broker's exam, I was convinced that I had not only flunked Florida's newly required and devised exam, but I had miserably failed it. Many of the questions on the exam I had never seen before although I attended the last two classes specifically geared with this test in mind. When I received word that I had a 'pass', I couldn't believe it but figured the grading must have been on the curve. One of my classmates later said he heard that only a portion of the subject was covered in class, resulting in many of the blank looks around the some hundreds of Salesmen taking the exam. I never was sure of this was the case, but neither did I have any further interest in finding out.

Stan Benjamin and I stayed in touch and when I needed backing to open a real estate office in Coral Gables, Florida, he came to my aid (once again) and invested in Out Islands Unlimited.

During the time I was working the island property market, I got friendly with Jess and Margaret Rice, who were operating an acreage development near Wildwood, Florida, and some 300 miles north of

Miami in a growing Central Florida. With a handshake, I started finding prospective buyers in the South Florida area, and enjoyed the weekend automobile trips 'upstate in the country!'

After a year or so of working with the Rices,'Margaret called and said, "Charlie, we we're getting ready to open a new project of 1,930 rolling acres in the Dunnellon, Florida area near the famous 'Rainbow River'. Now Jess told me he is going to Louisiana to put the final touches on his new invention, 'a portable steam pressure cleaner' and market it all over the country! I told him that if he goes we are going to have to sell the project and let someone else develop it, since I don't feel well enough to do it myself, even with my assistant, Vicky Nolte."

"Margaret, it's been nice working with you and Jess and I'll be sorry to see it end!"

"Charlie, Jess and I thought that since you enjoy country land sales, you might want to get some backing and take over the project. We don't need cash down for our interest and would be willing to take a second mortgage payable from the individual sales as they come in. I also need to pay Vicky her share with a third mortgage payable on sales. Are you interested and can you raise a little cash," she asked?

I got back to her a few days later after agreeing with (you know who to the rescue....again) Stan that we would take a look at the parcel and details of the deal. Excitement at the prospect of my own development would be an understatement and I was shortly on the road to Dunelleon.

This beautiful acreage had been a working cattle ranch until the elderly owner passed away creating a tax problem for the son and heir. The property fronted a mile of spring fed pond, full of large mouth bass and more acreage fronting on Big Lake Bonable and Little Lake Bonable with overlooking hills up to 98 feet. I contacted Stan and a few of his cronies form Cleveland with a 'thumbs up,'...

set up a corporation and signed the contract to purchase the deal for $1,500,000.

We followed the original developer's modus operandi and used a method called 'double escrowing', whereby we put a token amount down on a piece of property, giving us the right to access the acreage to survey and plat into parcels. When we closed with the full 20% down payment, we also receive a fee simple deed (property released to us free and clear in lieu of the down payment) for a pre-agreed parcel of the subject land. This released parcel contained a number of previously surveyed plots which had been pre-sold (at a discount) with deposits held by the title company in escrow. At the closing of the main property, the title company would take the deposited funds, both our original token deposit and the deposits in escrow from the early purchasers and pay the full 20% deposit to the original land owner, obtaining the agreed releases, pass title with a mortgage to us and pass title to the individual buyers from the released parcel. Did you get that? It sounds complicated but it works well and the main advantage is that you can close on a large piece of land with very little of your own money.

This first effort, Lake Bonable Estates, went very well and is now an area of mostly 20 acre mini-ranches on high, rolling land ideal for raising livestock and kids. My partner in the real estate sales end was Florida Broker Vicky Nolte and her husband Joe, who was very handy mechanically and good with road grading equipment. When we finished the Lake Bonable project the Noltes' and I bought 720 acres we cut up in sections (Victoria Acres after Vicky and Chris Acres, after my son Christopher), put in county approved limerock roads and sold it all in 5 acre parcels.

One of our friends, originally a biker bar owner from south Florida, who dabbled in the buying and reselling a plethora of inexpensive residential lots in the Dunnellon area, brought us a 240 acre deal near the Levy County seat of Bronson. The land was a square piece with a road on all sides making it easy to cut in 20 acre tracts (20 acre tracts did not require official roads thereby making it fast and cheap to develop). We called this one 'Flying C ranch' for our partner Bill Cox. This also sold out rapidly.

Happy, if not flushed with our success, Vicky and I moved on to 'North Star Ranch' of some five hundred plus acres, also in twenty acre tracts requiring only road right of ways with a little limerock over the sandy soil. No problem selling this one out either.

Riding a wave of winners, we felt infallible when we bought a strip of lovely, high rolling land along a paved Florida highway in Levy County, and had it surveyed into 8 lots along the road. Again, no road work required and all looked rosy until we had unusual resistance from the prospects we showed the property. After only one sale in the three months we were in escrow, we finally were clued in that a major county dump a short way behind the property was the sale-killing culprit. My partner and I knew there was a dump there as evidenced by a huge sign along the highway but we figured that it was far enough away that no smell emanated from the land fill, or moving equipment noise. What the hell could trigger this lack of response? Finally, I pinned down one of the prospects who originally loved the property but in the final analysis refused to buy and he unlocked the mystery by telling us, "I loved the land and would have bought it except for the county dump!"

I was taken back and expressed my opinion that the dump was far enough away to preclude noise or odor and therefore did not seem to represent a deterrent. He explained, "Good enough thinking, but you needed to go one step further and take into account that all sort of nasty stuff seeps into the ground from a land fill and into the aquifer with a potential to poison the water supply for a long way!" Since we were in a rural area with only well water available, we had over looked this serious issue and wound up paying the original landowner over $10,000 to cancel the deal. Shoulda been smarter!

Vicky and I bought a strip of commercial land along the main road in Dunnellon across the street from Sun Bank and sold a lot to Dr. Fox for a vet office. We then built some rental offices along with a bar and restaurant we opened ourselves (but soon sold) and our real estate office. We eventually sold the entire complex and were glad to get out of it.

Another time we bought a piece of land where two major highways merged a little north of Dunnellon (near where Wal-Mart built) and promptly sold the converging parcel for a 7/11 type of convenience store and gas pumps. On another part of the parcel, we started a mobile home sales business, carrying four of the major lines manufactured in Florida and Georgia. This did not turn out to be overly profitable and we finally sold the display models, paid off our lien holder and sold the property for the construction of a church.

Changing Florida real estate developer laws and requirements was making it more difficult in our kind of business, so when Stan called from the Bahamas in 1983 and asked me to come down and manage the hotel for four months (naturally, it wound up 6 months). I talked it over with Jean and son Christopher who was a sophomore at Dunnellon High, and of course, with Vicky, who would have to carry the brunt of running the real estate company. I guess they did not mind a little break from me and all agreed to hold down the fort, while I helped Stan out and got back to my beloved islands.

It seems that Stan had an English manager who did not see eye to eye with him and it came to a head one day when the manager said he did not trust Stan (not a sound job security move) and that was that! The main problem for Stan was that he was leaving to join his wife Jeanne on a around the world cruise and needed someone in the managers seat that hopefully understood the business and quick!

A few days later, on Christmas Eve, while walking down Bay Street in Nassau enroute the next morning to Exuma, I ran into old friend Bill Johnson, a talented American artist who once lived in George Town. He invited me home with him to have a drink and dinner. His mother, Lady Christie, was married to Bahamas real estate tycoon, Sir Harold Christie and resided in Nassau, where Bill was temporarily staying. We had a great evening renewing our acquaintance and chatting with Sir Harold, who remembered me from the days he flew into George Town on his sea plane during his real estate activities. On an interesting side note... when Sir Harry Oaks, the Canadian millionaire, was murdered in Nassau on July 8, 1943, Sir Harold, a friend, was over nighting at the Oaks mansion and discovered the partially burned body. This infamous Bahamian case was never solved.

It was great to be back at the Peace and Plenty where one of my first duties was to wear a snoopy-dog like baseball cap, have dinner with a group of hotel guests calling their informal club... 'Yellow Dogs,' play a kazoo and sing some song about a 'yella dog.' It was a little embarrassing, but what the hell... I've done worse stupidity. The members consisted of a group of Canadian and American winter visitors that fancied themselves as 'mad caps.' They had a large, stuffed yellow dog (complete with sunglasses) sitting at the table and a yellow dog flag on the flag staff (thankfully under the Bahamian flag!). Dinner was not too bad, but marching thru the hotel, playing the kazoo was a little much!

Finally, Stan returned from the cruise and asked me to stay a couple of months more until an Exumian lad he sent to Florida International University graduated with a Masters in Hospitality and returned to take over as manager. Return he did around the end of March, and took over the late evening shift while I opened early. All seemed to go well with our few months together and I left on Stan's Leer Jet (he had an air ambulance service out of Ft. Lauderdale) on crystal clear day May 1, 1984. It was the most spectacular high level view of almost the entire 700 Bahamian Islands one could imagine... from Grand Bahama to the North to Mayaguana to the south. Amazing!

Once back in central Florida I soon became restless and lost interest in doing additional land development projects. In November

1986 the phone rang and it was Stan inquiring if I might be interested in returning to the hotel for another stint at managing the place while he went on another around the world cruise? I couldn't help quipping, "don't tell me! You fired the manager! Is firing the manager a requirement of the cruise line?"

Stan explained that the young man he sent through FIU and whom I installed as manager had a problem with drug abuse and was reluctant to get out of bed everyday until after lunch. Not a great quality for a hotel manager, particularly in a small resort that required liberal 'hands on' participation by the manager.

I didn't realize it at the time, but I was embarking on another career chapter at the age of 55 and was glad to be back. To spice up my return, I met a lovely lady guest of the hotel in her mid-forties and after asking her to dance, we developed an attraction. She was of medium height, blonde, slim and beautiful in a Doris Day type look. The next morning we took the boat and went for a spin around Crab Cay, where she suggested a swim. I gave her a goofy, "we don't have suits!" I guess I was temporarily insane.

I recovered quickly by stopping the boat in a quiet cove and trying to beat her stripping off. She had a well toned body, but the one thing that stands out over these many years was her strawberry blonde public hair trimmed in the shape of a heart! She said she had electrolysis to shape it. It wasn't Valentine's Day, but you couldn't prove it by me.

It's an Ill Wind!

Exuma managed to avoid hurricanes that plagued the Caribbean and Florida since the Spanish were shipping gold out of Cuba 500 years ago. Prior to Lilly in 1996, the last storm that devastated the area was in 1926, when a hurricane demolished most of the old plantation houses, leaving only a few such as the 'Hermitage' at Williamstown, Little Exuma still standing. In August and September (the worst months) hurricanes tend to edge along the northern Caribbean islands of Puerto Rico and Hispaniola, seemingly to head directly for the southeastern Bahama archipelago and towards Exuma. One of the highest velocities ever recorded in a hurricane in the Western Hemisphere was 'Andrew' that skirted the Exumas' and slammed into northern Eleuthera and Harbour Island with winds clocked at 212 MPH by a British navel ship offshore.

One of the proposed reasons for this safety zone is credited to the shallow waters of the Little Bahama Banks, said to restrict the gathering of sufficient warm water needed to fuel hurricanes. This lack of fuel dictates storm movement toward deeper water to the north of Exuma that tends to provide the energy to steer the storm in a northerly direction. True or not, Exuma has had surprisingly few of these dangerous cyclones over the years.

It was fairly late in the year, October, when a storm in the Yucatan area was named Lilly. Little attention was given to it as it moved northward toward the western side of Cuba, packing winds of over 100 MPH. Since Exuma is rarely threatened by these punishing winds, particularly this late in the season, life at the Peace and Plenty, closed for a month's refurbishing, moved ahead. The Beach Inn had 14 out of 16 rooms occupied with vacationers who either for the lack of information or apathy continued their boating, beaching and fishing with no thought of an urgent need to flee to safe environs.

On October 18th, I called Bob Hyde my partner at the Bonefish Lodge who was following Lilly on the computer and advised, "this is a pretty strong but small hurricane that's moving over Cuba, so we need to keep an eye on it."

"I understood it was moving northward over Cuba, so shouldn't we be well to the east," I asked?

"Charlie, if that storm takes a hard right after it clears Cuba, we'll be dead in its path!"

I thought this was a very unlikely scenario, but went to bed around nine that night, figuring I had time to do some boarding up the next morning if it looked imminent. What we didn't know was Lilly had increased its ground speed to 26 MPH, moving twice as fast as previously reported, as it made that dreaded easterly turn, roaring in from the south side of Exuma.

A little after ten that evening, I was awakened by the wind rattling the shutters and when I looked out of the unprotected 8' sliding glass doors toward the pool, a howling gale had already bent the palm trees in the patio area almost in half. I raced to the front door of the upstairs apartment, but when I tried to open the door to scamper downstairs to a more secure shelter, I could feel the wind trying to wretch the door out of my grasp. I quickly decided to re-bolt the door and forget about trying to get out of the apartment, since I was sure at this point that the high wind would take the door and me with it flying into the turbulent night sky.

My portable radio reported that the sustained winds were over 100 MPH, with guests of 130, which did not give me a lot of confidence trapped on the second floor of a building well over 100 years old. Walking by the bowed-in sliding glass doors, I knew if they shattered in the heavy wind and rain, I would be picking glass out of my rear end for some time to come. Looking for a safer place, I grabbed a few pillows and went into the windowless laundry room and hunkered down (read... holding on the washing machine with one hand and sucking my thumb and whimpering with the other) to ride it out!

Around one in the morning, the whole building was rumbling and the noise of what sounded like a jet engine screamed in my ears. Momentarily freeing my death grip on the washing machine, I dialed channel 16 on my hand held VHF, a station normally monitored for general information and put out a shaky request for anyone that might have current information on Lilly. With relief I fielded a return call from the George Town police next door to the hotel, who answered with, "headquarters in Nassau advises that it looks like the eye will pass over us around 3 AM, when the wind will calm down and you'll be able to get out of the exposed upstairs." I thanked the officer for the news and stepped up my prayer program.

As predicted, the wind fell off to around ten MPH, at which I wasted no time getting my office keys and dash down the stairs right into a huge bougainvillea bush blocking the exit to the back area of the kitchen. Frantically, I weaved my way thru its long thorned branches, finally breaking free only to fall into three feet of backed up storm water in the garbage area, before I could get into the main building and the safety of the office.

In a few minutes Lilly came roaring back in all her fury to take another whack at me. This time it didn't seem so bad, once out of the shaky second floor. I actually fell into an exhausted sleep, waking after seven o'clock with a diminished wind, little rain and my first chance to review the damage to our self insured property.

A couple of large Tamarind trees near the laundry had gone down, along with the two coconut trees... one laying on the pool patio and the other with the entire top blown off (no surprise here after Richard's ministrations) and laying on the porch of upstairs room 8. Wave action on Elizabeth Harbor had knocked the planks off our dock, leaving only the upright piers still standing. All in all, we suffered little actual damage.

The Beach Inn, a mile to the west, also fared well with only one huge coconut tree that slammed into the second story roof sofitt. The Bonefish Lodge, 10 miles to the southeast at the bridge to Little Exuma, had considerable water damage in the rooms and main building and a huge loss of frozen lobster tails purchased for the coming season, when our outside freezer blew away. The tails were in 40 lb bags, most of which were washed into our boat dockage bay, but were not visible in time to be salvaged due to the murky water. Our final loss on all three properties was not crippling.

If there was a silver lining to this storm, it was that no one was killed, although a few local folks, including a pregnant lady on Harry Cay, Little Exuma, had to hold on to the tie beam of their roofless home for hours as the on rushing sea surged to over 12'.

A few days of fallen tree cleanup, finding and refastening dock planks, fishing out all the patio tables and chairs we threw into the pool for safe keeping, and it was hard to believe the Peace and Plenty had just suffered a major hurricane.

The Beach Inn had only minor sofitt damage… repaired in a few hours. The leaning coconut tree was pulled to an upright position and re-set itself. The room guests fared well and were pleased when the Inn's close proximity to Bahamas Electric's generators guaranteed an early return of power.

The Bonefish Lodge probably took more of a hit than the other two properties, mostly as a result of flooding rather than wind damage. By December, the Lodge was back in business and ready for another stellar winter fishing season.

The Shark Lady

For much of the forty plus years I worked with the Peace and Plenty Hotel group, I was friendly with a rough and tough, but charming woman called the 'Shark Lady.'

What in the world is a 'Shark Lady?' I knew, of course, what a shark was... and had little doubt of what a lady was... however, initially, I was baffled on what a 'Shark Lady' might be.

Gloria Patience was born on Hog Cay, the closest island southeast of Little Exuma, in the early 1920's, of Caucasian parents. Gloria spent her young adulthood in the thriving Bahamian capitol of Nassau, training as a masseuse, utilizing her sturdy frame and strong arms. While chatting, Gloria told me she loved giving massages and attended many clients staying in the major hotels, including celebrities, famous actors and public figures.

Later in life and with her children grown, she met George Patience, an ex-pat from the U.K. and a hotel maintenance chief. They fell in love, married and soon felt the allure of returning to Little Exuma to take up residence in Gloria's family home in the settlement of the 'Ferry.' The Ferry was named for the hand pulled, flat bottomed boat used to provide access across the cut from Little Exuma to Great Exuma. The ribs of the old ferry are still visible, lying in a few feet of water on the Great Exuma side next to the one lane bridge built in 1963, which rendered the ferry obsolete.

An enterprising Gloria soon converted the large front room of their house into a souvenir shop, offering various old Bahamian artifacts, bric-a-brac, hand-crafted jewelry, and (here it comes!) a wide selection of shark teeth and shark teeth necklaces. Gloria then explained how she got the 'Shark Lady' moniker... "When the word got out that I took my Boston Whaler skiff out into Exume Sound (with depths to 6,000 feet) and used a heavy hand line to hook huge sharks... some as long as the boat... bring them in and pump a couple of shots from my .38 pistol in their heads, tether them to the boat and slowly motor thru the cut and around to my dock... it didn't take too long before some fool writer came up the name."

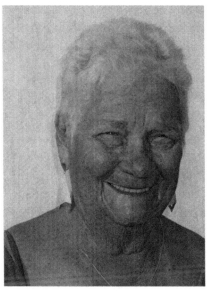

Gloria Patience,
'The Shark Lady'

She continued with, "Once at the dock, I had to take the jaw and teeth out to sell in the shop and then cut up the carcass for food... you know, shark is very good to eat... no bones and nice, flaky white meat."

"I would then have to clean the teeth and make what ever jewelry that seemed popular for sale. The whole jaw, with teeth in place was also a good seller!" At this point, I had a mental picture of this lady, in a small boat on a rough sea, spray flying and whose

309

muscled arms straining against a heavy hand line, pulling against a hundred or more pound vicious shark...what a painting that would make.

One idiosyncrasy she had was never wearing shoes! No... Not sneakers, nor boots, nor clogs... Nothing with a sole. Gloria went barefooted ALL the time, with the only concession to dress-up requirements... a beaded string from big toe around her ankle. I understand that while invited on a trip to Sweden by one of her visitor friends, she somehow managed to go bare-footed in the extreme Scandinavian winter weather to the utter amazement of the local citizenry.

Now, that's holding the line!

During one of our annual Bahamas Bonefish Bonanza fishing tournaments we were missing a guide; this disturbing last minute situation was solved when Gloria kindly volunteered.

Pleased, but puzzled that Gloria had the expertise to operate as a professional bonefish guide, I said, "I didn't know you were a bonefish guide."

She didn't blink an eye, "I've caught more bonefish than you've ever seen, old cock!"

This year I was teamed up with George Hommel for the three day tournament (George usually fished with Ted Williams who was unable to attend this year). The first day we drew one of the best professional guides in Exuma and as a consequence caught and released 37 bonefish for the tournament lead. Happiness abounded in the bar that evening as we crowed our success!

When we drew for guides on the second day, we pulled Gloria's name out of the hat.. Still riding the previous day's euphoria, we figured we were unbeatable, no matter who was guiding us. We were soon to be shattered on the broken dreams of competitive bonefishing!

Gloria, with a passing knowledge of the area (her main expertise was more to the south off Little Exuma), tried a number of various coves and bay with no results... I observed, that when fishing technique required the guide to quietly pole the skiff in deference to the easily spooked bonefish, Gloria, clad in a 'bathing costume' would jump out of the boat, grab the bow line and noisily pull us through the water... much like Humphrey Bogart in the 'African Queen.' As you might glean, we did not sneak-up on a single fish.

We caught nothing that day and subsequently watched our first day lead dwindle to an ultimate, ignominious third place finish..... What we did gain from that day on the water with Guide Gloria, was a wonderful experience that I wouldn't trade for a hundred first place trophies! We went from whining over the lack of fish to howling with laughter and rapt fascination, listening to Gloria's outrageous stories of her past exploits. George and I had to take a back seat in the swearing department and when having to tinkle, we discretely lofted a stream from the stern while Gloria did her impression of Bogart off the bow......That day give credence to the old adage of 'don't ask how many fish we caught... but ask if we had a good day!' And let me tell you we HAD a good day.... one that would stay in my memory long past a rusting trophy gathering dust on a neglected shelf. Looking back some thirty years, this day with Gloria was a absolute delight and the memory highly cherished.

During these years, we sponsored many fishing tournaments, writers' workshops, various magazine articles and such, on the hotel activities, alluring powder sand beaches, and the like. When the writers and video professionals arrived in Exuma (often staying on a comp basis at our hotel) nine times out of ten they wound up at Gloria's shop interviewing the 'Shark Lady,' recognizing a more interesting and saleable story when they saw it! I moaned to Gloria one evening, with mock anger, after she was finished doing an interview for television, "Gloria, how in the hell do you weasel almost every media person we bring on the island to do their major segment on you? Last week it was a French magazine and how I see this week you have cornered a television crew to do a piece on you? Have you no shame!"

We all had a laugh over this, and she knew we didn't mind a bit and in fact encouraged what ever publicity on Exuma we could get.... and Gloria could get it! Let me tell you that the bold print of 'Exuma Shark Lady' on an article, out sell the best celebrity pap.

On into her eighties, Gloria was still taking her little skiff out on the Little Bahama Banks, fishing no longer for monster sharks, but still a dangerous antagonist to the swarming schools of reef fish for the dinner table ... Tragedy struck one dark night, when some warped idiot stole the outboard motor off her little boat, depriving her of her main recreation and source of fresh fish. She was heartbroken until everyone chipped in and replaced it.

Gloria Patience, one of the Bahamian Out Island's most beloved and interesting characters in a host of island characters, passed away a few years ago at age 85, her strong frame carrying her almost to the end. Unfortunately, I was off island at that time and regretted that I wasn't there for a final 'goodbye' to an old friend who gave so much 'character' to her community. How do you replace a 'Shark Lady?'

Celebrities Visit Exuma

In the 1970's, I read an article in the Miami Herald that George Hommel of World Wide Sportsman and Ted Williams were looking for a new bonefishing spot in the Bahamas. I called Jim Hardie at the Herald and he put me in contact with George, who was part owner/manager of a large fishing tackle store and angling destination agency located at Islamorada, Florida Keys. I explained to George that Stan Benjamin and I wanted to start an annual bonefishing tournament at the Peace and Plenty in Exuma, to help promote angling tourism at the hotel and on the island, and asked if he would like to team up and give it a try.

George liked the idea that the Peace and Plenty would provide the accommodations and line up the boats and guides and George would offer the three fishing day package to his clientele and run the tournament. In addition, George would invite a celebrity for the sizzle factor along with a fishing magazine writer or two for publicity... The 'Bahamas Bonefish Bonanza' was born!

Charlie Pflueger and Ted Williams at the Bahamas
Bonefish Bonanza Tournament 1977

For a few years, we had the pleasure of having Baseball Hall of
Famer, Ted Williams; also renowned fisherman (and Sears's sports
spokesman) joins our tournament. He was very generous with his
time and mingled with his fellow tournament fisherman, all of whom
were keen to meet a celebrity of his caliber. Late one afternoon, after
Ted caught a 10 lb bonefish (which won the 'largest bonefish' trophy
a couple of days later), we all sat around the bar and lounge, having
a few drinks and swapping 'lies d'jour'. It was Halloween and some
of the local kids were coming in the hotel for 'trick or treating' and
asked Ted for some money....Ted looked at George and said, "give
the kid ten dollars!"....George grumbled, as this was the third time
that afternoon, Ted had been overly generous with George's funds....

"Next time, give'em your own damn money!" George groused, to a titter of laughter.

While this was going on in the bar, I was seating some of the regular guests in the dinning room for dinner. At one table a gentleman asked me, "Could that be Ted Williams from the Boston Red Sox in the bar?" I admitted it was the very same, at which he added, "my boss won't believe this! I'm from Boston and a great fan of Ted Williams, but my boss has to be the greatest fan in the world and when I tell him I saw his hero, he'll go crazy!"

A few minutes later, Ted was lurching out of the bar, sloshing in a sea of Doc's rum punches and walking through the dining room to reach his room in the west wing. When Ted neared the Sox fan sitting on the main isle, preparing to dine, the fan jumped up and shook Ted's hand, bubbling over with a greeting and an offer to join him for dinner. I was stunned when Ted, a little wobbly on his feet from too many rum punches after a sun baked day, instead of lurching on to bed, accepted the invitation and sat down with the fan for dinner. Ted seemed to be having a great time telling stories while the fan sat in rapture.... sucking up every word! Finally they finished dinner and Ted continued on to bed, leaving the fan in a state of euphoria. A few minutes later when I went by his table, he grabbed my arm and babbled, "This is the happiest day of my life! Spending an evening with my idol was something I could never have imagined! Wait until I tell my boss!" spewing me with a spittle spray of sheer joy. I offered my congratulations and left him talking to himself.

The next day at breakfast, I asked Ted how he enjoyed spending the evening with one of his greatest baseball fans. Ted looked at me strangely and said, "I don't remember a thing about last night, thanks to the Doc's punches!" I guess in the final analysis, only the fan really needed to remember it!

Fore!

The second year George and I put on the 'Bahamas Bonefish Bonanza' (1976) we were lucky enough to have Jack Nicklaus agree to join us. Jack turned down free transportation on our chartered DC-3 and opted for a more comfortable ride in his personal Jet Star aircraft (one couldn't fault him for skipping the flight down in our rattle trap, where I played the steward, dispensing as much beer and booze as needed to keep the participants from jumping off the plane).

Stan Benjamin and I had dinner with Jack a couple of the nights and enjoyed talking to him, not about golf, but fishing locations and techniques. Stan attended the University of Michigan while Jack went to Ohio State which started a good natured banter, finishing with a bet on the next football game between the two. I can't remember who won, but it was a lot of fun.

Jack Nicklaus and Charlie Pflueger at
Bonefish Bonanza Tournament 1976

Jack was kind enough to take a few pictures with Stan and me, which we eventually hung in the hotel bar. Since it was a month later when we had the pictures developed, Jack had not signed them, but he rectified that in 2008 when a stay at our Peace and Plenty Bonefish Lodge uncovered one of the old black and white photos residing in Bob Hyde's office. Jack was surprised, since he had probably long forgotten a couple photos in a life time of photo opportunities. He was pleased to oblige Bob's request and signed 'I wish we could go back to 1976'.... I do too, Jack... I do too!

You're Out

My friend and partner in the Peace and Plenty Bonefish Lodge, Captain Bob Hyde, is not only a skilled fishing guide and lodge manager, but in addition is a dyed in the wool baseball fan. Having lived in the New York area as a youth, he was a rabid Brooklyn Dodger fan until they broke his heart with a move to Los Angeles, thereby kindling a smoldering outrage lasting these many years. Since he couldn't murder the whole Dodger Organization, he turned to the New York Yankees and its hero, Mickey Mantle for solace. Bob must have had a Fairy Godmother, because a few of his childhood dreams did come true.

I guess it was a touch of the magic wand when a call came to our fishing lodge office that Mickey Mantle wanted to book a week to do some bonefishing. When Mickey arrived he certainly found a friend in Bob and they pounded the local bonefish population, talked baseball and had dinner together every night. I even had the opportunity of joining them one night and although I wasn't a baseball fan, I did enjoy, if only for a moment, basking in the reflected glory of a super sports hero.

Just before Mickey was leaving, he offered to sign a few articles for display at the lodge. Bob only had an old Brooklyn Dodger jersey displaying the number of arch rival, Duke Schneider....so what the hell ... Mickey signed it anyway with 'WHO THE HELL IS DUKE SCHNEIDER? Mickey Mantle!' This was, unfortunately the last year of Mickey's astounding life and he died of a liver disease a few months later. I have always been thankful that Bob (and I) had the chance to get to know that great ball player.

Charlie Pflueger, Mickey Mantle and Capt. Bob
Hyde, playing the 'hook' game in George Town

With the signed Dodger jersey safely displayed in a locked glass case at the Lodge, one of the dinner guests asked a stupid question, "what did Duke say to that?" That got Bob thinking that perhaps Duke would respond to Mickey's remarks. One of Bob's friends knew how to contact Duke and arrangements were soon made and a Yankee jersey with Mickey's number was dispatched to Duke. Soon the jersey returned with 'WHO'S MICKEY MANTLE? Duke Schnneider'! This jersey resides next to Mickey's. Another addition to the Lodge jersey Hall of Fame is the San Francisco jersey signed by the 'say hey' kid...Willie Mays.

A second flick of the magic wand conjures up Bob's childhood fantasy of playing in the famous Boston baseball stadium 'Fenway Park.' A couple times a year Bob takes a week off and flies to the

States to join a couple of baseball buddies to see a few games. On this occasion, he was invited to Fenway Park to spend a few days watching a Boston vs Kansas City series (one of his pals was coaching).

When Bob arrived at the stadium, he was instructed to put on a uniform to take batting practice with the KC team. The uniform was from the Boston team and especially prepared with 'Hyde' on the back over number '9' (the Boston superhero Ted William's retired number). When Bob went on the field to take batting practice he caught hell from the Red Sox players.... the nerve of this Hyde guy wearing Ted's retired number.... plenty of hooting and hassling. Finally, they all broke up laughing, having been in on the gag! Friends like these are hard to find! Sometimes dreams do come true... even taking batting practice at Fenway! Walter Mitty would be proud!

Don't Stop the Carnival

Bob called me from the Bonefish Lodge one day and asked if the Beach Inn I was managing had room for singer Jimmy Buffet and if he could tie up his Mallard seaplane to our dock. Jimmy was down for a little R & R bonefishing with Bob and Allston at the Lodge. Flying his seaplane further down into the less populated islands to the south offered fantastic virgin fishing from flats swarming with hungry schools of bonefish that had never seen a fly.

At the time, Jimmy was writing the musical score for the libretto 'Don't Stop the Carnival', written by the master story teller, Herman Wouk, who also wrote the 'Cane Mutiny', 'Marjorie Morningstar', 'Youngblood Hawke', the 'Winds of War', 'War and Remembrance,' among others. Jimmy told me he had a challenge finding Herman, who was then living in Southern California, and talking him into using 'Carnival' (a long time bible for island hotel managers) for the story line.

Early one evening, Jimmy found me hanging around the bar at the Beach Inn, grabbed me by the arm and said, "Do you have time

319

to listen to a few songs I wrote for the musical?" Upstairs we went to his corner room, where he played three songs on his keyboard. When finished, he asked, "What do you think?" One of the songs, 'Public Relations', blew me away and I told him that while I wasn't a music critic (I think he suspected that), in my opinion it was a sure winner. As it turned out... it was a show stopper!

Many months later, the production was ready for a try-out and booked an opening run at the Coconut Grove Playhouse in Miami. Jean Pflueger managed to get a couple of tickets and I flew over from Exuma for the opening night. We sat in the front row next to Jimmy (who didn't sit long) and a seat over from Herman Wouk. When the curtain came up, Jimmy addressed the audience with an introduction to the plot and musical numbers. At that time Jimmy also introduced me to the audience as the "real Normal Paperman" (the anti-hero in Carnival) and the General Manager of Club Peace and Plenty in George Town, Exuma in the Bahamas. This took me my surprise, but I stood up and magnanimously gave a 'Queen Elizabeth' wave to my fans (ok, the crowd ....which contained a lot of Out Island people over for the show). I lapped up the attention and was overwhelmed by Jimmy's kindness.

I thoroughly enjoyed the musical, especially 'Public Relations', which, as mentioned, was a hit. After the show, Jimmy introduced me to Herman, which was certainly a thrill... but alas, no camera was at hand.

I don't know if 'Don't Stop the Carnival' ever made it to Broadway, but I thought it was certainly worthy of a decent run. If I didn't thank Jimmy for that wonderful evening, I thank him now!

Pirates of the Caribbean

When we heard that Disney was going to shoot some segments of their fabulously successful film 'Pirates of the Caribbean' in Exuma, we were ecstatic, not only from the excitement of movie making on our island but also from the financial bounty it would bring. Our hotel and others, including the ultra-posh 'Four Season's, reaped a bonanza of food and lodging income. I rented my four bedroom house, Shalimar, on Master Harbor, to the production company who had some of the camera crew in residence. On an amusing side note: a month after they left the island, my yard man moved a decorative conch shell on the porch to clean and found a packet of what looked like marijuana jammed into the interior of the beautiful pink shell. Guess the boys forgot their stash when the shoot ended! Since neither my yard man nor I had any interest in it, he threw it on a pile of burning trash.

The big star, of course, was Johnny Depp, masterly playing Captain Jack Sparrow. He was reportedly staying aboard his yacht and liked the area so much he purchased an island in the Exumas. The best spot to mingle with the stars was, oddly enough, at Dee Dee's restaurant 'Santana's' at Williamstown, Little Exuma. The crew boats used the docks at Williamstown as the jumping off port for a small island called 'Sandy Cay' a few miles away. 'Sandy Cay' was a lovely small island with native Iguanas, picturesque coconut trees and pristine white sand beaches where, in the movie, the treasure was found.

When it was apparent that Johnny Depp was going to receive the Peoples' Award for most popular male actor, the network slated to carry the presentations on television, contacted the Peace and Plenty and arranged to shoot that clip from our hotel, since Johnny was filming and unable to accept in person.

We were pleased to close off our 'Slave Kitchen Bar' and had the TV crew shoot Johnny sitting in one of our booths with Bill Johnson and Mady Eisenberg's 'Regatta' mural in the background. Johnny accepted the award but refrained to mention that he was at the Peace and Plenty in Exuma (much to our chagrin).... only that he was somewhere in the Caribbean. Many of our regular guests later advised they saw the show and knew he was in our bar (they should have known, since many of them spent most of their waking hours there getting a buzz on!).

Not withstanding the lack of meaningful publicity, Johnny was kind enough to greet, chat and sign a few autographs for our guests when the show was over. I recently heard that 'Pirates #4' is on the drawing board... hope they shoot some of it in Exuma.

Over the 50 plus years Club Peace and Plenty has welcomed visitors from all over the world. While the vast majority is considered our valued guests, only a small number could be classified as celebrities... however, here are a few we have had the pleasure to meet:

Jackie Onasis had lunch at the hotel two seasons in a row in the 90's. She was with a friend who owned a yacht anchored in the harbor. She remained unannounced and wore her trade mark head scarf and large sunglasses. She was very accommodating, and we chatted before lunch and thanked us for the service when they left. A lovely lady.

Actor Raymond Burr, who played Perry Mason on TV, visited my air base in the Philippines in the early 50's with a USO group. I saw him again in the early 90's at the Peace and Plenty's bar, visiting from a yacht. He was a regular winter guest on Harbour Island off North Eleuthera and a long time friend of the Bahamas.

Sam Elliott, the actor with a deep, gravel voice, came into the Peace and Plenty to use the telephone one afternoon. I had the opportunity to briefly chat with him.

Al Roker, Weatherman with NBC Today show has stayed with us at the Peace and Plenty several times while filming. His paternal grand parents were from Exuma. Al has a property on Stocking Island.

Deborah Roberts, NBC TV personality, visited the hotel with husband, Al Roker.

Don Shula, the legendary Dolphin coach had lunch with Raymond Floyd and me, on the dining porch of the hotel, when Ray was laying out the original golf course for Emerald Bay and the Four Seasons Hotel.

Gene Hackman, a popular actor, with his wife spent two days at the hotel, flying in from Puerto Rico, to meet his hired yacht for a Exuma Chain cruise. I enjoyed talking with him mostly about the history of Exuma.

Ester Rolle, actress in a few hit TV shows, spent a week with us while visiting family and friends at Rolle Town, where she was from.

Vanessa Williams, actress in the TV series 'Ugly Betty' and 'Desperate Housewives,' visited the island several times, staying at the Out Island Inn. I chatted with her on the plane over and again at the hotel bar. A beautiful and interesting lady.

Charlie with the Doctor of Libations and Al
Pflueger, Marine Taxidermist, at the Reef Bar

Dusty Baker, Davey Johnson and a host of baseball players helped partner Bob Hyde put on fishing tournaments for a few years in the late 1990's. Their awards banquets at the Bonefish Lodge, attended my many of the Government Tourism officials, were classic, offering an opportunity to mingle with baseball's elite.

Hume Croyn, actor in many films such as 'Cleopatra' and his Academy Award winning wife, Jessica Tandy, owned for a time,'Children's Bay Cay' in the Exumas, leased a home on prestigious Goat Cay, a little over a mile from the hotel. Hume was an ardent fly fisherman and loved to fish the bonefish flats with Bob. When Jessica died, Hume continued to visit Exuma. He eventually proposed to his writing partner, Susan, and had the engagement party at the Bonefish Lodge, attended by actress Sigourney Weaver who was wintering in Exuma. Hume died a few years ago at 92. This friend of Exuma has been missed.

An Exumian son of sorts, David Elliot (Smith) was the lead character, Harm, in the long running TV series JAG; a tall, handsome man whose father was born in Exuma and still has family on the island.

Joe Namath, Jets great quarterback, spent some time at the hotel in the 80's and enjoyed the out island ambience of the 'Slave Kitchen Bar'.

Royalty also found their way to the Peace and Plenty. Prince Philip of England, his picture is on our hotel brochures, had lunch with us in 1963, escorted by Bobby Simonette, Member of Parliament for Exuma. Owners Stan and Jeanne Benjamin poised at the entrance to the hotel with King Constantine for a photo opportunity during his stay in mid-1980.

I have no doubt that I have forgotten some of celebrities that we were pleased to welcome to the Peace and Plenty and Exuma, but I am still amazed how many celebrities have actually found their way to our remote out island.

The Bonefish Lodge

In 1991, owner Stan Benjamin and I were in the Slave Kitchen Bar at Club Peace and Plenty presiding over the Monday night cocktail party when a salty character in shorts and T-shirt, asked Stan if he was interested in having him join the hotel and build up a serious bonefishing business to replace our step-child hit or miss operation He introduced himself as Bob Hyde, a Florida Keys fishing guide, who drove his 16' Dolphin Bonefish skiff, powered by an 86 hp outboard engine, across the Gulf Stream, thru the Bahamas, and down the Exumas to George Town.

I was impressed with Bob and figured anyone who could take off in a skiff for this kind of trip had to have a pretty good knowledge of the sea, so when Stan agreed to give Bob room and board at the hotel to see if it would work out, I readily concurred. This move turned out to be one of the smartest moves we ever made, since Bob not only turned out to be brilliant, hard working and well connected, but turned out to be a great friend and business partner.

Bob proved to have another important attribute... he was organized! He started by locating a core of reasonably competent adult guides and filling in with a few seniors from the local high school. Most of the trainee guides knew how to catch a bonefish on a hand line and where the fish tended to range, but very little about how to professionally guide the international fly fisherman.

326

Bob trained the guides, obtained the skiffs for those without, arranged transportation to the various fishing areas and promoted our hotel to the international fishing community. He created all inclusive packages that provided for the airport transfers, guides, boats, transportation to the fishing area, meals, hotel accommodations, and such. Phew! A logistic nightmare if not carefully executed!

Our first full year operating out of the Beach Inn, we were running a daily average of an astounding 15 boats, scattered over 55 miles of world class bonefish habitat.. When you stop to think how difficult it is to operate that many boats with cranky outboard motors, 15 individual guides, all with potential problems of their own (I still smile when I think of one guide we had whose grandmother died twice that year in Nassau, requiring his presence at the funeral... that poor woman must have taken one hell of a beating), and transportation by automobile to various boat landings all over the island, you have to spend a lot of energy to get it right. There was no room for screw-ups with rooms, box lunches and guide selections, with rabid fisherman paying thousands of dollars for a week's action. No time for illness, bad engines, leaky boats or a plethora of other excuses that can crop up in a normal operation from time to time. I don't know how Bob and right hand man, Alliston, pulled it off.... but with a lot of sweat and fanatical attention to detail, they did!

It wasn't all work! We had a few laughs along the way, including the afternoon when one of our clients was checking out after a five day trip fishing with his very masculine and butch type daughter. As he sat at the front desk, writing a check for the trip, Bob, ever keen to help future business, was promoting our special off season fishing program designated as a 'Father and Son' affair, said "we are having a father-son fishing tournament this summer. Why don't you bring your DAUGHTER down and join us?"

The client looking a little stunned and uncomfortable, but managed to mumble, "We'll check our schedules and get back to you."

Overhearing the exchange from my nearby office, I almost fell out of my chair and had to shut my office door to coke off a bout of hilarious snorting! Bob, finally realizing his gaffe, ignored the implication and raced to the end of his spiel to send the client off without further damage. No! The client did not bring his daughter down to the summer Father/Son tournament... Surprise! In addition, there was no truth to the rumor that we were going to change the name of the tournament to the 'Father and Whoever' Tournament.

Late one afternoon, I was working in the office, when one of our fishing clients, who was enjoying a Beach Inn honeymoon, came in, barely concealing his glee over catching a tremendous barracuda. Almost breathless, he sputtered, "The guide said it weighted 40 pounds! What a fish! Come take a look!"

I bounded out of my chair, eager to see that big a 'cuda, since I recently had a 25 pounder mounted for son Paul that he caught on the Little Bahama Banks, so I knew something about what a fish of that size should look like. The honeymooner dragged me to the guides open trunk and proudly pointed to the '40 pounder'. The guide stood by with a huge grin, mentally spending the big tip he was surely going to get from his skill (and luck) in putting his client on a fish of a lifetime on a fly rod.

I don't know what got into me, but as I looked down at that Barracuda, there was no question that the fish was not 40 pounds and probably less than 25 lbs. I could not hold it in and blurted out, "that fish is no way near 40 pounds!"

If you wanted to see a smile turn into a frown in the blink of an eye, you should have seen our fisherman! The guide, with a grimace in seeing his big tip start to disappear, shouted, "no way! That fish is at least 40 pounds!"

I don't know what made me continue this ill advised conversation, since I had no axe to grind nor anything to prove. I certainly wanted our guests to catch lots of big fish to ensure their return, not to mention the extra appreciation for our hard working guides. I guess there was an under-lying need to show off my expertise and how damn smart I was, when like a dog with a bone, I suggested we take the fish into the storeroom and weigh it. Stupidity at its finest! I read the numbers on the scale and proudly announced that his 'championship 'cuda' was a less than a rousing 22 lbs. At least I didn't scream out, 'I told you so!'… But it was close.

Needless to say, the fisherman was crushed over the discovery, evaporating a big tip and if the guide was impressed with my expertise, he did not mention it through his clenched teeth and barely concealed rage. Why I didn't jut congratulate the fisherman and suggest that he have the 'monster' mounted, I don't know. A little P.R. (and common sense) would have gone along way in this situation.

When Bob heard about the fiasco, he wandered over and said, "Congratulations, Slick! You can really screw up a great day on the flats!" After a passage of time, Bob and I can kid about this, but for the fisherman, who never returned for another dose of disappointment from a 'know it all'… it probably still smarts.

As the bonefishing operation became more successful, Bob and I kicked around some possibilities and decided we wanted to build a fishing club that would be a state of the art lodge strictly for all inclusive fishing packages. We talked to Stan who agreed to do the major financing of the project, while Bob and I bought our shares at a discount. I located a 3.5 acre hillside tract on the south side of Exuma, only four miles from George Town, with elevations up to 55 feet. At the foot of the property, a meandering stream led to a wide, saltwater river and open bay, providing quick access to a fantastic, island dotted bonefish habitat.

We quickly arranged for a set of plans prepared by a local architect, featuring all the innovations needed in a first class club. The hillside building site, overlooking the wide river to the west, promised to provide some sweeping sunsets on the veranda, to enjoy with libation in hand. We had a backhoe dig out a small boat marina off the creek and the electric company installed powerlines to the edge of the property. Things were moving!

It's strange that sometimes a chance encounter changes the course of all your efforts! Only days from ordering the building materials and laying out the site, I ran into Leslie Knowles, owner of the Blue Hole Bar and Restaurant, located near the bridge from Great Exuma to the settlement of the 'Ferry' on Little Exuma (on a side note: Les tragically died of a heart attack recently, while sipping a little Jack Daniels with his best friend Glen and son Michael, when coming in from a fantastic day of Dolphin fishing in Exuma Sound. If you have to go, what better way?).

Stopping to chat for a minute, Les, without preamble and in the way of a greeting said, "I've decided to sell the Blue Hole! Are you interested?" This came over like a bombshell!

My first question, as usual, was "this is quite a surprise. How much are you asking?" When Les named a reasonable figure, the wheels started to spin. Stan wasn't on the island, but Bob was and I spared little time in finding him, anxious to get his take on the situation. We both knew Les had not done well recently at the restaurant, partly due to the numerous potholes residing in the ten miles of the Queen's Highway between George Town and the Blue Hole. Although the terrific fresh seafood and rustic atmosphere was alluring, it was a long, pothole dodging trip, driving the ten miles back in the dark of night with a snoot-full of booze. No doubt, this kept the paying customers to a minimum. Another thorn in the side of economic prosperity was the universal difficulty in making a profit in a restaurant operation in the out islands, considering the cost of food and labor.

After quickly deciding that the Blue Hole location offered a step up from the previously purchased property, we called Stan in Cleveland and gave him the story. Although, I think he was as excited as we were over this sudden possibility, Stan was quick to point out, "let me remind you both that we have already purchased a darn good club site, and have spent over six thousand dollars drawing up the plans and more in dredging a marina. Now you've got me in a completely different deal!" We knew from his weak protest, he loved the idea and was hooked! And so were we!

We shelved the other project and started the new Peace and Plenty Bonefish Lodge, by moving Bob and Karen into the now closed Blue Hole. One of his first moves was to contact local heavy equipment guru Cyril Rolle, to cut and place giant, limestone blocks around the perimeter of the peninsula site, reclaiming low, unused land on the outer edges of the exiting building. Once the blocks were in place, Cyril provided truck after truck of fill to bring many areas of the property up to grade. This procedure was not inexpensive, but was necessary to define and reclaim the land to the legal property line. This allowed us to build our two stories, 8 unit, residential building, on a prime location, facing the main water way and bridge between Great and Little Exuma.

Cautious construction procedures required that when digging the foundation, we had to excavate 12' down to bedrock to insure no future cracking or sinking of the building. During this phase of the construction, Stan brought his son David, a Phd in architecture, out to look things over. David, a perfectionist, eyed the layout of the foundation, now walled up well above ground with concrete blocks and called Bob over.

"Bob, you need to move the building over a few degrees to more effectively utilize the view of the bridge and waterway," David explained.

Bob, not one to suffer in silence, responded with, "Perhaps you missed the fact that we have a deep hole in the ground full of a very expensive foundation. I think we are going to have to forgo the optimum utilization of the site in deference to the three weeks invested, not to mention $75,000 of your father's construction loan!" Bob then suggested to Stan that while he appreciated David's professional opinion, it might be time to take him back to town. As a side note, while David has a brilliant mind, he has little tolerance for the 'make do' mentality of our island builders.

As the deluxe units came online, we closed the fishing operation at the Beach Inn and moved to the new Bonefish Lodge. The interior was already what you might expect an out island bar and restaurant to look like.... mounted fish hung high on the walls.... a hammerhead shark, a large hog snapper, a huge bonefish, a grouper and lots of the usual photos of smiling fisherman and proud guides holding the obligatory trophy catch. The interior walls and ceiling were constructed of Canadian cedar, expertly crafted wooden tables, booths and unique bar; create a masculine, but elegant fishing club atmosphere. Later Bob added a 12' extension to the restaurant, matching the original décor and vastly increasing the seating capacity, while maintaining the ambience.

The original Blue Hole had very little in the way of office space or manager's quarters, so Bob's next project was to expand the front of the building to to allow for a spacious business office, a managers office and two bedrooms and bath. To increase our freshwater holding tanks, we built a large planter in the middle of the newly graveled parking lot, which is artfully concealed in tropical flowering shrubs and palms, and utilized to save the freshwater runoff from the hotel roof. Other eye-catching landscaping included a huge intertwined series of bouganvillea in a multi-colored burst, climbing up the side of the stairway to the top of our second floor.

The second floor not only contains the main kitchen, but the guest lounge boasts a self service bar, a fly tying table, satellite TV, a media corner with telephone, computer with internet connection, a fax, library, pool table and card tables. A wide sheltered walkway with lounge chairs, cool breezes and sweeping bay views complete this recreational area.

Another of Bob's most effective improvements was the vast, wooden planked back deck he turned into an exciting party area with dipping pool, waterfall, secluded seating areas, wood burning grilling hut, large boat dock and a unique fish pond. A beach, with relaxing hammocks, jet out into the rushing waterway. The rising sun comes up over the Ferry Bridge, and sets over a vast inland sea to the west, complete this picture perfect Bahamian out island resort.

Exotic tropical drinks and wood grilled fresh lobster, grouper or conch are, of course, a prerequisite to a successful evening at the Lodge, but many of the guests feel that the high point of the night is watching Bob's lady, Karen, hand feed a half a dozen ferocious Lemon sharks.... some as large as 7 or 8 feet. After dark, Karen will switch on the pond light to seemingly call the fish from the bay, through a narrow canal and into the pond. Once in the pond, Karen, sitting on the edge, feeds scraps of the evenings fish dinners, by hand to the snapping teeth and pounding tails. When you see how close those razor sharp teeth come to Karen's hand, you'll wonder where she gets the courage and how she has survived these years without losing a hand or arm… or worse! We have no applications for Karen's vacation relief.

On more than one occasion, she received a serious tail slap to her high thigh that left a red, bruised area for weeks. One night while Bob and I were watching the 'Karen Show' on the back deck, I noted how close she was working to the snapping teeth and murmured, only half seriously, "I hope you don't have to jump in to that swirling mass of sharks one of these nights, if Karen gets dragged in....we can't afford to lose you!"

Bob looked serious when he replied, "Don't worry! I'm going to run right into the office and make an urgent call!"

Knowing there was no 911 or even an open medical clinic at that time of night, I had to ask, "Who are you going to call for help?"

He looked at me like I had lost my mind, and laughingly said, "What do you mean 'who am I going to call for help?' I'm going to call the INSURANCE AGENT!" He got me again! Fortunately, no mishaps have required us to test our rescue procedure, or lack thereof.

While Karen managed to avoid being bitten by a shark, she did suffer a serious bite when she tried to go to the aid of her beloved dog, 'Nellie,' who was frolicking in the shallow water on a nearby island. Nellie thought it was amusing to snap at a cruising Stingray, who took exception and slapped its barbed tail deep into her rear flank. The dog, howling with pain and not ready to accept help, gave her a vicious bite, ripping open an extensive gash on Karen's hand. Eventually, Karen got herself and the hound, both bleeding profusely, to George Town and into Dr. Fox's office for group stitching. I later ask her if Dr. Fox had a two for one sale that day and she hit me on the arm for my trouble.

Over the years, we have had the good fortune of welcoming numerous celebrities, tournaments (including a couple 'World Bonefish Championships'), and major island social events at the Lodge. We are proud that we were able to initiate and maintain a first class fishing club in Exuma for all these years and have reveled in the many wonderful associations that have resulted.

Nearing the end of 2010, the Peace and Plenty Bonefishn Lodge under contract for sale..

Bush Medicine

Many of modern medicine's cures were developed from ancient remedies concocted by primitive people... gathered from the nearby bush... and driven by necessity. When I arrived in Exuma, I was fascinated with a few of the local people that practiced the art of 'Bush Medicine'.

Christine Rolle, an energetic lady operated a bus tour that exposed the visitor to the various indigenous flora and their medical applications. Another practitioner of the art was old, Joe Rohmer, who kindly prepared a whiskey bottle full of some kind of special brew to drive out a debilitating flu I had picked up. Gad! It was a tough guzzle... but I finally got it down and since it didn't kill me, I had to credit a rapid recovery on its application.

Laurel Pickey, a botanist from Miami University of Ohio, did extensive work in the Bahamas, and recorded that there were 140 plants used medically on Long Island and 163 on Cat Island, of which about 120 were common to both islands. Since these two islands, along with Exuma, were called the 'Cotton Islands' in the Loyalist plantation days, support the fact that slaves brought Bush Medicine to the islands from their African homeland.

Bush Medicine has treatments for many ailments… such as the common cold, diarrhea, headaches, flu and for more serious diseases, such as leukemia and cancer. The following touches on some of Exuma's medicinal plants and their applications.

One of the most versatile local trees is the Lignum Vitae (Tree of Life), the national tree of the Bahamas. Its resin, called 'guaiacum,' is obtained by distilling the wood and is used to treat 'weakness' and strengthen the back.

The Gumbo Limbo Tree (also called 'Gamalamee' or 'Sunburn Tree' for its peeling bark), provides strips of bark that's boiled and drunk as tea. It is used to treat backaches, urinary tract infections, colds, flu and fever. When used in connection with a few other ingredients, it's also used for an aphrodisiac.

The 'Gale of Wind/Hurricane Weed' is a popular treatment for kidney stones, poor appitite, constipation, flu and colds, with little side effects or toxicity. It may also be useful in treating hepatitis and the HIV virus.

Exuma residents use Picao Preto, a small annual herb with prickly leaves and yellow flowers. They grind the sundried leaves and mix with olive oil to make poultices for sores and cuts. Also leaves are balled up and applied for toothaches and plastered on the forehead for headaches.

The 'Aloe' (Bitter Aloe) plant is popular for treating skin for burns and cuts. The leaf is slit and the gel applied directly to the skin. Some use the gel to mix with water and drink for the stomach. The gel is also touted to remove face wrinkles.

Love Vine (Cuscuta) is used in tea as an aphrodisiac for 'sex weakness!' and as a soothing bath for prickley heat. One of my workmen, a man in his 50's, during the construction of my

Tropical Gardens cottage rental complex, used Love Vine to add to Gamalamee and an un-named leafy tree growing on the property, to prepare an aphrodisiac potion for the ages! He swore by the brew, which was usually accompanied by a detailed narritive of the previous night conquest. One time, after missing a couple days work and looking like death warmed over, he told me, "Charlie, I thought I was going to die! No, I hoped would die! I drank an exceptionally large dose of my brew for some extra fortification, looking to please my new, young girlfriend, and it went through me like a volcano!" Listening to this wreck of a man… I immediately crossed this elixier off my list!

The Pigeon-Plum Tree is not only a supermarket for the White Crown Pigeon (a locally hunted game bird that feeds on the small, plum-like fruit growing in clusters), but is used to stop 'free bowels' in humans.

In the old days, it wasn't only the children who chewed sugar cane… it was used as a remedy for Heartburn (reflux).

Obviously, this has hardly scratched the surface of all the available native remedys, many of which may actually work, while others invoke the power of positive thinking. In any event, as medical facilities and practices continue to develop in the out islands and when the old practitioners pass away, it's probable that Bush Medicine will soon fade into the history of the islands.

Calling Doctor Kildare!

Calling Doctor Kildare might be a little too much poetic license, but in the out islands any doctor is better than what we generally have. On Exuma we have a medical clinic located in George Town and another in Steventon, manned by a medical doctor and a nursing group under contract to the Ministry of Health. Dr. Fox, a competent doctor from Nassau has a branch office on Exuma, which he attends on Thursdays and that's about it. Dr. Fox, however, is currently building a small hospital about 3 miles west of George Town, which will house a modern medical facility, including digital X-rays, operating room, pharmacy, dental complex, optometrist, a live-in doctor, ambulance and most everything needed to offer relief from minor maladies. The hospital will also have facilities to stabilize the patient for air evacuation. The Bahamian Government has a regional island hub on the drawing board for major medical problems in the southeastern Bahamas.

Our present local clinic can handle minor illnesses and trauma, including a few beds for the odd overnight stays. It's hard to believe, that in today's world, the only X-ray equipment available on an island of thousands is in the animal hospital run by a Veterinarian from the United States.

A case in point occurred last year when a returning guest in his early 70's fell coming out of the supermarket and broke his femur near the hip. In terrible pain, he was transported to the George Town clinic before noon and laid there until after nine in the evening before being loaded on an evacuation aircraft and flown to the creditable Doctor's Hospital in Nassau. The next day he was evacuated to a hospital near his home in Boston, where after some rehabilitation, he had another fall which, unfortunately, proved to be fatal.

A few years ago we had a charming couple in their thirties at the Club with their six months old baby. Although the wife had a history of serious asthma, it was important to attend her father's wedding and share in this happy event. In the pre-wedding excitement, her asthma struck, manifested in serious breathing difficulties. The clinic doctor was called and after a check-up, he advised that it was no problem to relieve the symptoms, and she was removed to the clinic.

An hour later, we were advised by her distraught husband, clutching their squalling baby, that she had passed away.... so much for 'no problem!' It was certainly a shock to see a 37 year old die that swiftly from asthma. Had we had a modern medical facility the outcome would have probably have been more positive.

One night many years ago in the Club dining room, a wealthy Canadian Exuma home owner suffered a heart attack. We got him to one of the rooms and summoned the doctor who did his best to stabilize him, but urged his immediate airlift to the Princess Margaret Hospital in Nassau. While the premise makes sense, the execution is difficult, when you factor in that the airport had no night lights on the runway. Looking around the full dining room, many of which were expat home owners that had driven to the hotel for dinner, a quick announcement provided over a dozen volunteers to light the runway with headlights. A little risky perhaps, but doable, particularly for island pilots who were kin to the bush pilot in Alaska.

The rescue proceeded as planned. We assigned the available cars to each side of the runway, providing a flawless landing and eventual departure amid cheering that could be heard for at least a mile. Unfortunately, the victim died a short time after arriving at the hospital.

During the busy winter season, the George Town area boasts perhaps 600 sailing and power boats in residence in the vicinity. Exuma is the winter destination for nautical types.... running the gauntlet from wealthy business and professional visitors to ner-do-wells sailing in on a leaky tub with one pair of underwear and a ten dollar bill and not changing either during their three or four month stay.

Having access to channel 16 on the VHF radio net with its weather forecasts, daily and special events geared for the boaters, and individual contact facility, is responsible for the overall enjoyment of the area. One other advantage is conversations that usually begin with, "any heart (or whatever) doctors out there? We have a problem on 'Yacht Serenity' anchored near the Peace and Plenty Beach Club on Stocking Island. We'll standby on channel 14 (or pick a channel not in use)." In many cases, out of all the boats in the Elizabeth Harbor area, there will be at least one doctor that fits the bill and is willing to look into the emergency problems of a fellow visitor in a remote area.

Its obvious to most, that to live in an 'Out Island' without the benefit of adequate medical facilities to stabilize accident victims and the older more affluent visitors, more subject to life threatening emergencies, is a crap shoot at best. While its only 150 miles to Nassau and 300 miles to Miami... that's a long way when a life is in the balance.

Hopefully, proper medical facilities will soon be on the island and this threat to peace and tranquility will be a thing of the past!

It's Regatta Time in Exuma....Mon!

Every April during the last Thursday, Friday and Saturday, it's 'Regatta Time!' at George Town, the provincial capitol of the Exumas and Ragged Island, some 150 miles southeast of Nassau in the Commonwealth of the Bahamas.

Competing boats and rabid fans come from all over the Bahamas to celebrate the annual 'Family (or Out) Island National Regatta' since 1954. George Town was incorporated in 1793, when the area was one of the major contributors of fine cotton during the Loyalist years from 1783 to 1834.

The three day sailing event is held on beautiful Elizabeth Harbor (some theories suggest that Columbus landed here since it's large harbor fits the description by Columbus that on his first landfall he discovered a harbor 'that was huge enough to accommodate all the ships in Christendom!.' This pristine body of water is five miles long and over a mile wide, offering a world class sailing course, edged by miles of white sand beaches.

National Family Island Regatta Photo
Credit: Onne Van der Wal

Since sailing is the Bahamas national sport, other regattas are held through out the year on some of the other islands, but only the George Town Regatta is sanctioned by the government as the official 'National Regatta'. Hotels and private homes are booked from one year to the next with competing crews and fans in town to support their home island favorite. The always pleasing Bahamian Police Band performs a musical marching demonstration to the delight of the massive crowds.

Dining is a delight, featuring a multitude of food 'shacks' temporarily constructed by the local Exumian entrepreneurs and offering fresh island conch, snapper and crawfish (spiny lobster) along with 'pea soup and dumpling', 'Stew fish' (reported to be a good cure for a hangover), 'boiled fish' and other Bahamian specialties. Plenty of local 'Kalik' beer, rum and other spirits help one to relax after a tough day on the water.

The 'A' boats, 28' wooden sloops, are the largest in the competition and usually number 13 to 20 depending on the year and vie for the main trophy's and cash prizes. There are also a 'B' class and a smaller 'C' class that normally race in the mornings leaving the larger 'A's to compete in the late afternoon to close out the day's events. The Government and the Regatta Committee allocate funds to assist in transporting the boats to Exuma and to help maintain the crews while at the race. Many of the local businesses and hotel also contribute to help make the estimated quarter of a million dollar budget.

Rules dictate that the boats are of wooden construction to strict specifications (based on the old time Bahamian island traders and work boats) and be owned, built and sailed by Bahamians. Another rule demands that the boat must finish the race with the same number of crewmen on board that started the race, thwarting the practice of excess crew reducing the weight by jumping into the sea on the last leg of a tight race.

One regatta, Gloria Patience, the famous 'Shark Lady,' along with a mixed bag of local ladies, crewed one of the boats. As their boat crossed the finish line all stripped off their blouses and finished the race topless… much to the approving roar of the local aficionados!

There is dancing nightly at the popular landmark, Club Peace and Plenty ideally located on the harbor opposite the race start and finish line. A local band keeps the revelers on the floor until the wee hours of the morning. Lermon, the 'Doctor of Libation,' presides over the pool bar, while Glen Monroe, the islands Para-medic (he has to leave the bar periodicly to operate the island's only ambulance) is in charge of the main 'Slave Kitchen' bar.

By the Saturday night awards ceremony, the crews and fans are at a fever pitch and much cheering and some jeering, accompany the presentation of the hardware and the cash prizes, but to many of the winners, the satisfaction of bragging rights and the satisfaction of bringing the championship back to the home island, is of more importance than anything else.

By Sunday most of the visitors have gone and the shacks are being dismantled, to be stored until next year when new winners will crow and the new losers will eat crow and lick their wounds! Regatta Time, Mon! It's a great sport!

Fancy Meeting You Here!

Sometimes life plays strange games and orchestrates very improbable chance encounters. One such an event that will always remain in my memory was the outrageously amusing chance meeting with an old friend and former business associate in a very unlikely location.

As mentioned in the 'Egg and I' chapter Bob Williamson, my assistant with Pan Am in Venezuela in 1959 and later partner in the Bahamas Poultry Farm egg operation in Freeport, Grand Bahama Island, went his separate way when we sold the farm. The last I heard of Bob, he was going back to aviation school to complete his instrument rating with a view of flying corporation jets.

Ten years later wife Joan, son Paul and I decided to take advantage of her free Pan Am passes and spend a week touring Scotland. Joan's paternal grandfather was born a 'Fraser' in Fraser, Scotland, which figured in our motivation, along with an longstanding interest in visiting this beautiful country.

We flew into Preswick, rented a car, skirted Glasgow and headed for a first night at 'King's House Inn,' near Glencoe, the oldest licensed public house (pub) in Scotland. What a historical location... the original Inn, from the 1400's, was of white washed stone; great hewed beams supported the ceiling, with a well worn stone floor. A 14' fireplace concealed a 'Priest Hole,' where during the reign of Queen Elizabeth (1558), hiding places were built into Roman Catholic buildings, primarily for the safety of persecuted priests. A cold stream pounded down from the Scottish highlands and roared along the Inn to complete this picturesque venue.

In subsequent days we drove along Lock Lommand and Lock Ness, stopping at an observation area to peer out into the lake to see if we could get lucky and spot the elusive Lock Ness Monster (good luck there!). We continued thru Joan's grandfather's town of Fraser, on to Perth, and finally to the capitol of Edinburgh. Fortunately, we found a great, high-rise hotel, Esso 66, checked in and spent the afternoon exploring the famous hilltop Edinburgh Castle.

That evening Joan, Paul and I had dinner at the hotel's main dining room. While studying the menu, I glanced up to eyeball the large, crowded dining room, when to my jaw dropping surprise and amazement; I saw Bob Williamson and another man finishing dinner at a nearby table. Bob did not see me in his urgent need to wolf down a large bowl of ice cream.

With a quick inventory of options, I decided to drape my white napkin over my forearm, turn my face away from Bob's table and slip up behind him. Reaching over his shoulder, I started to remove his half full ice cream bowl... without looking up, he growled, "I'm not finished!" As if acquiescing to his warning, I stepped back and he resumed shoveling another heaping spoonful into his mouth. I reached in again...this time with a firmer grip on the lip of the bowl and started to remove it... to be met with a snarl and in a loud voice chastising this 'dumb waiter.' "Dammit...I told you I wasn't finished!"

This time he looked up and was struck with a look of absolute disbelief ... that the loathsome waiter in a hotel in Scotland was his old friend and business partner from the Bahamas. The look on his face was priceless as he sputtered, "Is it really you, Charlie?" I assured him it was indeed, and I was vacating with my family and not moonlighting as a waiter in Edinburgh. We both roared with laughter (I guess this was a puzzling evening to Bob's dinner companion) and after dinner spent a few hours reliving all our adventures and activities since we sold the egg farm. He had finished his training and was flying jets for an international corporation, hence the overnight in Edinburgh. This surely was a one in a million chance meeting... go figure!

Another unusual happenstance took place one afternoon on one of the main isles in the huge London Marks and Spence Department Store on Oxford Street. Joan, Paul and I were visiting friends in South Clapham, when we stopped in the store to purchase a sweater for Paul. As we walked down the crowded isle, I had a quick glance of a woman and a small child pushing through the shoppers, moving toward the main exit.

I quickly mumbled to Joan, pointing, "See that lady and child... looks just like Maria Teresa Johnson, Randy's wife." We stayed with Randy and 'Mary Terry' in Jakarta, Indonesia for a couple of weeks when Randy was Pan Am's Director for that country. More recently, we visited with the Johnsons' in Madrid where he was then the airline's Director for Spain. I had the pleasure to spend my 36th birthday with them 'out on the town' in Madrid, drinking 'chata's' (small glasses) of heavy red wine and stuffing ourselves with 'tapa's in lieu of dinner, as we worked our way around the city and through the evening. By two in the morning, we finally packed it in and retired to a major bout of heartburn!

I ran to catch up with a surprised Mary Terry, who let out a shriek and delivered a big hug and kiss. We arranged to meet the Johnsons' at their hotel bar for an hour before we were due at the theater for a performance of the old favorite, 'Show Boat.' Randy and I had a lot of catching up to do, accompanied by the mandatory couple of scotches before we reluctantly had to break it off and head for the theater. Once we settled in our seats and the music swelled, I started to doze off... rebounding with a start and jerk of neck. This went on until I thought at the next jerk of my head it would surely snap off. Intermission blessfully came and a splash of cold water allowed me to tough out the evening. Well, I reasoned to my disgusted family, it wasn't everyday that I ran into an old pal in London, and it's not like we hadn't seen 'Show Boat' before!

During the Korean War, while temporarily assigned at an overseas staging base in Oakland, California, I was standing by to catch a troop ship to Manila. Relaxing one evening while swilling a .75 cent pitcher of beer in the PX, I noticed an airman come up to claim a seat on the end of our picnic style bench. As our eyes locked, I was shocked to see my old neighborhood pal from Miami, a fellow Boy Scout and a member of my 'Seagull Patrol!"

As luck would have it, he shipped out with me and wound up in the barracks next to mine for the better part of the next two years. While it seems that these coincidents are really rare... I imagine that it happens more often then we realize... path crossing in strange places against astronomical odds and gives new meaning to the phrase 'it's a small world!'

The Twilight Zone

Growing up, I never placed any stock in the supernatural. I figured if Houdini couldn't come back from the 'beyond,' nobody else could either. Oh, it's interesting to watch a TV show with unexplained phenomenon and its hints of the shadows beyond, or a few bug-eyed aliens hot-rodding silly looking space ships around the Arizona desert... but to really believe it is another matter, indeed!

My first experience was in November 1963. My much loved Grandmother was taken to Mercy Hospital in Coconut Grove, Miami with a serious heart problem. I was home for a couple of weeks from managing my egg farm on Grand Bahama and accompanied my Mother to the hospital to await the outcome.

As I sat in the waiting room, my Mother suddenly came out of Gram's room, obviously distraught, and in answer to my question on her condition, sobbed, "She's gasping and saying crazy things! She asked me if I could see the black flag at half mast. She said the 'black flag means death... someone died! The flag is at half mast!' Charles, look at me! I'm still trembling!"

At this point, it's well to explain that my Grandmother spent the last 20 plus years of her life attending some sort of a mystics' church. As far fetched as it seemed to me as a young fellow, she had a metal horn (tin) and I was told that the parishioners worked at floating, or trying to float the horn. Unfortunately, I can't be more specific. I remember getting her agitated a few times when I made fun of the horn, spoofing its use as a megaphone at an imaginary football game. I did attend church services with her a couple of times when I was a kid and remember the female priest was purported to be a clairvoyant and would answer questions from the congregation... even about love ones that had passed on!

After my Mother took a few minutes to calm down, she went back into Gram's room and within a few minutes returned to hug me, sobbing that Gram has just passed away. At that moment a commotion erupted in the waiting room, with nurses rushing in, some crying... some shouting that President Kennedy had been shot and was dead in Dallas! Now it was my turn to get goose bumps and raising hair on my neck, remembering that Gram had, in her delusions and close to death from a coronary occlusion, just seen a black flag at half mast (half mast for the President, while in limbo between life and death herself?) I surely don't know if there was anything to it, but it was certainly creepy and at least food for thought.

The second thought provoking incident and one that probably saved my life and the life of my son Paul, friend Bob Castleberry and his son, took place in the summer of 1975 while on vacation at Steamboat Springs, Colorado. Paul and I few out to Colorado from Miami with Bob for a two weeks vacation to visit a son by his ex-wife Rosie, and to do some sightseeing and trout fishing. Rosie kindly lent us her apartment and moved in with her sister. To solve our transportation problem, she also let us use her pickup truck, which was ideal to tool around the area doing some camping and fishing for the frying pan. We particularly enjoyed a couple night tenting at Pearl Lake in a National Park, about twenty five miles out of Steam Boat. It was late May, but spotty drifts of snow remained under the trees and kept our food and beer cold. The first afternoon we caught 27 rainbow trout and had a fresh fish pig out. Deer were grazing all around, which was a special treat for the Miami boys. One item of concern was a posted warning sign to beware of the bears and we made a mental note to be 'aware to beware of the bear', and we were pleased to see no bears, at least close up.

One fishing excursion required riding horses up into the Rockies to a pristine, secluded lake where we were the only people within miles. The trout attacked our flies like hungry wolves, making the pain from my saddle pounded ass worth the effort. For guys living in the tropics most of their lives, this was bliss!

Yellowstone National Park, our oldest national park, beckoned and since we had a truck and a tent, we decided to give it a try. I checked the oil, and all that good stuff including the tires that appeared to have ample tread, loaded the tent, stove, sleeping bags and a ton of extra junk we would never use, and hit the road. After one night at a motel reroute, where Paul blasted Bob for sipping vodka laced beverages while we loaded all our stuff into the motel, all went well and we made it to the campgrounds at the park.

After setting up the tent, I had a few vodkas myself to catch up with Bob who was drinking while I was driving. This proved to be a poor idea when I tripped over a tree stump coming back from the bathroom in the dark and fell full length on my face. I must have cracked a few ribs as the pain overwhelmed the horse induced pain in my rear end. It was months before the wounded rib area quit hurting. I managed to crawl into tent where I told Paul, "I fell and think I broke some ribs!" Half asleep he grunted something like, "hang in there!" grabbed his bedding and retired to the truck, I guess to avoid listening to a grown man moan and groan all night.

The next day the boys fished some of the easy to reach streams, while I pouted and took it easy with the throbbing ribs. A few days later driving back to Steamboat Springs we went thru the lovely Estes Park in Colorado, winding around hairpin turns and narrow roads. All considered, we had a great trip and settled down to spend our last day fishing at Pearl Lake, so see if we could fish it out before we left..

Late that night I awakened with a frightening nightmare about a terrible automobile crash involving my mother and stepfather. It was so real that I was trembling and distraught and immediately went to the phone to call home. It was already early morning in Miami when my mother answered the telephone in good sprits and happy to hear from me she asked, "how come you're calling so early?"

I explained my bad dream and implored her to drive with special care. She promised she would and I finally relaxed with a cup of coffee and started making plans for the last day of fishing. Later driving out to Pearl Lake, I couldn't get the nightmare out of my mind. When we arrived at the lake parking area, the boys raced down to start flogging the water while I took a moment to walk around the truck. After checking the tires and to my surprise the front left tire was bald of tread! I had checked those tires before the Yellowstone trip and they all had tread and looked in good condition... now one was bald! I couldn't figure out how that happened so quickly, but when we finished fishing I told the fellows that the left front tire was bald and we had to take care going back and that, "instead of going 65 we had better take our time and keep it at no more than 40 in case the tire blows!"

It seemed to take forever at our slower speed, on the winding roads with precipitous drops off a narrow shoulder. Almost on script the left, front tire suddenly blew! A fuel tanker was on the two lane road at that moment and heading toward us as our truck swerved back and forth! It was unbelievable the difficulty I had in trying to hold the vehicle on the right side of the road and screamed, "Hold on! We're going to roll!" At that moment it felt that there was no doubt the truck would roll off the side of the road and down the deep slope to a pasture below. A further fleeting thought was that we would not live through it.

With all my strength I finally managed to steer to the shoulder of the road and bring the truck to a stop. We were all visibly shaken from the freighting experience, but I think I was the only one that actually realized how close we came to a fatal crash.

Since that day, I have often mentally followed the chain of events that lead us out alive. Every scenario starts with the nightmare that caused me to check the tires, which I would not have done on our last day in Colorado and only 25 miles left to return the truck. Of course, after I found the bald tire and again with the dream crash on my mind, I decided to take special caution and reduce my normal 65 miles per hour to 40. Since I almost lost control at 40 when the tire blew, I have no doubt that I would have lost it had I been going my usual 65. I also have no doubt that due to the steep terrain; we would have rolled multiple times with catastrophic results.

Some questions still remain with me. Did a higher power send the dream crash warning, or was it strictly a random event? If a higher power did send the warning, was it to save all four of us or was one special? If so, was it my son Paul who went on to become a brilliant orthopedic surgeon? Or perhaps Bob's son did something of great value in his life? I doubt if it was especially for Bob or me... Maybe it was just chance, but deep down I believe there was a reason we survived that day.

Adventures in Central America

After I sold my half of the Crow's Nest to Stan and Jeanne Benjamin, I returned to the real estate school, took the broker's exam and was rewarded with a Florida Broker's License, as mentioned in the 'Land Baron's' chapter. With Stan's participation, we incorporated a real estate firm called 'Out Islands Unlimited' dedicated to the brokerage of island properties primarily, as you might suspect, in the Bahamas with an office in Coral Gables.

In a search for an affordable way to advertise our island listings, including 'Pretty Molly Bay Club,' a 24 room hotel on a fantastic, five acre beach in Little Exuma, I decided to try a series of cheap ads in a 'penny Saver' nationwide publication. One of the issues in the Los Angeles area attracted the attention of Bill Isherwood who contacted me and said he thought he had an interested prospect and would try to hook us up. After an exchange of information, I met with the prospective purchaser at the Peace and Plenty and at 2 AM, after enjoying the Saturday night dance and a few drinks, he agreed to purchase the property. The price at the time was $150,000 and carried a nice commission of $15,000, impressive money in those days.

Bill was hired by the new owners to manage the purchase and immediately flew to Miami and much to his chagrin, had to cool his heals for two months, sleeping on my office couch, while the wheels of the legal system grinded out the sale and transfer in Nassau. Once in operation, Bill found promoting a small resort on a remote island with no public electricity and no telephones, a daunting proposition. The major stockholder had wanted to offer me a small percentage of the ownership to work with the management but the other partner, a lawyer from California, was interested in playing a major role and nixed that deal. I had suggested that the hotel join the Bahamas Out Island Promotion Board and the Bahamas Hotel Association to take advantage of the exposure without breaking the advertising bank. Unfortunately, the number two partner decided he could fill the hotel without my local expertise and assistance. I was curious and asked him to give me an idea of how he was going to accomplish this, as one should never be too old to learn new things. He looked pensive while replying, "We are going to get all the guests we need from California!" That revelation knocked my socks off and I wished him well in that enterprise... of course, it didn't happen and the small resort turned into a hang out for druggies and eventually closed.

At Out Islands Unlimited, selling small residential lots kept the wolf from the door; with a dollar here and one there, until I discovered a land development company on Grand Bahama Island. They owned a very large subdivision that had seemed to have petered out after the hayday of Freeport in the mid-sixties. They had invested in paved roads and a crisscross of electrical lines to their quarter acre lots. However, they sold very few when the Freeport bubble broke after Prime Minister Pindling's 'Bend or Break' speech in 1968, shortly after he came to power, where he reasserted Governmental control of the Freeport area.

I made a deal to represent the land company and registered their lots with the Florida Real Estate Commission. Going back to the Penny Saver Publications and a free Swiss church publication (strangely enough, the publisher called me and offered to advertise the lots free in European church circles). I offered the lots from $2,500 to $4,000 with 20% down and easy monthly payments. At the peak of this cash flow, I received a monthly check for $3,400 which represented a lot of cheap lots. It's a thrill to open your mail and have six or eight deposit checks fall out... and they say 'money doesn't grow on trees!'

While I was working on real estate sales, Stan met Mr. Jay Horberg, a Chicago attorney, who with a couple other partners built and owned a 32 room casita (cottage) development with 6 lighted tennis courts, a huge restaurant, bar, Olympic size pool and club house, located at Alejuela, Costa Rica's second largest city. Slightly lower than San Jose's 3,600' the Alajuela Racquet Club's 2,800' of elevation still offered a perpetual spring-like temperature, as opposed to the stifling heat of the Pacific and Atlantic coasts. Jay told Stan that he and another partner from Chicago teamed up with a Costa Rican surgeon and were just finishing the construction of the project and wanted to put together a management team to operate the club.

Around that time, Stan and I leased office space in a large, ground floor office complex operated by a friend, Bob Bond. His company owned a reported 115,000 acres on Costa Rica's Osa Peninsula on the Pacific coast near Panama. Their business plan was to engage a Japanese saw mill ship and eventually timber this remote area. This required the permission of the government to secure the permits necessary to cut the timber, saw it and ship the finished lumber to Japan. One of the snags in receiving permits was probably the necessity of having to remove hundreds of illegal squatters, who used slash and burn methods of clearing land to build thatched roof shacks all over the area. A future collision was brewing between the company and the squatters, with little help from the government to remove these illegal tenants. In addition to the timbering deal and agriculture, the company also owned a previously laid out, but largely undeveloped subdivision of residential lots on a small part of their acreage near the Golf (Gulf) of Dulce in an area called 'Rincon' (corner). At Rincon, there were a dozen houses, all owned by the company and housing local workers, including one harboring an informal restaurant. Little did we realize at the time, that one day we would be involved in their exciting, but remote country.

While Stan was visiting in the Coral Gables office, Bob Bond suggested that Stan and I might like to meet him in Costa Rica on his next trip and look the area over. This ideal appealed to Stan, since Jay Horbeg had also invited us down to inspect the tennis cub. We soon arranged to fly down to San Jose on LACSA the Costs Rican national carrier and checked into the Hotel Herradura (horseshoe), a lovely, new low-rise hostelry near the city.

Before moving on, I have to tell you about an amusing exchange on the aircraft just before arriving at an intermediate stop in Georgetown, Grand Cayman Island. I was chatting with a man and his wife flying into this well known vacation destination (and notorious island tax haven). Making chit-chat, I asked the man, "What do you do for a living?"

"I'm a doctor in North Carolina," he proudly replied, unconsciously fondling the handle of an attaché' case residing on the floor between his clutching feet.

Still making innocent conversation, I pressed on with, "How long will you be staying on the island?"

"Oh, only overnight!" the Doc shot back, earning him a hard kick to the leg by his loving (and cautious) wife, who figured her husband might as well taken out a billboard saying 'look everybody! We are over nighting on Grand Cayman to stuff our secret bank account with patient's un-taxed cash!" I kindly let this declaration slide with only a mild chuckle, as the relieved couple scurried off the plane. I would have liked to have heard the conversation between those two when they were alone!

Bond stayed in a downtown hotel and was pleased to show Stan and I around the city and bring us up to speed on Costa Rica as a U.S. citizens retirement mecca. We started to feel right at home since the country had one of the most liberal and inviting retirement programs in the Hemisphere, with an estimated 12,000 Americans residing there. When Jay arrived from Chicago, we were delighted to spend a few hours checking out the Racquet Club and when he offered the management contract we jumped at the opportunity. The completion date was a couple months down the road which gave us time to contact Hans Zahnmeyer, current manager of the Treasure Cay Club on the Bahamian Island of Abaco. Hans immediately expressed an interest in coming onboard as manager and made plans to fly his family down to Alajuela along with shipping his belongings and car by sea carrier.

While doing some of the advance planning, Stan and I met a young, local real estate broker who went to high school in New Jersey and spoke excellent 'New Jersey-ese.' Jorge had a listing on a prosperous pig farm up a river near the southwestern town of Palma del Sur, a little north of the areas largest city, Golfido.

The next day Stan hired a private single engine aircraft and pilot to fly the agent and ourselves... not to the 'Emerald City' to see 'Oz', but to Palma de Sur to visit a pig farm up a river located at what seemed like the end of the world. The flight thru the mountains took a little over an hour and was uneventful. We parked the aircraft near the small terminal where the pilot plopped on a bench to await our return, while we piled into a car Jorge pre-arranged, drove thru banana plantations and boarded a boat for the trip up the river.

With five of us aboard we were going at a snail's pace as the afternoon wore on. To add to the looming time restraint, a building tropical thunderstorm further up the river prompted the captain to call a halt and suggest we return to the dock immediately. The frustrated agent pointed to the far shoreline, now being inundated with a heavy squall and whined, "Well... the farms over there!" We all strained to see it, but only saw heavy rain, as we turned back. We thought it was a tad shy of a convincing real estate presentation.

The storm broke as we jumped into the car for the quick trip to the airport and a dash back to San Jose. Unfortunately, by the time we ran into the airport to connect with our pilot, the rain and howling wind created zero visibility, which was not encouraging for an immediate departure. Stan, keen to put the adventure behind him, almost yelled to be heard over the pounding rain, "let's get out of here!" A sentiment I wholeheartedly shared.

The pilot dashed our hopes with, "it's too late! The monsoon has set in and we can't fly into the mountains in this kind of downpour!"

Stan appeared to be outraged and shouted, "What the hell are you talking about... it's only 3:30 in the afternoon. It's urgent we get back to San Jose for important business!" Actually, the 'important business' was a nice room and a great steak dinner waiting back at the Herradura.

At this point, the old airport manager chipped in with, "Senior, the monsoon starts at 3:00 PM and does not stop until 8:00 PM." Stan, still hoping to get back to civilization today said, "Ok, we can leave at 8:00 PM and still arrive in time for dinner."

"Can't do it!" growled the pilot, not bending before Stan's onslaught, "it will be dark by the time we get in the middle of the mountains."

Nervously licking my lips at the thought of flying between those towering peaks blindfolded, sent a chill through my (yellow) spine. I threw in my two cents with, "Stan, lets not get killed tonight!" I thought this was a pretty solid suggestion.

Finally, Stan relented and gave into the logic of it all (and that we would probably have to hold a gun on the pilot to make him fly this night). His agile mind now moving ahead asked the terminal manager where to overnight, have dinner and maybe a little female companionship (this last part was surprising since I never saw Stan fooling around on any of our trips, so this question must have been for the instance of our agent and a couple of his friends who were still with us).

The old manager assured Stan that, "We have a very nice motel in Palma del Sur, with an excellent Chinese restaurant, but let me implore you not to go across the river to Palma del Norte where most of ladies are."

Now intrigued, Stan asks, "What's the problem there?"

"Well, Senior, if you stay in Palma del Sur, you have a 50/50 chance of not catching a venereal disease... but if you go over to del Norte, your chances are slim to none!" The unlikely thoughts of a little companionship for the evening went soaring out the window in one swoop.

Later that night at the Chinese restaurant, Jorge and his local driver and boat captain suggested that Stan and I would be most welcome to join them after dinner for a trip to the fleshpots on the north side of the river. Stan and I almost ran to our rooms and bolted the doors, ignoring departure pleas from the high-spirited lads.

Whooping and hollowing at 1:00 AM signaled the boys return from an evening sampling the flesh-pots of Palma del Norte. I hope it was worth it… if not, maybe it was time to dust off the old peanut can! The next morning the van had a dead battery (they probably left the headlights on while in Palma del Norte), requiring all of us to giver it a push. Finally we got to the airport and put the 'Great Pig Farm' adventure, thankfully, behind us.

The Racquet Club was finally finished and Zahnmeyer arrived and took over the management. My visits to Costa Rica increased, since I was the General Manager of Out Islands Unlimited and needed to keep an eye on the operation. In August 1977, Joan, son Paul and I were dining at the Club, when were informed that Elvis

Pressley had passed away. It was one of those disasterous occasions when you always remember where you were at the time.

On one trip to San Jose, I met Sarah, an attractive blonde young lady of German decent, who was employed as an English speaking telephone operator. We met at one of the hotel supper clubs in San Jose and danced the evening away. One particular song, 'Feelings' sung by an American girl accompanying herself on a guitar, was a terrific mood enhancer. Gliding (or stumbling) across the floor, cheek to jowl, relaxed from a libation or two, was indeed, magic!

Near the end of our third date Sarah, obviously overwhelmed by my manly charm, suggested that the evening would not be a complete success unless we gave some thought to a little hanky-panky. As one might imagine, I loved the idea, but hated the thought of having to drive all the way from San Jose to my casita at the Alajuela Racquet Club and back at this time of night. Sarah, no doubt experienced in these matters, explained that scattered all over the city were special 'hot sheet' motels that were convenient and protected fragile reputations.

She gave me a 101 course in how these motels operate... first find one (makes sense).

Next, look for an open garage door, which indicates the room is unoccupied. Drive in and close the garage door, which sent a signal to the motel office; open the interior door and make your way to the far wall, which contained a drawer to place the rental money... push it in sending the money to the outside of the motel wall for pickup and into the coffiers of the management... I never found out if there was a time limit on the room, since I must admit that I only lasted about 45 minutes... When finished, we went out the same way we came in. Talk about convenience, no one would ever spot Aunt Juanita going into a motel for al little anonomos action.

With Zahmeyer operating the Club, I spent most of my time when not in Costa Rica, back at my office in Coral Gables, trying to promote business. One morning, Bond came into my office and suggested that perhaps we should explore a joint venture with their property on the Osa Pennesula. His company had built an eight bedroom villa on a high hill overlooking the jungle to the west and their settlement of Rincon to the East. The Golf of Dulce was to the south and the private air strip to the north. Immediately surrounding the villa was an abandoned, but developed residential subdivision that the company would like resurrect and resume selling. A couple of crumbling houses put up by previous buyers, stood as testimony to management problems, a lack of appeal in a hideaway deep in the Central American jungle, lack of sufficient development funds, or all of the above, plus some I haven't thought of yet. All considered, we found the area strangely attractive.

The Company's villa was professionally done, with swimming pool, nicely appoinated rooms, a modern kitchen and a large, screened porch overlooking the rainforest from the top of a high hill. The villa was aptly named, 'Casa Loma,' or 'Hilltop House.'

Ralph and Connie Shultz, friends from the Florida Keys and I flew down to Golfido in the company plane. We had to wait at the terminal while barrels of diesel fuel was loaded and flown in thirty miles or so across the Golf of Dulce, unloaded at Rincon and returned for us. The short flight was not a problem, but landing on a short jungle strip was another matter. I guess sucking in my breath (or maybe it was the pucking of my rear-end) was a help and we landed without crashing into a nearby rice paddy.

That night we had dinner at Rosita's house cum restaurant, which boasted six tables nicely set up with tin pans and an oil cloth tablecloth; TV was a little snowy and had on 'Big Bird' pronouncing Spanish words... kind of interesting, but lacked the appeal, Ralph said, of Monday Night Football, which was on at the same time, but a thousand miles to the north. When dinner came out of the kitchen, it consisted of a slab of braised meat that looked good, smelled good and tasted good (no... it did not taste like 'chicken', but more like pork), but qualified as a 'mystery'meat that made one wonder what it looked like when it was alive. We finally was told that it was from the 'Rat' family and called something like 'Esquina', that was hunted in the area and was considered 'muy sabrosa'or very delicious. What the hell! I thought.

Rat or not, I've had a lot worse.

Ralph, Connie and I stayed at Rincon for almost a week, mapping out a few things we needed at Casa Loma and driving the roads of the defunked subdivision in the company Jeep. Actually, it was a very interesting rainforest and did have some appeal. With time on their hands, Ralph and Connie went down to the nearby river that ran thru the property to cool off. Like a bolt, a giant water snake swam between them causing a very frightening few seconds.

Snakes in the Osa were nothing to play with (figuratively and literally) since the Osa provided a habitat for some of the most deadly in the world, including the feared Black Mamba One day at the airport in Golfido, waiting for a flight to San Jose, we chatted with a couple of American finca (farm) owners, who were taking their German Shepard to the capital for medical attention. The dog had been bitten on the neck by a poisonous snake that had taken refuge on a banana leaf and struck as the canine passed by.

The waterways of the Osa offered some interesting gold panning opportunities. I met an old prospector panning the river from deep in the interior. He carried a bag of small nuggets, flakes and gold dust. I purchased a few hundred dollars worth, put it in a clear, plastic vial and gave it to Joan to wear around her neck, making an unusual and eye catching necklace.

A Canadian lad once told me that at one time he was part of gold recovery crew working a barge on the rivers of the Osa, dredging for gold similar to the methods used by the gold dredging barges around Fairbanks, Alaska in the 1920's.

For some months we tinkered with the proposed lot subdivision and a jungle tourism operation with Bond, but in the final analysis, the local employees were uncooperative to hostile, making tourism development problematical. In addition, most of the employees were involved in ripping the company off with unreported agricultural production, use of the company's huge landing craft to transport cattle to market, delivery of fuel and supplies to outlaying settlements, and God knows what else. The last thing these rip-off artists needed was a bunch of Gringo tourists running all over the area, so we opted out of the development and wrote it off to a grand, but failed adventure.

Back at the Racquet Club, which was slow going, Stan was approached by a very fat fellow American called...you guessed it!... 'Tiny.' He built a very rustic fishing camp on the Tortugara River on the Atlantic side of Costa Rica. This river steretched from the Nicaraguan boarder to the city of Port Limon to the south and was as wild as any imagined. This fishing club was currently closed and for sale. Its location across the river from the University of Florida Turtle Station on a world famous turtle hatching beach, was interesting enough to have Stan ask the third partner in the Racquest Club, Dr. Ferrero, a local surgeon, to fly Ralph and me down to Rio Colorado, a settlement north of the fishing club, that boasted an airstrip, a small population and a well known U.S. managed Snook and Tarpon fishing operation. Dr. Ferrero and his wife, joined Ralph and me on a pre-arranged inspection trip down the river in a dugout (a giant Cottonwood Tree) canoe, complete with a 25 hp outboard motor and native guide (most of the locals on the Atlantic side were originally of Jamaican ancestry and spoke passable English).

We had a pleasant flight down from the Central Plateau, in Ferrero's single engine Piper Aircraft and landed at the postage stamp airstrip. The guide was waiting and after a couple of minutes to close our flight plan in the office, we boarded the boat (read 'log') and after a 'sit still' warning we headed down the river. During the two hour trip, civilization was only a memory. The guide had to steer the canoe and bail at the same time with a rusty Hunt's tomato can to compensate for the long crack in the bottom of the hull where the river flowed... well, like water!

Howler Monkeys were everywhere in the thick forest, while Parrots and beautifully colored Macaws flew low overhead from bank to bank. Occasionally, the guide slowed down to point high in the trees at a Sloth or other animals.

When we arrived at the thatched roof camp, we took over bedrooms complete with plenty of nasty looking spiders and shooed one snake out the door. Sleeping with one eye open, certainly looked llike the order of the day (or night). The kitchen however, was in reasonable shape and allowed for the preparation of a reasonable meal for the five starved travelers, who could eat a shoe at the drop of a hat... and probably eat the hat too!

The guide and I discovered a heavy duty trolling rod at the camp and decided to try out the local fishing before dark. We trolled a shniny spoon lure along an opening of the river to the sea, near the turtle reserve. In minutes I had a tremendous strike and fought something very large for about twenty minutes before the spoon pulled free. I never saw the fish, but it was one powerful fighter.

During the night, we could hear all kind of jungle noises, but nothing seemed like it would breakdown the door and get us and since we were not going outside short of burning the building down, we fell into an exhausted sleep. The next morning, after a quick breakfast, we boarded the log and returned to Rio Colorado, the aircraft and back to the welcoming arms of the Racquet Club, with its unlimited scotch and sodas in a tall glass... not to mention a gourmet dinner. It didn't take long to convince Stan that 'Tiny' had a bonafided 'dog' on his hands and we would be out of our minds if we bailed him out... and we didn't.

The only situation of interest during this Rio Colorado expedition was an offer by the airstrip manager of acreage for sale along the

Tortugara River at the cost of $8.00 per acre. It sounded like a great deal, but the remote location and what the Government would allow you to do with the land, including, but not limited to timbering, was a big question mark. For those reasons, we reluctantly gave it a pass.

On one trip to Costa Rica, Bond's Public Relations chief wanted to introduce me to the President of the country, who was giving a speech at a school in Guanacaste, the northern peninsula on the Pacific coast. The firm sent a station wagon to take me down from the Central Plateau, hell bent on baldish tires. This caper scared the hell out of me and I was still a little shaky when safely seated at the school. A chair in the front row was held for me as I hunkered down for over an hour's speech in Spanish by the President… the contents of which I hadn't a clue (but I nodded a lot in agreement).. After the speech, I did get to meet the President, shake his hand, mumbling a 'Con mucho gusto!' and was whisked back to Alajuela, scratching my head and wondering what the hell that was all about. I never found out why this trip was necessary.

We operated the Racquet Club for a few years, but eventually opted out of the contract when the owners declined to continue financing the operation and sold the property to a U.S. University for its Central Anerican campus. I enjoyed the lovely and interesting country of Costa Rica and valued the time spent there.

It's a Tie!

I regularly attended a weekly luncheon meeting of the Coral Gables Ponce de Leon Association, a business club dedicated to the improvement of one of the main streets in this upscale city, a suburb of sprawling Miami. Christie's Steak House, a posh restaurant, welcomed our Monday business lunches, where we enjoyed a few hours of stimulating conversation and an excellent meal charged to our respective companies.

I was living at the time in Coral Gables, running the Out Islands Unlimited, Inc. real estate office Stan Benjamin and I set up to sell off- shore properties. In addition, we operated the 32 room Alajuela Racquet Club, a tennis resort near San Jose,' Costa Rica as mentioned and a few other foreign real estate activities... so getting out of the office now and then was a welcome diversion.

At one of the meetings I sat next to a gentleman who owned 'Islandia', an island inside the Biscayne National Park, which he was trying to set up as an independent territory. Obviously, it was an uphill battle with state and federal authorities, who were not noted for relinquishing power or potential revenue for that matter. Marty, was very dedicated in his efforts to pull this off and since it was a very interesting premise, he and I developed a friendship which led to an invitation to visit and inspect the island.

The island itself was beautiful, with a few buildings that served as a club house of sorts, causing one's mind to swirl with potential, should he actually be able to accomplish this uphill battle.

The following week, Marty invited me to lunch at an expensive French restaurant to meet with two of his investors, to debrief my visit to 'Islandia.' I dressed carefully in blue blazer, gray trousers, white shirt and a dark blue, silk tie, and black, tasseled loafers... along with my silver hair and toasty suntan... Gad! What a vision... Beau Brummel couldn't have done better!

Marty was having a Martini with the two other guests when I arrived and joined them for a libation. Normally, I don't drink during the day, but at an affair like this (and since I wasn't paying), it seemed like a sound idea. The air was full of chit-chat, mostly on the merits of the island and the challenging prospects of separating it from the rest of the park.

As lunch was served, we continued in deep, animated conversation, each trying to make some obscure point or another, while shoveling in the Haut cuisine. As luck would have it, I chose a lull in the conversation to wipe my mouth of the heavy cream sauce I slopped from the feeding frenzy.

In itself, this was not an earthshaking move... the unfortunate part was that I mopped the cream off my mouth with my TIE... witnessed by the aghast ensemble! Everyone suddenly looked in a different direction in an obvious effort to avoid involvement in the faux pas.

When the horrible realization struck home... I looked down at the cream incrusted tie (still in my hand, like a hot poker or better, a smoking pistol at the scene of the crime), and with a confused look on my face, I lamely mumbled, in defense of my stupidity, "the tie is very slick and felt just like my napkin!" This brilliant confession brought grunts of agreement, a chuckle or two, a tad of shared pain and continued conversation... signaling the close of the incident!

Needless to say, I waited in vain for my next invitation. I later heard that Marty lost in his attempt to develop the island and decided to relocate to Denver, Colorado, a broken man.

But as the wacky wand of fortune sometimes flicks stardust on mortals... within a few months after moving to Denver, he won the state lottery of a reported several million dollars. How about them apples! Sometimes you have to remember... 'It ain't over until it's over!'

Club Peace and Plenty Turns 50

On January 14, 1958, heir to the Henry Flagler railroad fortune, Lawrence Lewis, opened the charming, colonial style 24 room Club Peace and Plenty Hotel, on the then undiscovered Bahamian Island of Great Exuma. The main building was originally a sponge warehouse and the bar a cookhouse, dating back several hundred years to the Loyalist cotton plantation days. With early success in offering a safe, relaxed out island atmosphere, pristine water on sheltered Elizabeth Harbor, white powder sand beaches, and world class fishing, another wing of 12 rooms was added to the Club for a total of 32 rooms and suites.

Lawrence Lewis with Exumian Bonefish
guide Sam Rolle 1955

In 1969, when manager George Franks moved to Nassau, Mr. Lewis sold the Club to a group headed by Paul Swetland, Armanad Angelone and Charles Pflueger. Also in 1969, a vacationing Stan Benjamin, a Cleveland industrialist and family, fell in love with Exuma and its people. A few years later he and his family purchased the hotel and began a long, successful association stretching to this day.

The hotel experienced many remodeling efforts over the years, including the addition of three 'Bay View' suits as an addition to the West Wing, and the conversion of six rooms into three deluxe Harbor View suites. The owner decreed that in any remodeling, the original character of the buildings must be maintained as to preserve the old colonial style as first envisioned by Mr. Lewis. Today's visit will provide proof that although the entire hotel has been upgraded, it visually appears as it did when first constructed by Tippy Lightburn and his Cavalier Construction Company's first job in the mid-1950. Probably the most significant change is from the original concept of a first class out island fishing club to the present day family vacation Mecca.

Over the years Stan Benjamin, the Peace and Plenty and its management team have been singled out for Bahamian tourist awards, including Stan's lifetime tourism award presented by the Deputy Director General of Tourism a few years ago. The hotel also received the 'Silver Jubilee Award' in 1998, by the Commonwealth of the Bahamas for out island hotels.

Other positions of Bahamian Tourism influence were held by former Manager Valerie Noyes as President of the Bahamas Out Island Promotion Board in the early 1980's and Charlie Pflueger, President in 1989/90. In addition, Charlie won the prestigious Bahamas Hotel Association's 'Hotelier of the Year 1991, and was presented with the Ministry of Labor's 'Distinguished Citizen's Award in March of 2010. The Peace and Plenty can boast of over 50 years of active participation in promoting the Bahamian Tourism industry around the world.

Charlie accepting Bahamas Hotel Associations 'Hotelier
of the Year 1991' with Jean Pflueger, in Nassau

This 'Queen of Out Island Hotels' celebrated its 50th Anniversary
on January 17, 2008, in the company of Government, Tourism, and
Hotel officials, along with a throng of invited guests. A program
commemorating the fascinating history of the hotel and owner Stan
Benjamin's contributions to Exuma and Bahamian Tourism, was
presented. A cocktail party with 'open bar', a junkanoo rush around
the pool (native costumes and Music), a dance band, commemorate
T-shirts and souvenirs...complimented the ceremony that stretched
far into the night.

The program featured Chamber of Commerce President Reggie
Smith as M/C, comments by the Bahamas Minister of Tourism, the
President of the Caribbean Tourism Organization, the Exuma MP,
the Administrator, the former Exuma MP, the Executive Director of
the Bahamas Hotel Association, the Peace and Plenty owner Barry
Benjamin, the Peace and Plenty GM Charlie Pflueger and other
distinguished guests.

32 Room Club Peace and Plenty - Queen of Out
Island Hotels — Photo: Mady Eisenberg

The highlight of the afternoon however, was the presentation
of the 'Bahamas Historical Site' plaque by the Minister of State
for culture, the Hon. Charles Maynard. This bronze plaque is now
proudly displayed at the entrance to the Club Peace and Plenty, and
now takes its place as the oldest, continuously operated hotel in the
Bahamas Out Islands.

I Thought I Saw a Pussycat!

The Bahamian Islands of Little and Great Exuma are blessed (or cursed) with a startling lack of wildlife... there are no Rabbits, Skunks, Possums, Raccoons, Fox or Cougars, or so we thought!

Norman Wells and his then wife Jan, were telling me one day of the 'Wildcat' she saw lapping water from a puddle in the rough road that lead to their development, 'The Cay's on the south side of Great Exuma. I brushed off the 'Wildcat' description with, "it's probably a large domestic or feral cat that's loose in the bush, since Wildcats are not indigenous to the islands."

Jan was insistent, "no, it's bigger than that! Its some kind of a wildcat!" she injected, "it was huge with a long, droopy tail... certainly not a domestic cat! It bounded into the bush when my car approached."

This was a tall tale (no pun intended) indeed, although I thought she did sound quite sincere, but no 'big' cat had ever been reported that I knew about. Since I lived in the general area and had only seen a few chicken snakes, Peacocks brought to the islands in the 1960's, and one Green Iguana that lead us a merry chase over the rooftops at Tropical Gardens, I dismissed the illusion and prepared to leave the country on a promotion trip.

As luck would have it, shortly after I departed, Roslin, one of our tenants, was riding his bicycle on a road in front of our Tropical Gardens rental complex, when a 'huge' cat bounded out of the bush and attacked him. Keeping the bike between himself and the snarling animal, Roslin managed to fend off the attack, while screaming at the top of his lungs! The cat was frightened off and disappeared back into the bush, leaving him rattled and concerned for his future safety and that of others at our complex. Roslin told Evie Bixby, who was living at Tropical Gardens and the other tenants of his encounter and warned them to move around the premises with caution. Evie, who is squeamish when it comes to snakes, wild animals and creepy-crawlies, promised to keep an weary eye, although not fully believing the farfetched story of a huge, vicious wildcat rampaging through the neighborhood.

Three days later, Roslin was in enroute through the same area on the way to his fishing hole carrying a machete' just in case, when he heard a groaning in the bush. Cautiously he approached and saw the big cat on the ground withering in considerable pain from a distended belly, probably attributed to some kind of poison. It was probable that others had seen the beast and taken steps to protect their families by using malathion or another such insecticide poured over a piece of meat (reported to be a favorite local method of removing nuisance animals) which the cat had found and devoured

Roslin quickly dispatched the suffering animal with a few well placed machete blows to the head and marveled over its huge size... something he had never seen before.

When I returned to the island, Evie told me that Roslin had dispatched a giant 'cat' while I was gone. I asked her, "Did you actually see it?"

"Well, no, he wanted me to come out and see the dead animal, but you know how I hate to see snakes and this kind of stuff!" she retorted defensively, dashing my hope of a reliable eye witness.

My last resort was to call Roslin, who was from Haiti and not completely responsible for his interpretation of the English language, for his version of the situation. "Big cat, Mr. Charlie! Long, long (hands held as far apart as he could manage) tail and big teeth! It must have weighted over 100 pounds!"

"Ros, show me where you left the body!" I instructed, keen to see this thing for myself.

"Sorry, I dragged it into the bush and threw it down a deep sink hole so it wouldn't stink up the neighborhood," Roslin replied, proud of his calculating intellect.

I threw up my hands in complete disgust, as my last chance to satisfy my curiosity on this anomaly, get a few pictures for a little P.R., and have a great cocktail party story.... went down the tubes!

I don't know about you, but I have to believe there actually WAS a Cougar or Florida type Panther roaming around the wilds of Great Exuma, but Lord knows how it got there and how to prove it!

Tropical Gardens

In the early 1990's I had the opportunity to buy a residential lot of 120'X222' on the south side of Great Exuma, some three and a half miles from George Town. At the time the road was barely passable (and has not improved much since) and had no electrical power from the Queen's Highway three quarters of a mile away. The lot itself was level and had a plethora of tropical hardwoods, including some huge Gumbo Limbos, Pigeon Plums, palmettos and such. We used a backhoe to cut a 10' trench, and were delighted to find ample good, fresh water.

At the time, I was managing the Peace and Plenty in George Town and living the good life from the company's comfortable two story, two bedroom apartment overlooking the pool with a fantastic view of Stocking Island a mile across Elizabeth Harbor. I hadn't given much thought as yet, where I would one day retire (Stan kept telling me never retire or you'll die... he was a living example of that principle).

When I finally received the Bahamian Governmental approval for Permanent Residency with a right to work, I took the opportunity to buy the lot at a very reasonable price. I could feel my 'I love a deal' juices start to flow. Since I now had legal residency, I knew that after all these years in Exuma and the many friends both local and visitor that in the future I would want to spend at least winter seasons on the island. Once I came to grips with this premise, I went ahead and started to build a three bedroom, two bath cottage on a site friend Ralph Schutz and I hacked out of the bush.

Stan gave me four heavy cedar beams left over from the Beach Inn construction that Ralph installed on concrete blocks for the foundation and I started building the cottage. Lack of available island electricity presented a problem, so to operate the saws, drills and other electrical equipment, I borrowed a small gas generator from the hotel which provided just enough power. Electrical power remained a problem until Bahamas Electric Company strung some wires out my way some five years later.

As I wasn't planning on retirement in the near future, I paced the construction of the cottage and wound up taking eight years to complete. One wag suggested that the partially constructed house would rot down before completion. One of my first local 'contractors' was a fellow named Haywood, who would show up walking to work with a level in one hand and a hand saw in the other as his only tools. He would borrow any other necessary tools from me. The good news was that he was a decent carpenter and a pleasant guy. Before the doors and windows were installed one of my workmen killed a huge Bahamas Boa snake, who was happily ensconced in a partially filled box of kitchen utensils. I was glad he found the snake instead of me.

Nearing my scheduled retirement date, Stan asked me to stay on awhile longer until he got some things sorted out. Having completed the cottage at Tropical Gardens (a name I pilfered from an upscale flower ship in Coral Gables), and with retirement postponed, I had the opportunity to rent the cottage to a builder working on the island. This arrangement seemed to work so well that with retirement still looming, I built another cottage to move into while protecting the original cottage's rental stream. When I completed the second cottage, Stan wasn't ready to send me on the retirement road... so the second cottage was rented to a Mrs. Lopez, who would come over from south Florida every other week to supervise the construction of her beach house on Little Exuma. Finally, when I was actually retired and having grown overly fond of the income from the two rentals, I had to build the third cottage to get in out of the weather.

From this humble beginning, I built six cottages units for Stan (he wanted to get in on the action) on a lot he purchased next door, and another two units for myself. The timing was right. Exuma was poised for development with the commencement of the Emerald Bay complex, featuring a five star Four Seasons Hotel, with casino and 18 hold Greg Norman golf course. The expected influx of foreign and Bahamian tradesmen materialized and for a few years we filled all the available cottages, creating a nice retirement income and a pleasant place to live.

The property was landscaped and all electric and telephone cables placed underground. As many of the natural trees were left as possible and others such as royal palms, coconut and a sprinkling of orange, lime, mango and flowering shrubs, were added to the ambiance. Literally two pieces of Bermuda grass, left over from the Beach Inn, were also planted and grew into the ground cover, making a lush, green carpet over the whole property. A few exotic tropical apple trees, a peach tree and a nectarine were also planted to lend a little diversity, but grew very slowly in a tropical and alien environment. Unfortunately, the nectarine was eventually the only survivor and recently produced its first fruit. Hang in there!

On my side of Tropical Gardens, I have a three bedroom cottage, 1 two bedroom, and 3 one bedroom, all furnished. In addition I built a large storage building which is always crammed full of junk we will probably never need. On Stan's side we built 5 one bedroom units, 1 studio, 1 caretaker's cottage, a laundry building and a couple of storage buildings.

Our original plans included continued development of a couple of cottages per year on some of the contiguous lots we purchased some years before. The prosperity of Exuma at that time however, created an unprecedented building frenzy of rental units by Bahamians and foreigners, which soon outstripped the demand. With all these excess units on the rental market, coupled with the sudden world financial crisis dictatied no new building projects were coming on stream and the departure of personnel from the now completed projects, further deluted the rental potential. Any thoughts of further rental cottage development obviously became a dead issue.

A number of years ago, Stan and I had the idea of using one of his lots for a fruit grove. We secured a permit from the Ministry of Agriculture thru the local office at the packing house in Mt. Thompson and ordered fruit trees to be shipped from a Ft. Lauderdale nursery. We decided on twelve mango trees of three species, selected to produce fruit at different times of the year. We also purchased four different kinds of avocado, a few assorted limes and some exotic bananas. We looked forward to having all the fresh fruit we could eat within a few years. Unfortunately, the following year, with the trees growing nicely, we had a hurricane that went thru Andros Island, creating 70 MPH winds on Exuma and pushing saltwater from a nearby river over the grove for only a few hours on one high tide period. Try as we might in removing the salt soaked soil and replacing fresh soil around the roots, we had little success and eventually all these expensive trees died. It was so heartbreaking that we had no stomach for another attempt, although we have never had another bout of saltwater intrusion. A few of the orange and mango trees planted on higher land around the cottages did survive and flourish.

In 2010 the our cottage rental market was almost non-existent until rental rates were cut in half... more in keeping with salaries... to finally attract local renters. None the less, it was very satisfying to be able to develop such an interesting rental property in a lush site on an island straddling the Tropic of Cancer. I enjoyed all the time I spent on this endeavor and wish I had started it earlier in life.

This 12 unit rental complex would be an exciting life project for a younger couple that wished to be involved in Bahamas tourism with the potential to become truly a lush tropical paradise. Three extra lots provide ample future cottage expansion opportunity and extensive fruit grove potential.

Retirement Looms

During the demanding winter months of 1999 my thoughts went to the possibility of retiring from the active management of the Peace and Plenty. I was 68 years old and had been collecting Social Security for a few years. I was also operating Tropical Gardens Cottages that brought in enough to supplement some of the lost wages.

I approached Stan Benjamin the owner and ran it by him...We explored just what the hell I would be retiring from? I was living on a lovely tropical island, in a comfortable two bedroom apartment with fantastic views of Elizabeth Harbor, upscale hotel cuisine, a well stocked bar and interesting guests popping in and out before we tired of each other....What could retirement offer that I didn't already have?

I had no plans to actually retire... no indeed! Retiring to sit and stare at a television screen on my rapidly expanding rear end had little appeal, nor did the prospect of soon dropping dead from shear lack of interest... Stan's warning of 'never retire' was echoing in my brain!

Stan Benjamin, island benefactor and long time owner of
Club Peace and Plenty surveying Stocking Island 2004

We came to the conclusion that a major plus was to spend more
time with my children, visiting for longer periods and perhaps taking
a few cruises together. Plans were also in the mill to purchase a house
in a senior community in Plantation, Florida west of Ft. Lauderdale.
The community, Lauderdale West, had attractive two bedroom/two
bath detached homes with lake view, a few minutes from a major
hospital, Broward Mall and ten minute to the famous Sawgrass
Mills shopping center. Major restaurant chains and theatres were
also minutes away.

Another consideration was the availability of a good primary
doctor and HMO health plan supported by my Social Security. I
had already had polyps in the bladder removed with the distinct
possibility of more to come, including a mandatory quarterly
checkups.

With additional consideration that the Peace and Plenty Hotel, although only 32 rooms, demanded full time management, I came to the conclusion that after a long and happy run, it as time to hang up the hotel manager's hat.

Stan proposed that he would throw one hell'va retirement party at the hotel in August 2000, a few weeks after our replacement manager, Neville LeeChoy came onboard. Good to his word, Stan organized a great party, with food, an open bar (once again a very popular concept) and music. I wasn't sure the huge turn out was a tribute to my popularity or for the free booze and food (I was kidding myself... it was surely the freebies)... but it really didn't matter! We had a great time and I appreciated the wonderful send off, even if was only a few miles down the road to our cottage development.

To help wean me from the action of the hotel operation, I was invited back to every Monday evening Manager's cocktail party and every Friday's diner's cocktail party... all held on the pool deck. Remaining in the hotel loop, chatting with returning guests and meeting new people, while sipping one of Lermon's rum punches and joining the manager for dinner, was a weekly ritual that I looked forward to with relish. Since I held a Permanent Residency with a right to work, I was able to reciprocate by standing in for the manager, to enable him to take a break every few months to visit his family in Lake Worth, Florida.

A few years into this program, Stan's son Barry assumed ownership control of Peace and Plenty Properties for he and his brother David, after Stan had two strokes and was physically unable to continue active management. Barry, living with his family in West Palm Beach contacted me and asked me to re-join the Peace and Plenty as General Manager and look after the ownership interests. Since this position did not require a fulltime commitment and I was living most of the time on the island anyway, it looked like a good fit. It took little time to agree and I was pleased to be officially 'back in the fold.'

When I originally retired from the hotel, it took a little getting used to. Staying busy however was not a problem, since I was fully occupied building the Tropical Gardens complex for Stan and myself as reported in the previous chapter. Every day was filled with construction decisions, ordering materials, shipping, clearing customs, trucking to the site, securing materials, paying workers and a myriad of details. No lying around watching TV and trying to figure out what to do for the day when running an out island construction team.

On the home front, I continued my quarterly cysto (passing of a cystoscope through the urethra into the bladder for inspection purposes) exams with my urologist. When I first saw a droplet of blood in my urine...a rattling discovery when living in an out island (or anywhere else for that matter), I erroneously passed it off with 'not to worry, it's probably nothing.' I had no further problem and quickly put the episode in the back of my mind, until a repeat performance occurred while overnighting at a motel in South Carolina on a vacation trip to Washington, D.C.

This time the situation screamed for attention and the next morning we headed back to Miami and an appointment with my newly selected urologist. After a cursory exam, he sent me for a sonogram, which turned up 'negative!' I was relieved until the doctor reminded me that I had reported a droplet of blood, not once but twice and a negative report from the sonogram was not necessarily the end of the story. He asked, "Do you really want to find out if there is a problem in your bladder?"

Warning: You know how people like to talk about their health problems! Well, I'm no exception... so if you're squeamish about medical procedures... skip the next six paragraphs!

Faced with the reality of the situation, I reluctantly admitted that I did, indeed, have a serious interest and as frightened as I was... I had no intention of walking out of his office without some sort of definitive answer. "Okay," he cheerfully replied, as if my decision had made his day, and with a quick "follow me!" we trooped to one of the treatment rooms, where the equipment would do a medieval dungeon proud. At this point, my subconscious screamed run! Run like the wind! But before I could engage my trembling legs, the doctor said, "Drop your pants and shorts and jump on the table!" I guess the doctor knew that I couldn't run with my pants around my ankles.

Realizing that the door was shut (bolted?) and I was trapped with an obviously mad doctor, I abandoned the flight mode and went to plan 'B' … for a series of silent prayers. It looked like the nurse licked her chops as she inserted a tube of pain killer suave directly into the penis. I howled with surprise, discomfort and indignation, temporarily halting the prayer marathon. Marshalling all my courage, I did the only manly thing I could think of... and shut my eyes.

With a deft hand the mad doctor slipped the camera tube in through a protesting prostate, increasing the pressure until he reached the bladder! I picked this time to do my best impression of a hooked flounder... flopping around the table... while clutching the nurse's waist in my version of a Vulcan death grip!

The doctor, busy watching the screen monitor, mumbled, "Mr. Pflueger, take a look at this!"

If you had a chisel and hammer you couldn't pry my eyes open! The nurse, trying to wiggle out of my death grip, made the astute observation, "doctor, I don't think he wants to see it"

The doctor, apparently still studying the screen pointed out, "I saw two smallish polyps in the bladder that need to come out!" I was not amused to hear that, but was relieved to feel the pressure dissipate as he removed the tube. "There may be a few more in there, but no use causing you anymore discomfort since we have to go in anyway at the hospital under general anesthesia." General anesthesia sounded like a dandy idea, as I staggered out of there.

The outpatient surgery at Baptist Hospital went well as did the other five or six surgeries, as the polyps returned again and again. Apparently this disease is caused from smoking (I had quit 35 years ago, but the doctor said the carcinogens remain in the fatty tissue) and seems programmed to reoccur numerous times. Later, in the summer of 2007, hoping to derail this condition, the doctor gave me a series of six weekly treatments of T.B. vaccine directly into the bladder. The medical profession has not yet figured out why T.B. vaccine would slow down or eliminate the cancerous polyp's reoccurrence, but apparently it works 65% of the time. Fingers are crossed as we enter the third year.

Moving on to more pleasant pursuits, I had the opportunity to attend another travel promotional trip to London for the annual World Travel Market. I went to the U.K. five days early and stayed with our Peace and Plenty Representative, Pam McCarthy, to enjoy the Windsor countryside, while I waited for our pilot and marketing representative Walt (Mongo) Stewart to arrive. Walt planned to join me for exposure to the international marketing opportunities this kind of a travel show can offer. While waiting for Walt, Pam and her friend Jeff were kind enough to take me to the countryside to visit the magnificent English manor house of the Rothschild family. Some may recall that the Rothschilds' were French Bankers originally from Eastern Europe, and made many fortunes financing wars, among other enterprises. The huge complex contained many priceless art works, including Gainesbough's 'Pink Boy' painting that hung, unpretentiously, in one of the living rooms. 'Pink Boy' is an almost exact likeness of his more famous 'Blue Boy,' which I understand is hanging in the museum in Los Angeles.

Another day, when Pam found out that of all my trips to England, I had never visited the famous 'Stonehenge' site near Salisbury where her daughter lived. Arrangements were quickly made and we had an exciting day tramping around Stonehenge, topped off with a delicious dinner at the Daniel's home in Salisbury. Hospitality at its finest.

When Walt arrived, Jeff invited us to an Armistice Day Celebration at famous Eaton College, where 'Die Requiem' was being performed by a full orchestra and a choral group of some 150 singers from the Netherlands and the U.K. Jeff, the organizer of the event, drove us in early with him, giving us time to find a pub where a couple of quick pints of 'bitter' beer might possibly get us in a musical mood.

After some searching we finally located a pub sign and entered to find that... yes it was a pub, but it was on school grounds for the use of Eaton students! A smashing idea... getting sloshed on campus certainly cuts down on DUI and other problems however, for grown (some say 'overgrown') men asking for a couple of beers in a student beer joint appeared to be pushing it a bit. At first the manager refused, while giving us a careful look-over for any sign of sexual predatation. I guess we looked decent (coats and ties didn't hurt), that and our explanation that we were shortly attending the celebration at the college, finally got us a table and a couple of well earned pints. The students, for whatever reason, chose to avoid sitting at any table near ours, creating a standing room only at the huge bar. The students were, obviously, excellent judges of character, so we soon finished our beer, thanked the bar manager and proceeded to 'face the music!'

Jeff had reserved two seats in the front row, precluding any attempt to sneak out, but to our amazement, we actually enjoyed the program, and hope to return one day.

While still spending most of my time in the Bahamas, I have had the opportunity to take a few cruises. A memorable trip was out of Barcelona in early Spring a few years ago, when my youngest son Chris, wife Marnie, granddaughter Madison and grandson Chase, joined me for a twelve day cruise to Italy, Croatia, Athens, culminating in Istanbul. We were welcomed aboard the NCL line with flutes of champagne, of which I immediately took a huge swig! The bubbles hardly reached my throat when I choked and it came back up with a blast that propelled used champagne all over the hair of my lovely 12 year old granddaughter. She coolly mopped her hair and observed that she had hoped the cruise would have started with a little more class. I told her that I thought spitting champagne in her hair was classier than say, spitting beer!

It was a great trip until we visited Naples for a tour of Pompeii. It was an interesting and educational tour until we were crossing the cobblestone street to re-board our tour bus when, arm in arm with Marnie, who topped the scale at 100 lbs, tried to beat a light change. We tried to rush across when my bad left leg gave out! Poor, little Marnie courageously held on for dear life... as I plummeted, top heavy, faster and faster until I fell flat on my face in the middle of the street.

Even the Italian drivers waiting for the light change, were aghast and held up their usual mad dash, as Marnie enlisted the help of one of our husky fellow tour members. Together they pulled me to my feet, while I patted various parts of my body to see if they were still attached. That evening at dinner, with only minor scrapes and bruises to show for the horrendous fall, I bravely announced to the family that 'Marnie pushed me!' Nobody bought into this declaration!

Another cruise I enjoyed was the ten days from Ft. Lauderdale to the Panama Canal and into Lake Gatun. I was particularly keen to take the city tour, since I had been stationed in Panama with Pan Am in 1956. During the tour I continuously strained to see anything I might remember from those days long ago... but I saw nothing remotely familiar. I was impressed however, with the huge high-rise buildings that had sprung up in the interim years and was surprised to hear of Panama's newly implemented foreign retirement program rivaling if not surpassing Costa Rica's.

While son Paul was working on the South Island of New Zealand as an orthopedic surgeon and not available, I took a cruise to Alaska, again with Chris and the family. We were amazed by the majesty of Glacier Bay, the scenic observation train to Denali, and gold panning near Fairbanks. The opportunity to spend quality time with the grandchildren was priceless.

During the stock market crash a few years ago, oldest son Tom and wife Giana, joined Jean and me for a wonderful cruise from Bayonne, New Jersey to Quebec City. We were wining and dining on the high seas, without a care in the world, when the world's financial system went to hell in a hand basket! It seems when I got on the boat I was financially sound... and when I got off the boat, ten days later I was in the proverbial barrel! In any event, we had a good time and cried later!

While my brand of retirement has suited me, I finally realized that when I turned 76 that there was a distinct possibility that I was getting old and perhaps it was time to sell my Bahamian holdings. My house Shalimar on Master Harbor, and my five rental cottages at Tropical Gardens were not particularly stressful to operate, but there would a time in the coming years that living on an out island with sparse medical facilities, would not be practical.

Bob Hyde and I had hoped to buy the Peace and Plenty shares and keep the Bonefish Lodge, unfortunately, economic realities dictated that we needed to sell the entire property. It was a great run while it lasted. I will seriously miss those balmy nights on the outside deck watching a golden sunset and enjoying Chef Martin's succulent, fresh seafood cooked on a wood grill. Ah! Bliss!

At this writing, due to the world's economic recession, Exuma has been hard hit with the real estate market slowing down to almost nothing. My properties are still for sale, but in the meantime I plan to carry on as usual, and enjoy the island life as long as I can.

As my Father was dying of lymphoma cancer, he told me, "remember, it's the journey in life that counts and if this is it... I've enjoyed it!"......Me too, Dad!

Epilogue

It's been a great ride. I have been lucky to have been able to live life as I wished and manage to stay reasonably healthy and financially sound. Interesting jobs (and some not so interesting) have come... and gone...sometimes creating wonderful prospects and other times, bitter disappointment... but always enjoying the challenge of the moment.

Charlie Pflueger receiving Ministry of Labor
award 2010 from Leslie Curtis and the Peace
and Plenty award from Neville LeeChoy

As my career(s) come to a close, it was with great satisfaction that in March 2010, the Exuma branch of the Bahamas Ministry of Labor's longtime Chief Representative, Mr. Leslie Curtis, presented me, with a Lifetime Achievement Award plaque 'For Contributions, as a Businessman, promoting Occupational Health and Safety For the past Forty Years'...signed by the Honorable Dion A. Foulkes, Minister of Labor and Social Development for the Commonwealth of the Bahamas. I thank them for this recognition.

An additional plaque was presented by the Manager of Club Peace and Plenty, Mr. Neville Lee Choy, from the Ownership, Management and Staff, honoring a 'Lifetime of Service' to the hotel. I thank them for this honor and for the forty-something years I have had the pleasure of being associated with this outstanding organization.

Sons Tom, Chris, and Paul with Charlie at Ministry
of Labor Awards Ceremony, Exuma 2010

The frosting on the cake was a surprise visit from all three of my sons, Tom, Paul and Chris, who managed to attend the Awards Ceremony, away from their busy schedules, to spend a few days with me at this important time. Jean Pflueger arranged this wonderful surprise and I was proud to have her join me at the head table for the Awards Ceremony. I can't thank her enough for her thoughtfulness.

This autobiography would not be complete without a heartfelt 'thank you' to my dear friend and mentor Stan Benjamin, now sadly deceased. For forty years Stan stood behind me with his friendship and support, allowing me to enjoy the many amazing adventures we able to share over those exciting years. Stan, your favorite toast...'l' chaim' ... 'to life' ... until we meet again one day! Also a warm thanks to my friend and Bonefish Lodge partner Bob Hyde, who shared what seemed like a lifetime of laughs... some of which, I'm amused to confess, were at my expense.

As I wrap it up, I look back over the years and if I did not do all the things I wanted to, I came close... and those I missed were, as Jimmy Buffet's Margaritaville said... 'It's my own damn fault!' At this stage of the game, accomplishments are not as important as the love of family and friends. The real 'lifetime achievements' are my three step-daughters, three sons, twelve grandchildren, three great-grandchildren and the two exceptional women, Joan and Jean, who made this possible.

A thanks also to my friends and acquaintances that helped to brighten my life over the years, and a special thanks to the wonderful people of the Bahamas... who allowed me to share their lives for over 45 years... its been a blast!

A final thought... at this stage of the game... dying young is fortunately, not an option!!

Charlie Pflueger
George Town, Exuma
Fall of 2010

CPSIA information can be obtained at www.ICGtesting.com
Printed in the USA
268263BV00004B/48/P

9 781450 287920